The Voice is the Story

Conversations with Canadian Writers of Short Fiction

The Voice is the Story

Conversations with Canadian Writers of Short Fiction

. Laurie Kruk .

mosaic press

National Library of Canada Cataloguing in Publication

Kruk, Laurie, 1962-
        The voice is the story : conversations with Canadian writers of short
fiction / Laurie Kruk.

Includes bibliographical references and index.
ISBN 0-88962-798-3

        1. Authors, Canadian (English)—20th century—Interviews. 2. Short
stories, Canadian (English)—Bio-bibliography.   3. Canadian fiction (English)—
20th century—Bio-bibliography. I. Title.

PS8081.K78 2003   C813'.0109054   C2003-903867-X

Published by Mosaic Press, offices and warehouse at 1252 Speers Road, Units 1 and 2, Oakville,
Ontario, L6L 5N9, Canada and Mosaic Press, PMB 145, 4500 Witmer Industrial Estates,
Niagara Falls, NY, 14305-1386, U.S.A.

Mosaic Press acknowledges the assistance of the Canada Council and the Department of
Canadian Heritage, Government of Canada through the Book Publishing Industry Development Program (BPIDP) for their support of our publishing activities.

Printed and Bound in Canada.
ISBN 0-88962-798-3

Mosaic Press in Canada:
1252 Speers Road, Units 1 & 2,
Oakville, Ontario
L6L 5N9
Phone/Fax: 905-825-2130
mosaicpress@on.aibn.com

Le Conseil des Arts   The Canada Council
du Canada   for the Arts

Mosaic Press in U.S.A.:
4500 Witmer Industrial Estates
PMB 145, Niagara Falls, NY
14305-1386
Phone/Fax: 1-800-387-8992
mosaicpress@on.aibn.com

www.mosaic-press.com

For my three families
(of birth, of love, of luck):

the story of my own voice.

Acknowledgements

I began these interviews as an earnest Ph.D. candidate at the University of Western Ontario, turning my natural inquisitiveness (nosiness?) about women writers and the Canadian short story—and many, many other subjects—into a growing fascination with participating in such conversations, then polishing and pruning their recorded transcripts into enlightening historical and intellectual documents. I am grateful to Professors Stan Dragland, Tom Tausky and Catherine Ross of the University of Western Ontario for helping me find my own voice in this fluid yet disciplined form. Equal thanks are due to the authors with whom I first created these conversations: Edna Alford, Sandra Birdsell, Joan Clark, Elisabeth Harvor and Carol Shields. Financial assistance was provided in the form of Social Sciences and Humanities Research Council of Canada Fellowships, Doctoral and then, Post-Doctoral, as I extended my interest in this type of "hands-on" research beyond my thesis topic. During 1993-94, I met with and interviewed Timothy Findley, Alistair MacLeod and Jane Rule. A few years later, Nipissing University provided research funds which allowed me to meet and converse with Jack Hodgins and Guy Vanderhaeghe. A six-month sabbatical in 1999 also proved crucial in permitting me to pull this manuscript together. Special thanks to Jan Ross, Research Analyst, and Nipissing's Research Services, for essential assistance in this process. I am also indebted to Janet Calcaterra, both for her rigorous research abilities and for her generous enthusiasm for this project in particular, and Canadian literature in general.

Again, I must point out that the conversation is a two-way reflecting mirror, and that the writers were also readers, critics, scholars and reviewers of their own, and others', work. They were also unanimously helpful collaborators in this project—not just in taking time from their busy schedules to meet and talk with me, but in following up with essential information, suggestions and assistance. I value the warm feeling of entering the Canadian literary community that this project engendered.

Happily, my life has progressed along with my career, and this project ... I need to thank my husband, writer Ian McCulloch, for his help in transcribing the Jack Hodgins interview, and in picking up the parental duties during the winter weekend I was in Saskatoon, interviewing Guy Vanderhaeghe. *And for much, much more...* Thanks, T. C.

*****

All of these interviews—with the exception of those done with Hodgins and Vanderhaeghe—have been previously published in Canadian journals, albeit in a slightly different, unedited form, and are reprinted here with their kind permission. The journals are: *Quarry, The Wascana Review, The Antigonish Review, Room Of One's Own, Studies in Canadian Literature, Canadian Literature.*

Table of Contents

Acknowledgements   vi

Introduction:

Voices of Story … Stories of Voice   1

Conversations:

. **Edna Alford:** Writing "for our Psychological Survival"   28

. **Sandra Birdsell:** Falling into the Page   48

. **Joan Clark:** Letting it Rip   63

. **Timothy Findley:** "I Want Edge"   77

. **Elisabeth Harvor:** "A Humiliation a Day"   100

. **Jack Hodgins:** "The Voice *is* the Story"   126

. **Alistair MacLeod:** "The World is Full of Exiles"   159

. **Jane Rule:** I Don't Need Other People to Say What I Feel" 172

. **Carol Shields:** "Inhabiting the World"   192

. **Guy Vanderhaeghe:** "A Vernacular Richness"   207

Notes on the Authors   233

Index to the Conversations   253

Introduction:

Voices of Story ... Stories of Voice

"Finding your own voice is a writer's first duty."
—**Timothy Findley**

"I find short stories have a lot to do with where I am and who I am—who I've been—in a way that a novel doesn't."
—**Joan Clark**

"I write in both male voices and female voices, and I maintain the right to do that. To have that scope of voice ... that choir...."
—**Edna Alford**

"I think it's sort of an intense moment, and I don't know if I would compare it to the lyric poem, but [the short story] allows you to write a letter to the world."
—**Alistair MacLeod**

Story; voice. These appealingly, deceptively simple terms are inevitably intertwined for the short story authors cited above, for their six colleagues also featured in this book—Sandra Birdsell, Elisabeth Harvor, Jack Hodgins, Jane Rule, Carol Shields, Guy Vanderhaeghe—and for many other writers, readers, critics and theorists of the literary story form. Mavis Gallant, one of Canada's pre-eminent writers of short stories, has declared, "Voice is everything. If I don't hear the voice, I can't write the story."[1] But to start with an apparently "simple" question, what *is* a "short story"? To his important cross-cultural study of Canadian and New

Zealand short stories,[2] W. H. New appends a glossary of terminological definitions—intentionally reductive, he acknowledges. The entry for "short story" itself is a case in point: "a short form of prose fiction (usually 500 to 15, 000 words long) which in English developed during the nineteenth century; generally it creates a unity of effect through one or more elements of plot, character, tone, theme, or style, but no restrictive rules govern its protean nature."[3] Thus, New first replays the modern story's accepted origin: the literary story associated with early practitioners such as Poe, Hawthorne, and Melville in America; Thomas Chandler Haliburton and Duncan Campbell Scott in Canada. He then invokes Poe's venerable dictum, "unity of effect," and lists the standard formalist ingredients, but abruptly subverts his own taxonomic authority with the addendum, "no restrictive rules govern its protean nature." Simplicity deceives us as absolute definition eludes.

I think it is this tension between formal expectations of brevity or economy, and the continual shape-shifting possibilities of "content," what is contained within or conveyed through the "small" word count, that fascinates me, as it fascinates other followers of the short story. Susan Lohafer and her colleagues in *Short Story Theory at a Crossroads* (1989) decisively demonstrate this point, revealing a range of different ways in which to discuss this new-old form—historical, psychological, typological, cognitive, to list a few approaches—both its slippery "shortness" and undeniable "storyness."[4] Yet as Gerald Lynch, another writer on this "at once oldest and newest of the genres," wryly points out, these scholars "can justifiably be said to arrive collectively at a tautological definition of the short story as a story that is short."[5] Although preceding their heavily theorized discussion by thirty years, Norman Friedman's meditation offers a final position that is still useful:

A story may be short because its action is intrinsically small; or because its action, being large, is reduced in length by means of the devices of selection, scale, and/or point of view. No one can tell in advance that, if a story is short, it is short because it has a certain number of words, or because it has more unity, or because it focuses upon culmination rather than development. All we can do, upon recognizing its shortness, is to ask how and why, keeping balanced simultaneously in our minds the alternative ways of answering these questions and their possible combinations. [6]

In other words, the "voice" of the story determines its own "telling," and its own time, length or duration, although we acknowledge the relativity of *short* as modifier to *story*, and recognize too that "the historical variability of attention spans might well make us wonder what experience of duration inspired Poe's 'single sitting'."[7] More literary "dissection," however erudite, cannot escape this insight: the story, no matter how brief, is always more than the sum of its parts. Thus critical consensus is finally reached on the maddeningly fuzzy observation that to tell stories, by voice or by paper, to listen to or read stories, is a definitively cultural, maybe even "universal" activity, since it appears that "Story is the human frame for experience."[8] To recognize the existence and endurance of "story" in its different ways of telling, its sliding scale of economy, its range of ideas, attitudes and events, is one thing; as numerous diligent critics and scholars have shown us, to define and circumscribe it any further with authority, not just the ingenuity shown by many, is another. The very fluctuations in story length; historical variations in presentation, publication and reader reception; innovation in its subject matter, tone, style, and literary mode—all of this change fuels my fascination with a form that escapes being pinned down, shifts audiences, tests generic borders while revealing their provisional nature, and encourages regular reassessment, re-evaluation and rethinking.

Perhaps in its relative brevity, ephemerality and fluidity of outline, the short story is free to take risks, to experiment, to explore new forms and new perspectives, and to challenge positions of authority erected on various fronts, be they academic, literary, or political. Mary Louise Pratt, in her landmark essay, "The Short Story: the Long and the Short of It," addresses some dearly-held convictions. One conviction she considers arguable is that the short story has greater potential for experimentation, what with less time commitment, less chance of rejection or ridicule. She writes, "just as it is used for formal experimentation, the short story is often the genre used to introduce new (and possibly stigmatized) subject matter into the literary arena."[9] Does the short story question authority or pose another vision of "reality"? Does it, in relation to the novel, occupy the adolescent's position relative to the parent's—much like Canada's vis-à-vis first Britain and then the United States? The short story has in fact been famously described by practitioner Elizabeth Bowen as "a young art: *as we now know it,* it is the child of this century."[10] Her qualification of the short story's "youthfulness" obviously underlines the threshold position occupied by this flexible artwork, which is both "traditional" in its storytelling origins of myth, legend, ballad, tale and forwardly "modern" in its nineteenth-century reincarnation as a written-down story of some compression, associated with such literary movements as Modernism, Realism and Impressionism. Short stories usually appear with other works in a literary journal, a popular magazine, an anthology, a newspaper, and so on. The short story has also been compared with lyric poetry, the essay and of course, the novel—forms it frequently and fluently engages. Cultural critic Frank Davey feels that the Canadian short story has a history of invoking "mixed genre codes," for example.[11] Yet despite the permeability of genre classification, to which many scholars, including Pratt, have drawn our attention, the short story continues to exist and evolve independently—inviting my "organic" turn of phrase, here and elsewhere—putting forth new readerly expectations, codes, challenges and pleasures on top of the old storytelling roots.

This paradox leads me to raise another: if the short story is an elastically youthful-old "threshold" form, is it also a "marginal" one, as New and others have suggested? And is that part of its attraction for Canadian writers? Certainly there have been ups and downs in its artistic status, corresponding to the huge social shifts in Western civilization over the past two hundred years, especially in the areas of cultural literacy, leisure time, gender equality and disposable income. The "Rise of the Short Story in the Hierarchy of Genres," as Suzanne Ferguson puts it, is tied in her view to the influence of Modernism's vision of "fragmentation as an accurate model of the world." [12] Other esteemed short story authors have echoed this insight—Nadine Gordimer from South Africa and Alice Munro from Canada, both of whom, arguably, share "marginal" perspectives through gender, class or political position within their cultures. While each and every short story generalization has been carefully critiqued in the growing area of its theorizing, there is logical consistency in associating a brief(er) work with Munro's fictionally-earned intuition that people live "in flashes." [13] However, even as the short story form has been intellectually elevated within high culture, deemed artistically appealing and socially relevant—no longer simply "popular" [14] but suitable for academic study—it has also become, ironically, less commercially viable. Lynch states, "Everyone wants a novel, and publishers' declarations that story collections do not sell, and therefore cannot be successfully published (that is, marketed) become self-fulfilling prophecy." [15] He wonders whether Canada now sees itself as intrinsically "less marginal" in a world of ever-increasing global trade and internet links. Perhaps this trade-off is inevitable for the short story writer, the result of exchanging crass commercial popularity for lonesome artistic integrity? Joan Thomas pointedly underscores the present economic situation for today's practitioners, emphasizing that from "a writer's point of view, short stories are a testament to pure aesthetic impulse. No one (almost no one) gets rich writing them."[16]

Meanwhile, as we enter a new century, the storytelling obsession with beginnings and endings offers an opportunity for reassessment on the Canadian cultural front. For a culture officially responsive, in our own historical and political creation myths, to a plurality of artistic voices, Canada can justifiably claim, without false modesty, to have nurtured—by good planning, good timing and probably some good luck—a rich, sophisticated, and multi-voiced literary culture. The distinguished Canadian critic George Woodcock wrote in 1987, "a literary landscape once sparsely inhabited by writers of real individuality [has] become visibly and thickly populated by scores of novelists and poets, dramatists and critics of high and idiosyncratic talent. Canadian literature, in others words [has] reached maturity."[17] And since our print beginnings, the short story has been part of this development.[18] As Gerald Lynch reminds us, "our first internationally acclaimed author was a writer of short stories: Thomas Chandler Haliburton."[19] In his introduction to a discussion of the short story cycle in Canada, Lynch provides an insightful overview of the development of the short story, including key practitioners and innovators, from Charles G. D. Roberts, Sara Jeanette Duncan, Stephen Leacock, Morley Callaghan, Margaret Laurence, Alice Munro, and Margaret Atwood, up to and including the ten critically-recognized authors treated here, who have cumulatively produced twenty-five volumes of short fiction.

Recognition of this submerged yet sustained practice in Canada is important and long overdue, coming at the end of "Canada's century," so dubbed by our seventh Prime Minister, Sir Wilfrid Laurier.[20] Two *fin-de-millennium* story anthologies, *The Oxford Book of Stories by Canadian Women in English* (1999) and Anansi's *Turn of the Story: Canadian Short Fiction on the Eve of the Millennium* (1999), amply demonstrate the variety and vigour of this art form, and of Canadian literature as a whole. Oxford collection editor Rosemary Sullivan observes, "It has only been relatively recently that Canadians have taken for granted the presence of great writers in their midst."[21] Anansi's Joan Thomas also draws attention to our literary growth spurt: "The time has passed when an active reader can expect to be familiar with most of the interesting reading in Canada. What is astonishing is that many Canadian readers can still remember a time when such a thing was possible."[22] Only fifteen years earlier, Robert Weaver wrote, "[I]t could be argued that in [the 1970s and 1980s] the short story became the most interesting and varied literary genre in this country."[23] Weaver himself, as Sullivan notes, was an early promoter of the Canadian short story; he created the influential CBC radio program, "Anthology," in which stories were broadcast on radio, and then helped found the literary journal, *The Tamarack Review*, another forum for Canadian stories.[24] If Robert Weaver cites writers of the 1970s and 1980s as actively pursuing this direction, Geoff Hancock describes "an extraordinary flowering in the 1980s and 1990s: hundreds of single-author collections and dozens of anthologies were published."[25] And in her 1988 study, Michelle Gadpaille describes the short story as perhaps our "strongest and most distinctive literary genre," and states that the "present condition of the Canadian short story is one of forward movement."[26]

Michael Ondaatje's *From Ink Lake* (1990), a collection of forty-nine stories selected by this celebrated novelist and poet, was designed as much for international readers as for Canadians, yet as he admits, could "only reflect half the country, possibly no more than a third."[27] There is an admission of a similar problem—an overabundance of material—made in Margaret Atwood's Introduction to *The New Oxford Book of Canadian Short Stories in English* (1995),[28] with forty-seven selected by Atwood and Weaver. The 1997 inauguration of an annual prize exclusively for Canadian short fiction, the Danuta Gleed Literary Award for "the best first collection of short fiction in the English language" published that year by a Canadian,[29] is another indication that the art of the story continues to attract, challenge and inspire writers and readers in Canada. *Globe and Mail* journalist Val Ross observes that over the last twenty years, Canadian short story writers have appeared regularly on the bestseller lists and literary prize lists; since 1978, "roughly a third of the country's oldest and most prestigious literary awards, the Governor-General's awards for fiction, have gone to short story collections."[30] In his 1999 survey of Canadian fiction, Neil Besner observed that "a disproportionate number of first books of fiction by Canadian writers this year ... are books of short stories of various kinds." Practice defies theory, he muses: "This is worth thinking about, given what editors and publishers know about the difficulty of selling short fiction." [31]

Which brings me to the practice of the ten story writers celebrated here: Edna Alford, Sandra Birdsell, Joan Clark, Timothy Findley, Elisabeth Harvor, Jack Hodgins, Alistair MacLeod, Jane Rule, Carol Shields, Guy Vanderhaeghe are all contemporary English Canadian writers with careers still very much in progress; they are novelists, poets, playwrights, essayists, teachers and editors who also have special achievements within the short story form. If that last fact seems an incidental or trivial footnote to each author's bibliography, that is precisely the point I wish to make: this perceived "marginal" form that writers continue to create, despite its lesser status and/or saleability, relative to the novel, actually has a lot to say about, and to, the mainstreams of Canadian literature, culture and society. Yet these ten authors remain individuals, not a school or a movement, and are inevitably diverse in regional affiliation, writing style, subject matter and career path. One area of mutual concern that emerged in the interviews is their shared resistance to "being labelled," "pigeonholed," or in Alford's evocative term, "compartmentalized." Perhaps this stubbornness (or evasiveness?) says something about their implicit, ineffable Canadian-ness, and our growing comfort with keeping our national "identity" fluid, open to discussion, subject to review (or Royal Commissions). A brief preliminary survey—full profiles of each appear in the Authors' Notes—proceeding geographically from West to East, with comments selected from our conversations, will suggest both their areas of common ground and divergence of approach.

Jack Hodgins and Jane Rule are claimed "West Coast" writers with many novels to their credit. In their work, both return to the importance of finding, or creating, "community" that will sustain stubborn individuals and their often thorny visions, although Hodgins is more spiritual in emphasis, Rule more political. David Jackel, surveying Canadian short fiction for *The Literary History of Canada* in 1990, observes that Rule's first collection, *Theme for Diverse Instruments* (1975) "presents a variety of personal relationships, with careful attention to their complexity and considered attention to the tensions between freedom and restraint."[32] Edna Alford, Guy Vanderhaeghe and Sandra Birdsell all capture Western prairie landscapes and peoples in their fiction with rigorous honesty and unfailing compassion. Alford demonstrates concern, thematically, about the "compartmentalization" of people, ideas, and language, while Vanderhaeghe and Birdsell do so implicitly, through choice of character, situation and conflict. Birdsell and Vanderhaeghe also share a special sympathy for members of the often invisible working-class. Jackel has this to say about Vanderhaeghe: "[his] stories show a keen attention to the patterns of speech by characters from different classes, a skilful use of dialogue, and an indirect but effective attention to the essential qualities of various settings."[33] Carol Shields, formerly of Winnipeg, now Victoria, is deeply concerned with the inner journeys of characters who are seduced, made and *un*made by the voices of their culture. She remarks, "I suppose there's nothing about existence that interests me more than language does. I think it's what makes us human." Timothy Findley, like Jane Rule, writes in a world which takes as its starting point the diverse possibilities of love and community—males and females, gay and straight, human and animal. Originating from the presumed "centre" of the country—"WASP" Ontario—he has gone on to champion the vulnerable and voiceless. He declares, "I'm perfectly happy to have it said, 'He is a homosexual.' I just don't think I want to be collected exclusively in gay anthologies.... I want my world to be wider than my sexuality." Elisabeth Harvor's wounded "mother-haunted" women travel everywhere, for they offer us wry, painful yet funny reflections of ourselves, searching for healing and love in a new-old world of alternative medicines and unmet yearning. Joan Clark, like New Brunswick-born Harvor, has roamed the country, though Clark has lately settled in Newfoundland. She has written for adults and children, and dismisses the patronizing cliches about children's literature, loyal above all to the narrative process. Her preoccupation with "relationships" makes her work "strongly female" in her opinion—and proud of it. And ending in the Maritime region ... perhaps no Canadian writer is so strongly identified with this place and its predominantly Scots-Canadian settlers than Alistair MacLeod. For while he was born in Saskatchewan, and lived and taught in Windsor, Ontario, he spent his creative "dream time" as a boy in the Inverness country of Cape Breton, Nova Scotia. His fidelity to this lost time and place is evident in eloquent, elegiac stories which celebrate the stoical men and women who live, work and die there. David Jackel acknowledges this celebration of a specific region and its community: "Few contemporary writers of short stories have conveyed so effectively the way in which the sense of place haunts people even in another environment."[34] Each author has written at least two story volumes each, collections which have claimed a large share of attention and interest in Canada and beyond. Depending upon definitions, three or four of the writers have put together collections that could be considered "linked" or "short story cycles,"[35] artfully arranged wholes not to be confused with novels.[36]

Still, I acknowledge, it is the novel which is considered the "mainstream" or "dominant" genre in Canada, as in other English-speaking cultures. Why focus on the story, fascinatingly contrary though it may be, and not the novel, which is often considered both more "serious" by critics, and more "popular" by readers— if number of reviews, and sales, count for anything? I asked the authors for their views on this modern opposition. To draw such a distinction reveals a "hierarchy of form, the perception of one form as more worthy [than another]," Edna Alford reminds us. She herself is attracted "by the possibility of compression [in a short story]—by that I mean I'm attracted to its poetic potential." Story remains the basic unit, the atom—less scientifically, the breath—of imaginative writing. It remains, as was suggested earlier, an especially rich place for encountering challenging voices, and a *variety* of voices—presented through the collection of stories, linked *or* unlinked—with a relatively small time commitment. Claire Wilkshire returns us to the initial connection of *story* with *voice*, in its multiple functions—formal, but also biographical, thematic and more—by arguing, "While the interplay of voices in a novel may generate many subtle effects, the short story allows voice a prominence it rarely achieves in the novel, where plot drives the narrative forward."[37] The sense of in-between-ness created by our reception of each story, within its volume, as something both completed and added to, challenged, questioned, is another intriguing aspect which causes some readers to wonder if the short story is especially appealing to Canadian writers. Casie Hermansson thinks so: "Since to be diverse means to be multiple, short stories create a relational identity ('diversity') in a way that is inherently intertextual"[38] –and, perhaps, especially Canadian in that potential opening for other voices. There is a sensible ring of truth to the observation, made by Pratt, that the short story may also be the easiest place to experiment, or as Jane Rule puts it, "to pose parts of questions, rather than whole visions." More philosophically, Carol Shields approvingly cites Munro, a writer whose influence in this genre is widely recognized among the ten authors, about why "she hasn't written a novel. And her belief is, that isn't the way life is, life is much closer to the structure of a short story: life is anecdotal." At the same time, the story quickly reveals its inevitable restrictions for a writer who creates *both* long and short narrative. Jack Hodgins muses, "I think the older I get, the more difficult it is for me to imagine how something as complex as life can be captured in a short story." He adds, "But occasionally it can, and when it does, it's a wonderful feeling." Guy Vanderhaeghe, an admired story writer who ironically feels he isn't truly a "natural," observes that "good short stories operate by subconscious associations," and enthuses, "in the hands of a master, there's a kind of explosion of understanding." As further reason for seeking out the "voice of the story," I declare that each of the writers featured here has touched off exactly that explosive effect in me. Reading them, I wanted to get closer to both the voice of the story ... and the story of the voice *behind* the story.

***

Does every voice also have a story to tell? In a self-reflexive caveat concluding his essay "Back to the Future: The Short Story in Canada and the Writing of Literary History," W. H. New posits that meaning is partly in the eye of the perceiver: "Any age, our own included, is subject to bias and preconception. What literary history valuably records is less a set of verifiable facts and universal principles than the perspective of the time and place in which it is written."[39] The thoughtful critic must consider the weight of time and place on her analyses, then must listen to her own "voice," acknowledge where possible its debts and deficiencies, identify and tell her own "story." Here is mine: I write as an admirer of the contemporary Canadian short story, both in its varieties of formal elegance and subtle engagement with the concerns, issues, attitudes and histories that contribute to the making (and remaking) of Canada, and especially its ability, in a society in which we are bombarded regularly by new media and new outlets for self-expression and self-invention, to stand between yesterday and tomorrow, the marginal and the mainstream, demanding time and respect for both. These ten Canadian writers so deftly weave the narrative voice into the story, that I "fall into the page," as Sandra Birdsell aptly encapsulates her ideal reading experience. The creation of a convincing and absorbing story "voice," whether conveyed by narrator or character, is necessary, it seems to me, to begin the activity of breaking down barriers of distrust and miscommunication between the worlds of "us" and "them," wherever they appear, and to move towards the process of understanding. The powerfully realized voices created by these ten authors are vividly marked with differing shades of "otherness" or distance from the cultural mainstream. This marking may be seen, in probable order of significance, through five key categories of identity: difference of gender, of sexual orientation, of class, of ethnicity, and of region. Absorbed by these fictional voices, we realize just how illusory, how defensive, is our belief in the Canadian societal "mainstream" and its day-to-day dominance.

The interviews bear this out, as the writers insist on complicating my original simplifications of authorial and narrative identity in various interesting ways. It is my contention that every story offers us an encounter with some degree of "otherness"—not far removed from the "mystery" that some associate, still, with story, the lingering legacy, in one literary history-telling, of Poe's psychological-supernatural tales. Even with Poe's super-rational-yet-mad narrators, it is the story voice that still draws us in, even if held in the mind's ear, to willing consideration of a tale that we might dismiss or disdain, presented via flat exposition.

Speaking of the story's "voice": my initial interest, as I began this project, was in the voice of the woman writer, telling stories of personal and political self-questioning inspired by their difference from the *male*stream. Since this "difference" was one I shared, it was an obvious entry point. But it didn't provide the fuller challenge of "otherness," and with time, I moved beyond the mirroring comforts of sisterhood to consider further differences—the marking of literature, in perspective or content or something else, by the awareness of sexual "otherness," gay or lesbian experience initially unconsidered—and the effects of previously invisible male socialization. Why, I wondered, do we assume that men are the uncomplicated norm, and women always the shadowy second sex?[40] As an illustration of men's growing awareness of what some have dubbed the "masculine mystique," Guy Vanderhaeghe explains why he writes so frequently about men: "I think I write a great deal about fathers and sons, because of failed expectations that at least I sense on the part of my father and my uncles and all the rest of the males around me, in terms of how I should behave and what I should be." While I admittedly drew up a very partial, very selected sample of writers (ten), I decided to test my assumptions about gender by including four male authors in my study, one self-identifying as gay.

Although I was now prepared to discuss perspectives on gender difference and the possibility of lesbian and gay traditions of writing, I was surprised by the introduction of class identity as a shaping experience, a circumstance which clearly uncovered my "voice" as a middle-class Canadian. The previously unexamined factor of class, its limitations or privileges, first arose during this project when Birdsell pointed out that Canadian literature of the 1970s was dominated for her by stories of middle-class women: "I couldn't find myself, I guess. When I was writing *Night Travellers* (1982), I was reading Income Tax forms down at the Taxation Data Centre, and that place was just filled with women who were working for microwave ovens, or groceries. It was such a mind-numbing sort of job; I just realized that they could never go home and write about what they were doing or thinking...." Vanderhaeghe insists that class is "much more important than gender" as a determinant of identity. And MacLeod's stories focus on the work that may become increasingly exotic, I suspect, for Canadians in this new century—mining, fishing, subsistence farming—a "lower-class," physical work that depends upon a certain blend of strength, necessity and courage. Ethnicity would appear as irrelevant as the non-existent shade of these same people of "no colour," or those descended from the early, dominant White Anglo-European tradition of immigration to Canada. Yet it is a mistake to homogenize, or generalize, I learned, for the fissures in our identity can so easily be papered over by an unobservant glance. Birdsell, for instance, has Metis and Mennonite ancestry, and struggles with the amalgamation of two conflicting, marginalized cultures. Danishness "afflicted" Harvor as a child, an Irish background has inspired Hodgins, and the Celtic influence is clearly alive for MacLeod. Finally, the attachment to place or region may appear pre-modern, cliched or taken-for-granted, but it continues to be a major link between Canadians from all geographic zones. As MacLeod says, "I just think landscape has an awful lot to do with all literature." Until we no longer have "regions" in Canada as well as provinces—geographically distinct and culturally recognizable—we will continue to value regional identification as a lived Canadian reality. All five identity markers shaping "voice"—gender, sexual orientation, class, ethnicity and region—appear as threads within my conversations with these ten writers, and are woven into their stories of complex truth and simple eloquence, complicating our understanding of what is "mainstream" or "marginal"— even "Canadian."

In making my selection, obviously I chose writers whose stories I genuinely enjoyed, admired and recognized as enriching the growing history of the Canadian short story. I also focused on authors whose short fiction was read widely by Canadians, writers who could point to the diverse regions of Canada, in origin if not in long-standing residence. At the same time, I wanted comparability of age or generation—historical context, if you like—and literary mode. Born just before or at mid-century, these ten authors may be deemed mid-career at least; but they published after the generation that brought Canadian literature to its modern prominence around our centennial year. Their work has been published and recognized in the last quarter of the twentieth century, and though associated with the "mainstream" of educated, putatively middle-class Canadian society as professors, editors, researchers and literary spokespersons, their stories of voice are quick to undermine attitudes of social and political complacency, privilege or smugness. Finally, the stories themselves, stubbornly self-made though they are, may be brought together in that all of them rest on a common hope of potential connection with a willing reader. Sandra Birdsell, for instance, summarizes her desired experience as a reader of fiction as follows: "I've learned the most important things about myself through fiction, and they always come from being able to crawl into that world, and live and breathe and walk around in the world the author has created for me." All ten writers, I maintain, share this crucial ability to create fictional worlds their readers "fall into." As Timothy Findley expresses it, we are dealing here with writing that puts "an anchor in the *real* heart, the *real* spirit and the *real* turmoil of *real* life."

Thus, these ten writers fit relatively comfortably within the "realist" tradition, although one person's reality may include magic, as Birdsell's and Hodgins's does, or Shields's "various miracles" or the disturbing mental experiences of Alford's fiction. Realism is the dominant tradition in Canadian literature, Vanderhaeghe argues, supporting Wayne Grady's 1980 assessment, in his Preface to *The Penguin Book of Canadian Short Stories,* that "realism is the most characteristic feature" of Canadian short fiction.[41] Nearly twenty years later, Joan Thomas, introducing *Turn of the Story*, states that realistic writing is "the daily bread of most people's reading," but ends with this shrewd reflection:

> The emergence of postmodernism and metafiction has made us more aware of the fact that realism in fiction is a literary convention like any other. But this hasn't dimmed our passion for stories, a passion that flows from *the way we use narrative, every day, to shape our experience.*[42]

Thomas's defence of realistic writing as supporting and addressing "our passion for stories" is significantly linked to her assertion, self-evident though it may be, that narrative-creation is not restricted to writers. This insight is borne out in the interviews that follow, each of which could be seen as a enacting a fascinating collaborative dance, creating a space for the writer's own self-narration or self-creation. These ten authors and their careers are very much "works-in-progress." No attempt has been made on my part to render final statements on careers that are still unfolding, or to revise their interview comments in the light of later developments, political trends or shifts of career direction.

These conversations are thus historical narratives, and will of course show that a writer's life is an act of "revision," for as Harvor puts it, "You revise and re-think and invent and re-invent your life by telling stories." I remain interested in the authors' creation of their (multiple) imaginative "voices" through the shaping events and narratives of their own life "story." These interviews—or conversations, as I also call them, to highlight the interviewer/reader/critic's equal participation[43]—offer insights into the poignant, exhilarating journeys of intelligent speakers, readers and writers who reflect on their unfolding awareness of their continuing creative process, as authors of their stories and, in some measure, authors of their biographical voices, invented and embodied. John Rodden declares the literary interview to be "a postmodern form newly emerging into a full-fledged genre." Rodden further argues that the interview is "an act of self-invention" which demands attention to the "psychology of authorship, to autobiography as a mode of literary performance, and to the shaping linguistic patterns and relationships (dialogue/monologue/speaker/listener, etc.) in the interview as a rhetorical act."[44] There is much more that needs to be said, elsewhere, about these rhetorical acts; sensitivity to narrative-, character- and voice-creation, is appropriate in discussion of the author interview, it seems to me, just as in discussion of the author's published fiction.

"The voice *is* the story," insists Jack Hodgins, pushing his description of narrative development to its essence. I borrowed Jack's insight for the title because I see now that these conversations between short story reader and writer show that personal identity, personal "voice," may be as much a narrated performance as the literary story. And it is a story whose ending is always open; as Rodden says, the interview is a "dialogical form" that "resists closure: instead it generates patterns of interaction that 'de-centre' and 'de-authorize' " as the participants alternate between roles of speaker and listener, and new questions are spontaneously generated.[45] Our lively, fluid conversations offer the reader a truly narrative satisfaction, for they allow for a (re)telling of the latest "life story" of the writer, woman or man ... suggesting the ways in which they came to claim, and be claimed by, the distinct voices which define them, regularly confounding critical platitude or academic generalization. The original informal "tellings," stopping or stretching to contain pauses, interruptions, rethinking, the dailiness into which I intruded with tape-recorder and deceptively "simple" questions, have obviously been revised, edited, ordered and constructed by the interviewer/writer into another kind of "story of voice," if an open-ended one. This critical-creative exchange has not always been accorded respect in all quarters; like the short story, the interview too has been seen as an ephemeral or "marginal" work. Yet this view may be giving way to new ideas of knowledge-creation, as Rodden suggests in his survey of the history of literary interviews. In 1996, critic Jean Royer wrote, "[T]he interview is a very important form of journalism, in the same class as the literary essay. Today, thanks to mass communication, the interview has become accepted as a critical genre. The interview has become an integral part of the literary and socio-political history of our era."[46]

The Voice is the Story participates in a serious project of published collections of interviews with Canadian authors beginning in the 1970s, contributions to this "critical genre" or "postmodern form" which enhance our understanding of our literary, cultural and historical moment.[47] Yet unlike any of the Canadian interview collections mentioned, this book centres on the short story. Many story anthologies celebrate the authors I have chosen to interview (see the four mentioned here, for a start), but sustained discussion of these ten authors' contribution to the short story is difficult to find. These interviews should be viewed as both timely tributes to the authors as storywriters, also Canadian writers, and the filling of a glaring critical gap. Finally, the interview itself can enact a subversive gesture, appearing as a breath of fresh air within our sometimes over-heated, windowless libraries and classrooms. As Janice Williamson, a contemporary interviewer-theorist, puts it "[In] a textual universe where critical work on a limited group of writers can proliferate while others starve for public attention, the interview can make space for the writer's revenge."[48]

These conversations with ten Canadian writers of short fiction offer perspectives on both the voices of story *and* the stories of voice. They survey the writer's story of claiming the vocation, becoming a storyteller in print. They give voice to women and men, gay and straight, who have something to say about gender and sexual orientation and how these markers do or do not affect the creation of literature. They examine the stifled expression of class division in Canada; the subtler shadings of ethnic, religious, and linguistic heritage which may inspire moments of alienation from the dominant culture; and the difficult loyalties to places and people we are often compelled to abandon. They provide observations on Canadian literary life by authors engaged with a "marginal," "threshold" and "protean" form; and most importantly, they amplify the voices of individual thinkers who defy easy "comparmentalization."

Why tell stories, in the end? And conversely, why read—or listen to—these voices? Each author has his or her own way of addressing this fundamental question, as the conversations reveal. Perhaps Elisabeth Harvor expresses it most poignantly, describing her motivations with characteristic and moving candour: "One of the main, and possibly not very honourable, reasons I want to write is that I need to throw some version of what I think of as 'my story' down before the World Court of Readers. And to be acquitted." The jury is no longer out: these ten Canadian writes have created stories that invite our compassionate consideration of all the (other) voices that participate in the conversation about our time, our place, our people, and our collective narrative-in-progress.

Notes

1 Cited as epigraph to Claire Wilkshire, "'Voice is Everything': Reading Mavis Gallant's 'The Pegnitz Junction," *University of Toronto Quarterly* "Images of Canadian Short Stories" 69.4 (Fall 2000) 891-916.

2 See W. H. New, *Dreams of Speech and Violence: The Art of the Short Story in Canada and New Zealand* (Toronto: Univ. of Toronto Press, 1987). For another Commonwealth comparative study, see Bruce Bennett's "Short Fiction and the Canon: Australia and Canada," *Antipodes: A North American Journal of Australian Literature* 7.2 (December 1993) 109-14.

3 New 253.

4 See especially Lohafer's Introduction to Part I, "The State of the Art," in Susan Lohafer and Jo Ellyn Clarey, eds. *Short Story Theory at a Crossroads* (Baton Rouge: Louisiana State UP, 1989) 3-12.

5 "Introduction: The Canadian Short Story and Story Cycle," *The One and the Many: English-Canadian Short Story Cycles* (Toronto: Univ. of Toronto Press, 2001) 3, 4.

6 "What Makes a Short Story Short?" in Charles E. May, ed., *Short Story Theories* (Athens, Ohio: Ohio UP, 1976) 131-46, quote p. 146.

7 Lynch 8.

8 Lohafer, Introduction to Part V, 209-16, quote. p. 211. For other scholarly studies of the short story, see Lohafer's *Coming to Terms With the Short Story* (Baton Rouge: Louisiana State UP, 1983), Wendell M. Aycock, ed., *The Teller and the Tale: Aspects of the Short Story* (Lubbock, Texas: Texas Tech Press, 1982), *Re-reading the Short Story*, ed. Clare Hanson (Houndsmills, UK: Macmillan, 1989) and May's updated volume, *The New Short Story Theories*, ed. Charles E. May (Athens, Ohio: Ohio UP, 1994). However, the focus in these valuable works remains predominantly American (or occasionally, British). Valerie Shaw's *The Short Story: A Critical Introduction* (London: Longman, 1983) and Ian Reid's *The Short Story* (London: Methuen, 1977) offer in-depth critical analysis of the form, yet, again, omit any consideration of the Canadian short story.

9 In May, *The New Short Story Theories*, 91-113, quote p. 104

10 "The Faber Book of Modern Short Stories," in May, *Short Story Theories*, 152-58, quote p. 153; my italics.

11 "Genre Subversion and the Canadian Short Story," in *Reading Canadian Reading* (Winnipeg: Turnstone, 1988) 137-49.

12 In Lohafer and Clarey, 176-92, quote p. 191.

13 David Jackel, *Literary History of Canada: Canadian Literature in English*. 2nd ed. vol. IV. Gen. ed. W. H. New. (Toronto: Univ. of Toronto Press, 1990) 46-72, quote p. 64.

14 See Allan Weiss, "Rediscovering the Popular Canadian Short Story," in *Dominant Impressions: Essays on the Canadian Short Story*, ed. Gerald Lynch and Angela Arnold Robbeson (Ottawa:

Univ. of Ottawa Press, 1997) 87-97. Weiss defines "popular short story" as "works published in general-interest magazines and designed to appeal to as broad an audience as possible. It also encompasses certain genres like romance, detective, and science-fiction stories that have been traditionally distinguished from 'mainstream' and 'literary' fiction" (87).

15 Lynch 13.

16 Introduction, *Turn of the Story:Short Fiction on the Eve of the Millennium*, ed. Joan Thomas and Heidi Harms (Toronto: Anansi, 1999) vii-xv, quote p. vii.

17 Introduction, *Northern Spring: The Flowering of Canadian Literature* (Vancouver: Douglas and McIntyre, 1987) 9-17, quote. p. 9.

18 For an informative survey of critical attitudes to the Canadian short story, see New's "Back to the Future: The Short Story in Canada and the Writing of Literary History," in *Australian-Canadian Studies* 4 (1986) 15-27.

19 Lynch 9.

20 This famous pronouncement was made in an address to the Canadian Club of Ottawa, January 19, 1904.

21 Introduction, Rosemary Sullivan, ed., *The Oxford Book of Stories by Canadian Women in English* (Toronto: Oxford UP, 1999) xiii.

22 Introduction, *Turn of the Story*, xiv.

23 "Short Stories in English. To 1982," *The Oxford Companion to Canadian Literature*, 2nd ed. Gen. ed. Eugene Benson and William Toye (Toronto: Oxford UP, 1997) 1058-61, quote p. 1060.

24 See the recent publication , edited by Weaver, of *Emergent Voices: CBC Canadian Literary Awards, Stories 1979-1999* (Fredericton: Goose Lane, 1999).

25 "Short Stories in English. 1983 to 1996," in Benson and Toye, 1061-64, quote pp. 1061-62.

26 *The Canadian Short Story* Perspectives on Canadian Culture Series (Toronto: Oxford UP, 1988) backcover and 118.

27 Introduction, *From Ink Lake: Canadian Stories Selected by Michael Ondaatje* (Toronto: Lester and Orpen Dennys, 1990) xvii.

28 *The New Oxford Book of Canadian Short Stories in English*, selected by Margaret Atwood and Robert Weaver (Toronto: Oxford UP, 1990).

29 The Writers' Union of Canada, *www.writersunion.ca/ compete.htm*

30 Val Ross, "A Quick Eloquence," *University of Toronto Quarterly* Images of Canadian Short Stories 68.4 (Fall 1999) 921-22, quote p. 921.

31 Neil Besner, "Fiction," Letters in Canada 1999, *University of Toronto Quarterly* 70. 1 (Winter 2000/01) 175-86, quotes p. 175.

32 Jackel 69.

33 Jackel 71-72.

34 Jackel 62.

35 Alford's *A Sleep Full of Dreams,* Birdsell's *Night Travellers* and Clark's *From a High Thin Wire,* are given special notice by Robert Weaver in his entry on the short story, due to their appearance within the same year (1981/82), their Western publishers and their "linked collection" format. Second collections by all three suggest a further attempt to write a unified collection of stories—either thematically or dramatically. Less obvious contenders for the "linked collection," or short story cycle, category are Jack Hodgins's two, *Spit Delaney's Island* and *The Barclay Family Theatre.* Gerald Lynch considers the "short story cycle" to be a distinctively Canadian form.

36 For instance, in our conversation Alford notes that *A Sleep Full of Dreams* (1981), her series of compassionate portraits of elderly women in a nursing home, was written with a deliberately non-novelistic reading experience in mind: "The form fits: it was like walking down this corridor, and you would walk into each separate room which had a separate door."

37 Wilkshire 892-3.

38 Casie Hermansson, "Canadian in the End?" *University of Toronto Quarterly* Images of Canadian Short Stories 68.4 (Fall 1999) 807-22, quote p. 808.

39 New, "Back to the Future" 22.

40 The end of the twentieth century saw an explosion of studies, essays and memoirs debunking the "normality" of the male gender

role. For two important texts addressing male identity, its psychology and politics, see *Men and Masculinity*, ed. Joseph H. Pleck and Jack Sawyer (Englewood Cliffs, NJ: Prentice-Hall, 1974) and *Beyond Patriarchy: Essays by Men on Pleasure, Power and Change*, ed. Michael Kaufman (Toronto: Oxford UP, 1987).

41 Cited in Jackel 50.

42 Introduction, Thomas, quotes both ix; my italics.

43 John Rodden is the author of an intriguing new study on the theory and practice of the interview, *Performing the Literary Interview: How Writers Craft Their Public Selves* (Lincoln and London: Univ. of Nebraska Press, 2001). He offers a typology of interview subjects as performing as *traditionalists, raconteurs,* and *advertisers,* or from the most self-effacing to the most self-promoting. I will leave it to the reader of this work to decide how well these descriptions apply to the writers presented in conversation here. Rodden also suggests that interviewers themselves may be described fairly succinctly as performing as *stagehands, supporting interviewers* and *intruders.* I consider my approach to be the intermediary one, or a "supporting interviewer."

44 Introduction, Rodden, quotes 18, 1.

45 Rodden 235, note 47.

46 "Preface: The Interview as Literary Genre," *Interviews to Literature*, trans. Daniel Sloate Essay Series 19 (Toronto: Guernica, 1996) 7-12, quote p. 7.

47 As Rodden shows, the "Paris Review" interviews with British, European and American writers, which were created in the 1950s, brought a new respectability to the popular interview form. About

twenty years later, these in-depth interviews began to be published in a series of volumes known as *Writers at Work,* which now extends to ten volumes. *The Voice is the Story* participates in a serious tradition of published collections with Canadian authors which started around then, in the 1970s. See Donald Cameron's *Conversations with Canadian Novelists I & II* (Toronto: Macmillan, 1973); *Eleven Canadian Novelists Interviewed by Graeme Gibson* (Toronto: Anansi, 1973); Alan Twigg, *Strong Voices: Conversations with Fifty Canadian Authors (*Madeira Park, B.C.: Harbour, 1988*);* Bruce Meyer and Biran O'Riordan, *In Their Words: Interviews with Fourteen Canadian Writers* (Toronto: Anansi, 1984). More recently, Janice Williamson's *Sounding Differences: Conversations with Seventeen Canadian Women Writers* (Toronto: Univ. of Toronto Press, 1993), has introduced a self-reflexive, and feminist, focus, as has Jeanette Lynes in *Words Out There: Women Poets in Atlantic Canada* (Lockeport, N.S.: Roseway, 1999), by combining poetry selections with brief interviews with twenty-three poets. *The Power to Bend Spoons: Interviews with Canadian Novelists,* ed. Bev Daudio (Toronto: Mercury, 1998), a compilation of interviews taken from *Paragraph* magazine, focuses on novel writers of recent years. The fascination with the literary interview continues into the new century with *The Notebooks: Interviews and New Fiction by Contemporary Writers,* ed. Michelle Berry and Natalee Caple (Toronto: Anchor, 2002). This list is by no means exhaustive, though it is indicative of a strong national interest in, and support for, literary interviews.

48 Williamson, "Entrevoir: Interviews as Intervention," *Sounding Differences* xi-xx, quote p. ix.

Edna Alford:

Writing "for our Psychological Survival"

Kruk: I'd like to start with your first collection, *A Sleep Full of Dreams* (1981). It focuses on older women and their daily existence—often grim—in a nursing home. How autobiographical is it?

Alford: I'm not really sure how to answer that, except to say that I had a fair amount of experience in this field, so that some of the events are autobiographical—or at least they're certainly based on experience—and some of the characters are composites. I guess I began working with older people first of all at the Weyburn Hospital in Saskatchewan, which is a provincial hospital for psychiatric patients, and then at the Sanatorium in Saskatoon, in the extended care ward. And then later, in homes for the elderly, etcetera. It's psychologically autobiographical, certainly.

Kruk: You played a role similar to that of Arla [the young nursing assistant who appears in each story], then?

Alford: Yes, at times I did: as a practical nurse. One of the things that I was very concerned about was, Arla really was not qualified—for example, to administer medications, and that sort of thing. I was very concerned that because these people were elderly, that in some way it made it all right to have people who were not—properly qualified, to care for them. And there still are lots of areas in Canada where lodges and homes for the elderly aren't really as well regulated as most people would like to see. But a lot of this has changed, or at least, the attitude of society has changed toward this field, because since the book has been published—actually, while it was being written—there were many developments in gerontology. And because of the fact that the population is aging, this will almost certainly become increasingly an issue.

Kruk: You say you had a fair bit of experience with psychiatric patients as well?

Alford: Well, I worked for a number of years as a co-therapist ... in fact, in Calgary I worked as a psychiatric worker, a mental health worker, actually. I'm also very interested in groups, I think you can tell—groups of people, obviously, but also groups of stories. I think that is part of how I look at people.

Kruk: You wrote *Sleep* out of a concern for the way the elderly were being treated or mistreated, then?

Alford: Yes: the compartmentalization of them, the institutionalization of them. This is changing, as I say, to some extent; I think we're going back to the idea of trying to keep people in their homes as long as possible. Home care. And a lot of things have changed: the attitude of older people towards themselves, their identification with each other. There's a great power in numbers.

Also, I had a very personal connection: The book is dedicated to my grandmother, Hanna Robbestad and I was *very* close to my grandmother. In fact, when I grew up, I spent a lot of time with her and her friends—a group of older women. She lived with us for a number of years, and we shared a room. And the writing of the book almost exactly paralleled her decline. I wasn't aware of that consciously when I began the stories, but they were a way of "being with her" throughout her ordeal as well. The motivation was both individual and collective; it wasn't very difficult for me to transfer the way I felt about my grandmother—that identification with *her* difficulties—to other people in the same circumstances.

Kruk: When you started to write the stories of *Sleep*, did you see them as a linked collection, or did you write one, and then another, in a disparate fashion?

Alford: It was actually conceived as a group of stories. The first one was "Fall Cleaning," and then I actually wrote the titles for the following nine. Some of the working titles changed.

Kruk: You wrote the titles before you wrote the stories? That's interesting—

Alford: Well, that's partly because I often work from trigger images—associatively, I guess.

Kruk: Could you explain what you mean by "trigger image"?

Alford: It might not *only* be an image, it might be a piece of conversation or something like that. But eventually, I think, for me, for the story to come together, I have to have that gathering image. For example, the hoyer, which is one of the major images in that book. To me it's the informing image of the whole book. Around that machine, and around the experiences I had with people, gathered this story ["The Hoyer"], as it were. That was the trigger image: that sense of dependency with the hoyer. And the pendulum, the effect of being neither in life nor in death, swinging somewhere in between in this state of dependency which is very much Miss Bole's experience. It's the swinging of her personality, but it's also the physical swinging. I mean she's in a state of hostile dependency; this is the way she defends herself when she has no defence. The hoyer had this canvas diaper, so it had that quality to it too—the dependency of infancy. And it represented this sort of no-man's-land or purgatory that we had created in these institutions, partly because of the nature of the institution and partly because of the circumstance of their physical decline.

The institution doesn't necessarily create that state; Mrs. Dawson [in "Companionship"], for example, isn't the same kind of character at all, but with Miss Bole, that's one of the ways she copes—she's also an artist—and I was interested in her duality. She swings as an artist as well; she tells the stories in a much different way from the way she paints. So she has both the light and the darkness of life in her expression, and she swings back and forth. The paintings are very beautiful and full of light, while the stories, her other "medium," as it were, express the darker side of her nature. But this is also the state of these elderly women: sometimes they would feel better, both physically and emotionally, and sometimes they would swing, regress. Sometimes they would be like that [gestures], in a state of limbo.

Kruk: Do you think of *A Sleep Full of Dreams* as a novel at all? It has so many novelistic characteristics, like continuity of place and recurring characters.

Alford: No, I don't. Although I can see why some people might— I'm not saying that it couldn't have been a novel, but I conceived it, certainly, as a group of separate, self-sufficient stories.

Kruk: As opposed to chapters in a novel—

Alford: As opposed to chapters in a novel. The form fits: it was like walking down this corridor, and you would walk into each separate room, which had a separate door.... It's possible that could be done as a novel.... But I certainly didn't see it as a novel. To some extent, it has novelistic continuity, but there are some stories that take place outside the lodge. In fact, some of those are ones that move into the kind of thing that I'm doing more of in *The Garden of Eloise Loon* (1986). Like the story about the bingo,

"Under the I". I see them as a group, like a family of stories ... I see the stories in *Sleep* as interacting with each other.

Personally, I think that it can be argued that the relationship of the stories one to another is not necessarily linear, that's the other thing. It's possible to do this with a novel too—create the illusion of multiple vision, multiple voice.... We're getting into the hierarchy of form, the perception of one form as more worthy, or whatever. And I don't believe in the hierarchy of form.

Kruk: I find your stories, especially those in *The Garden of Eloise Loon,* very hard to read. I'm sure they must have been very hard to write, too. It seems to me there must be a kind of catharsis achieved in both the writing and the reading process, for you.

Alford: Certainly a healing process.... That may not be *all* the work does, but it's certainly within the power of the arts to confront pain and to provide a healing model. Yes.

Kruk: Could you talk about how you got into your second collection, and the "healing process" of writing *The Garden of Eloise Loon*, then?

Alford: The process was different, I have to say, though both *A Sleep Full of Dreams* and *The Garden of Eloise Loon* are linked collections. With *A Sleep Full of Dreams,* I had, conceptually, most of the stories before I began—

Kruk: Though *A Sleep Full of Dreams* is more obviously linked—

Alford: Well it's mimetic, the links are much more easily perceived, whereas *The Garden of Eloise Loon* is associatively linked, linked imagistically. For me, it's equally as linked, but in a different way.

The Garden of Eloise Loon developed in a different way ... for quite a long time, I was obsessed with certain things; I guess that's fairly obvious. But really the central concern, I think has to do with ... madness certainly. The loss of long distance vision, inner vision. And it's treated differently in different stories, but it's both individual and collective. I see a connection between the two, I saw common characteristics between say, an individual closed delusional state, and what I perceived as collective madness, the kind of self-destructive abilities we have....

Kruk: Is that how you came upon the idea of nuclear war—I mean, you didn't "come upon it," but you made that issue such a central theme in the book.

Alford: I was very much preoccupied with it through the whole writing of the book.

Kruk: In a way, it seems to me that's almost taking a chance.... Now, in 1991, with the Cold War supposedly over, do you wonder if that dates it at all?

Alford: Well, as far as I know the nuclear capacity is still what it is, and what it was before, and if not that, then there's chemical-biological warfare.... It's not just exclusively discourse about nuclear warfare. It's the nuclear issue, but it's also a major metaphor for our capacity for self-destruction. For example, the Cruise Missile: I was living at Tulliby Lake, which was just south of Cold Lake, Alberta, when the tests began. Every night on TV (I'll never forget this) there would be a big map of Canada on "The National," and an arrow would come down from the top of the screen, tracing the path of the Cruise, and land right on my house! I had an intense personal reaction to that. And to the disassociation, the ability we have to disassociate ourselves from things like that.

Kruk: It's a compartmentalization again.

Alford: Exactly. It's not just our capacity for inflicting pain on each other, individually or collectively, but on the earth itself. A central story is the title one, "The Garden of Eloise Loon".... Eloise Loon herself is in some sense the earth, so it's an environmental destructiveness as well. So I don't see these issues as topical, fashionable, or transient. To me, there just were no greater concerns; I just was obsessed with them.

I guess I'm just as opposed to compartmentalization of the language; I mean I think that's what's happened: "No, this particular issue is in the domain of the sociologists or psychologists or whatever." I don't like the separation of art from the rest of the world. We have all these different specializations and they're not speaking to each other; the arts, I think, have the capacity, have the power, to do that. In former times, that's exactly what art did: it drew together associations.

Kruk: In this second collection, you appear more experimental, in style and theme; previously, you'd been pegged as a "realist" writer.

Alford: Oh ... in some quarters. I mean, I'm sort of in this no-man's, no-woman's-land! [laughs] This is what's happened to me, for a number of reasons, because what I was doing demanded different treatment. So initially, yes, I was identified as a realistic writer. But you see, to me—those categories really blur for me. Because realism obviously isn't restricted to superficial treatment of the material, right? But to me, for example, dream, all of the things that happen psychologically to people, or psychically to people—all of those things, to me, are real. I think one of the characters in this book [*Garden*] actually says that. "In Case of Rapture"—well it's actually Jim Gilchrist, the old companion, who says that just because people think the Turtle Lake monster is in the head doesn't make it less real. Why would they think that, just because it's in the head?

So I have a little difficulty with those distinctions.... But I understand, roughly, what they're getting at, and that I'm working differently, technically, in a number of the stories in *The Garden of Eloise Loon*....

Kruk: For example, with "The Bid", where the voice of the character comes in and introduces itself—rather jarringly and unexpectedly. This is what we call metafictional, and it was a real departure for you, wasn't it?

Alford: Yes, it was, but I had been doing rather unusual things in stories like "Head" (*Garden*) and "The Garden of Eloise Loon"— various other stories too, before that. Obviously, even within the imaginative construct of the story, the logical ending would have been: had she made a bid. And that's where I thought it was going. But when I got there—it's difficult to explain the process—it was a completely unacceptable vision. And I found it so abhorrent, that that was my authorial voice, as it were—it was necessary to circumvent the individual, singular narrative voice.

Kruk: To what extent have you felt, as a woman writer, that you don't have the same type of entrée to the world of literature that men have?

Alford: I think, statistically, it's impossible to argue otherwise. For example, in Canada, with women writers, the case is quite the contrary. Because we *have* models, we have wonderful women writers in Canada. Although I have to say that while I was growing up, and while I was in school, I really didn't have access to those people, or other Canadian writers. I don't think I thought of it as a career—writing.

In fact, what actually happened was, writing became part of the process of my life, like a companion to me. I started when I was in my teens; Saskatchewan had a summer writing school [Saskatchewan Summer School of the Arts]. I went there when I was in high school. I'm not from a literary family at all; I was given that early encouragement in school.

Kruk: Generally we think of the women writers—Margaret Atwood, Margaret Laurence, Alice Munro, Mavis Gallant—as some of our best Canadian writers.... Who would you mention for yourself?

Alford: All of those people; not as much Mavis Gallant, but certainly Alice Munro ... Margaret Laurence, absolutely. Audrey Thomas, Sheila Watson, Ethel Wilson, Adele Wiseman, Marian Engel....

Kruk: So, it was fitting you won the award named in her memory in 1988....[1]

Alford: Yes ... it was appropriate in a number of ways. I have also had a continuing interest in Russian writers, partly because of the landscape, the affinity with the landscape.... It's absolutely astonishing. My husband and I were there in 1974, and flew from the Edmonton International Airport and, to make a long story short, it was as if we'd flown all the way around the world, and landed back at the Edmonton International Airport, when we set down at the Moscow Airport, outside Moscow.

The other group of writers who have been most influential for me have been the women writers of the Southern United States: Flannery O'Connor, Carson McCullers .... phenomenally confrontational psychological writers. They use the language, especially Flannery O'Connor, in a very powerful, muscular way. I think she had access to part of the human imagination which maybe a lot of people don't see all the time, but which I was very familiar with, because of my psychiatric work.

Kruk: I'd like to continue in this vein, and ask you: has being a woman writer made any difference to you?

Alford: You know, that's one of those questions.... I haven't been a male writer [laughs], so it's really difficult to say!

As a woman writer, part of the excitement for me is that women haven't been able to express themselves in the way that men have, for so long, that there's this incredible energy—and material. But also still a lot of work.

For example, Claire Harris—she's a poet—and I are collaborating on editing a book called *Kitchen Talk*.² We were trying to examine attitudes, to see what was there, what Canadian women had actually expressed, about the kitchen as significant site, both positive and negative. It becomes quite a subversive act to write about it, in some ways, from *either* perspective. We had tremendous response, actually—and the work I looked at, all Canadian, was also very exciting. There's hardly a major writer in the country who hasn't addressed this in some way or another, creatively. For example, in *The Fire-Dwellers*, Stacey's experience in the kitchen: burning herself. In *The Sacrifice,* the murder occurs in the kitchen. Joan Barfoot, in *Dancing in The Dark*.... And wonderful poetry too. But initially the response was—even from a lot of the women—"Gee—I really don't want to have too much to do with something that is domestically oriented, that has to do with the kitchen." It was almost like a fear of contagion.

Kruk: Well women are just getting *out* of the kitchen, in a way—

Alford: That's what the irony was, and I understood that, I knew that—I thought, "Well this is actually a fairly healthy sign"... in some ways. But on the other hand, I was also really concerned about the acceptance of the devaluation of nurturing, and the trivialization of the energy that surrounds that, specifically in this case related to the kitchen. We wanted to hear the voices of as broad a spectrum as possible—hence the interviews with women who had significant things to say about "the kitchen" but who did not write. That was a very interesting experience ... it even meant examining myself. For example, "At Mrs. Warder's House" (*Garden*) is a very subversive story in that sense. I mean, the woman actually physically has her hands *in the kitchen sink* from the beginning of the story to the end.

Kruk: So the subversiveness comes in subverting the theme of women in the kitchen?

Alford: No, it was in reaction to people who were criticizing writers, especially women writers, for "kitchen sink realism."

Kruk: You're reclaiming the kitchen, in a way....

Alford: Yes. Hopefully that's partly what the anthology is about. This has something to do with my work as a woman writer and always being worried about self-censorship. And always having to re-examine yourself—and you do; maybe all writers have to do this anyway—not to accept messages that are given to us about what our experience is. From the traditional patriarchal system....

I think there still is a tendency to expect women to function only subjectively in writing, and to work from the "I" persona, in spite of the tremendous success of people like Atwood. Say you have a continuum, and you have the intellectual extreme, and the subjective extreme ... any writer will fall somewhere along the continuum. And it seems to me that there should be just as much of a variety of visions, and an array of women's visions, all the way from the intellectual to the subjective. But I don't think that's yet happened; I don't see it. I hope it will.

Kruk: Do you see a female perspective operating in your writing?

Alford: In one of the reviews—I'll have to check it, but I think it was a man—the reviewer said "One of the things that's never explained in *A Sleep Full of Dreams* is why these characters are all women." It really didn't occur to me that people in the country wouldn't know that older women—this is, *before* single parent mothers—represented by far the poorest, the most disadvantaged group in the country. I learned that. This was a case where the experience preceded the analytical confirmation, as it were. In the same way, Phyllis Chesler's *Women and Madness* showed that the majority of psychiatric patients are women.

When you ask about a female perspective, I think of "At Mrs. Warder's House" again, or "The Bid," where this voice— which is both male and female—at the end, says that humankind is the "literal handiwork" of women thus far. I guess there are many specific examples.... And in "At Mrs. Warder's House," a lot of the imagery is obviously from a female perspective: all this business about a ball of yarn. The doily [in "Companionship", *Sleep*] is another example of that. I was very much influenced by that whole thing of Judy Chicago's ["The Dinner Party"]; I saw it here in Calgary. Not just that, but influenced by the women in my family, who are very fine craftswomen. They haven't thought of their work as lesser, but—my mother, for example, just finished this enormous bedspread of embroidered birds. It's taken her years to do this, and it's beautiful. And I could tell that she had no idea what it was worth, either monetarily, or–

Kruk: It's the high art/low art distinction, isn't it ... and women's work so often falls into the low art category.

Alford: That's absolutely right; precisely. So I think I often use imagery related to so-called "women's work" deliberately—it's "woven into" the text.

There are bound to be differences [between male and female writers]; we know that there are differences. There are hormonal differences, there are physical differences, we give birth....*Vive la diversité*! as it were. That's what I would rather see: an emphasis on the wonderful and complex differences ... among *all* writers....

However, I still think it's quite ironic that the subjective attributes which are denigrated, or which for so long have been given a subservient, or at least a lesser, value in women, are the very attributes which have been often praised and preserved in the arts of patriarchal cultures.

Kruk: How would you say feminism has affected your writing?

Alford: Feminism: there just is no turning back.... It's fundamental to my work. I think it's the most important thing that's happened to the species in the last 2000 years....To me, it has always been a blasphemy, a second guessing of God, to place women in subservient positions. It doesn't matter what my position as a feminist writer does to me critically, it doesn't matter what that does to me commercially... I have no choice. Other than lying! [laughs]

You mentioned the fact that I write in both male voices and female voices, and I maintain the right to do that. To have that scope of voice ... that choir. After all, the male writers preceding us always had that scope.... Yet you have to examine your motivation. With "The Garden of Eloise Loon", for example, I made a very deliberate decision that the central character would not be Native. I was uncomfortable with the use of a Native *inner* voice, certainly, but the most important reason for the selection of the Caucasian voice, lower socio-economic class, had to do with my feeling that, given similar circumstances, people often *do* react in similar ways; in this case, the cycle of poverty, of physical, psychological and spiritual destitution takes virtually the same toll on the young Caucasian woman as it would on a young Native woman.

But in some ways—in some ways, all writing is appropriation. I guess as an artist, as a writer, I don't want to be told what to write about, or how to write it ... and I don't think any writer worth reading wants to be told what to think. Whether they're male or female.

Kruk: How do you feel about postmodernist literature?

Alford: My deepest concern about it is the loss of affect. The belief that the work with the language is only play, or it's all illusion.... You see, I have this other perspective, I'm looking at the language in many different ways.... I guess what I'm saying is, from my work experience—for example, when someone cannot think metaphorically, it causes disturbances in language, and indicates thought disturbance. People who experience this phenomenon cannot function in the world.... Obviously I was working with that in *The Garden of Eloise Loon.* In "Transfer," Elspeth Gardner says "Maybe this appears playful to you"—you know, when she talks about the confabulations. It's not the confabulations I have problems with, or the rich, imaginative word play ... it's not that. It's the attempt to limit the language, which I think is dangerous; I object to an autocratic attempt to control the language.

Of course, language can be playful, wonderfully playful and entertaining, and give great pleasure. But to say that's all it is; that's so restrictive—it's creative. These people [postmodernist writers] were initially very revolutionary, and subversive—they were subverting the traditional forms of language, etcetera. And that's one of the things that the arts do: they turn things around, create a new way of looking at things. Now they're saying, "No, there's this *established* way of using deconstruction." It's the old story of the avant garde becoming the establishment, you see? I feel that once something innovative has come into existence (say with language in this case), you really can't control what it will do! The language is mercurial in that sense, and human beings are very good at being creative with language.

I would use the analogy of water: water, obviously, can be a medium of great pleasure (i.e. swimming, bathing, etc.) but it is not only that—it is absolutely necessary for our survival; language too is a source of great pleasure for us but it is necessary for our psychological survival and well-being. So I guess with the literary-political part of this issue ... I have reservations.

I think all healthy human beings relate to one another affectively, and one of the fundamental ways of doing that is through the language. But—for example, in the work of feminist writers—the concept and practice of deconstruction has been most useful, extremely important. To me this is one of the most extraordinary contributions postmodernist theorists and writers have made. And I use it.

Kruk: Yes: the fragmentation you evoke in "Transfer", for example, is a marvellous example of how women are trapped and coerced by society—

Alford: Seen through her own dysfunction, her own fragmentation—

Kruk: So you are interested in experimenting with language, but not necessarily interested in giving up character, and psychological realism, at the same time.

Alford: No, because I think that if it works, it works at all those levels. You see, there are so many fundamental problems I have with, for example, the abandonment of metaphor, the stripping away of metaphor, which is part of the postmodernist thing.... Concretization, they call it in other specialized fields. I've actually done it in the second book [Garden]—

Kruk: Can you give me an example....?

Alford: "Head": the man leaves his head on a stone pile, out in the middle of the prairie. And he comes back to it.

Kruk: His head is a metaphor for society, the question of "Where our head is at," so to speak.

Alford: But in the actual reading of the story, the text, it's a *head*.... On the other hand, the deconstruction of apocalyptic paradigm or myth seems to me essential to our survival. I guess I think that metaphor has a place in the "reconstruction" of what one would hope will be a "healthier" mythology.

Kruk: Have you given much thought to writing as a Canadian? Or as a regionalist? As far as I can tell, you've been labelled a regional writer, because you've been in Saskatchewan for so long.

Alford: I don't know—I've had work in translation; I've had far more critical response from other parts of Canada, really, than my own region.... A number of the stories have been translated, and anthologized in national and international anthologies. And a lot of the critical response has come from Eastern Canada, not my region ... so I have no idea. I've spent roughly half my life—more than half, really—in urban centres, and less than half in rural areas, in two provinces, both in Western Canada [Alberta and Saskatchewan], so I guess if anything, I'd have to be considered a Western Canadian.

If you're asking what my position is on regionalism, that is significant, I think, in that I work from the premise "from the particular to the universal." That seemed to be what people like James Joyce and William Faulkner and Flannery O'Connor–definitely regional writers in that sense—did, so my feeling about being called a regionalist, if in fact I am, is that it's a compliment.

Kruk: What is your sense of Canadian literature? And the national identity?

Alford: Meaning that a national identity has already been established? I don't think that can be said, certainly not between the English and French writing communities. I don't think enough has been done, for one thing, to make them accessible to each other—the two major literatures. Although there is much of literary merit in both places, and very rich Quebec literature that hasn't really been made available, for the most part, to English Canadians....

Kruk: You've established yourself by writing short stories: how important is the form to you?

Alford: I love the form, I love to read it. I enjoy other forms as well. I think that I am attracted by the possibility of compression [in a short story]—by that I mean I'm attracted to its poetic potential....

Kruk: So what is the difference between the novel process and the short story process, for you, so far....?

Alford: Well, I'm not finished my first novel yet, but—some things seem to be similar to me, and some quite different. With short stories, you get immediate reinforcement; that is, satisfaction is realized more quickly, with each story. Not necessarily from publication; just from the completion of the work, that sense of closure. Novel-writing is much more extended—in that sense....

Kruk: How conscious are you of your style, as a prose writer?

Alford: I do a lot of doubling back; what I call "associative scanning." Probably all writers do this—but I began to realize that it was a process I went through. Especially with the linked stories, where I would go through, and there would be associative clusters that reappeared in different stories. And so I will do that with the stories: when I'm working on one, I will often, in my mind, be scanning the others in the group. Sometimes the images just reappear, or sometimes an image will remind me, or make me aware, of a link, a link between images which I might amplify. But I did that through the whole process of writing both books, particularly *Eloise Loon*.

In "In Case of Rapture"—in fact, I had this happen to me a couple of times in this book [*Garden*]—Jim Gilchrist was once named Jack, and Jack Lune of course appears in "The Lineman".... I realized you can't have all kinds of characters in the same book named Jack; it becomes very confusing. Nevertheless, I was also aware I was striking the same "note" within the context of certain patterns of images. I was working with *jack*fish in that story as well.... And I had other variations of what I came to realize was the name "John." Once I suspected the link, I checked it out— rather an odd process, don't you think—deconstructing and constructing simultaneously! So you have Ian and John and Ivan, etcetera. Well, when I went back through that story, as I was writing it, it became apparent—particularly because of what I was writing about—that one of the things that was setting off this trigger in me was the business of John, the apocalyptic Book of Revelations's John—of the vision.... Then it came to me that really all of the men in the group would be named the same name, but different variations, nicknames, derivations, etcetera. So that worked really well for me because that was one of the things I was after: that all of these men were one, in a sense. As Jack Lune says in the end, we're all in this together.

Kruk: We've discussed Canadian writers: are there any American, or European, writers that have influenced you?

Alford: There are all kinds of people.... Heinrich Boll, *Children are Civilians Too*.... Isaac Bashevis Singer.... I go through these phases. Doris Lessing, I'm really a fan of hers.... Toni Morrison, Alice Walker, Louise Erdrich .... I read a lot of Canadian women ... not because it's Canadian work, but because I *like* it.

Kruk: Do you have a sense of yourself as possessing a particular voice? I just wonder whether our affection for people like Margaret Laurence is due to the fact that they have a recognizable voice leading us into their fictional world.

Alford: I'm interested in voices. And I'm confident that whatever I write will have my voice, at some level, because I'm the person who's using the language in that way. But I'm not sure that I want to be seen as someone—and it's not necessarily a *bad* thing—but as a writer who has, who works with, only one voice that's clearly identifiable as the *same* voice every time.

Kruk: You told me about writers you admire; is there anyone you particularly like to read—just for pleasure? Canadian and otherwise.....

Alford: All kinds ... though I read a lot of Canadian work. Particularly since doing the jury work for things like the Marian Engel Award, and doing *Kitchen Talk*—I've done *quite* an overview of Canadian women's writing in the past several years, which has been good, very interesting, and I discovered some new people....
    I think I've been upbraided for never reading for pleasure; but in some ways, I never really read for any other reason, either!

Calgary, Alberta: June 1991

Notes

1 The Marian Engel Award was established in 1986 by the Writers' Development Trust to honour the memory of one of Canada's most beloved and respected writers. The Engel Award, a $10, 000 prize, is given once a year to a female Canadian writer for a body of work, in hope of her continuing contribution to Canadian literature. It is juried by three Canadian writers, usually including a previous recipient. Past winners include: Alice Munro, Audrey Thomas, Edna Alford, Merna Summers, Carol Shields, Joan Clark, Joan Barfoot, Sandra Birdsell, Jane Urquhart, Bonnie Burnard, Barbara Gowdy, Katherine Govier and Sharon Butala.

2 This book was published in 1992 as *Kitchen Talk: Contemporary Women's Prose and Poetry,* eds. Edna Alford and Claire Harris (Red Deer, AB: Red Deer College Press).

Sandra Birdsell:

Falling into the Page

Kruk: Congratulations on winning the W H Smith/*Books in Canada* First Novel Award for *The Missing Child* (1989).[1] Are you going to continue to write short stories, or, now that you've got the time to write novels, will you concentrate on the longer form?

Birdsell: I've been really thinking about that lately.... I think what I've been discovering with the novel is, that I'm able to be away from home for so long, in a sense, that the work engages me and I am able to enter into the world that I am creating for much longer periods of time, and sustain it. With a short story, I'm in one and then I'm out, and I'm in another and then I'm out—and novel-writing is far more intensive and much more enjoyable for that reason: that the whole pleasure is in the process and that process takes longer.

Kruk: Do you distinguish between the two forms when you actually begin writing?

Birdsell: It seemed about a year ago, everything I started I thought was going to be a novel, and it didn't even turn out to be a short story: it was just busy work. I made a whole list of stories that I was going to write after *The Missing Child* because I thought that the novel had exhausted me, and that I was going to write short stories.

I took some—there were about half a dozen that I had started—and looked at them, and realized that my heart just wasn't in any of the material. Then, at Christmas time, I went to see Denys Arcand's film "Jesus of Montreal," and I was so overwhelmed by it—not necessarily as a story, but by the whole composition. I came home and was compelled to sit down and write, and what emerged, I knew, was exactly what I had to do now. Now I'm finding that elements of what I wanted to write in some of those short stories are coming up in the new novel.

Kruk: When you were writing the stories of *Night Travellers* (1982), did you have a sense of their unity?

Birdsell: Actually, when I first started writing, one of the first stories I wrote was this tiny, wee one that's stuck somewhere in the centre of *Night Travellers,* called "Stones." And it sort of came out like a prose poem. I wrote that in my first creative writing class, with Robert Kroetsch, at the University of Winnipeg. I put it away, and then tried to discover the short story form through a lot of sort of artificial stories that I thought were the kinds of stories writers like me wrote. When I went to Robert Kroetsch's class, I was still very engaged with language and it seemed that whenever I wrote anything that was close to me, it just came out poetic, with run-on sentences, and all that. Whenever I thought, "Now I'm going to write a short story," it became this very clunky, beginning-middle-end, plotted sort of story, and I hated it.

In that class a young woman read a poem about wild plums, and the poem triggered for me a series of stories, including "The Wild Plum Tree." All the stories were like that one ["Stones"] in form—the narrative came later. I brought them to Robert Kroetsch; he said, "You should write a series of sister poems." And because I was a little more interested in trying to tell a story, I pushed it further. I then started to write the Maurice stories ["The Flood," "Boundary Lines," "Journey to the Lake"], thinking that I would write a novel, and that I would incorporate the sisters into the novel. At about fifty pages, I realized I wasn't going to write a novel. I just didn't want to do the "Once upon a time, and then, and then, and then Lureen, and then Betty"—

Kruk: There's still a feeling that the novel has to be linear, to some extent....

Birdsell: Yes. I think my initial short stories struggled to be very plotted, to have that very traditional structure. I had experienced such frustration with the whole idea that you could actually tell a story in twenty pages and have an ending. I was more interested in the process than in the ending, in where the person was actually *going to.* So I think that *Night Travellers* worked well because I didn't always have to say "And she lived happily ever after" or "She didn't live happily ever after." I didn't have to really impose anything on the stories because you could always show this person at another time of her life, in a different situation.

You know, when I was writing *Night Travellers* I was so aware of their connectedness that I think when I showed the manuscript to Turnstone, I only had about seven stories. I met with David Arnason [of Turnstone Press], and he said, "Well, fine, go ahead, but write so many more." So I quickly signed up at the Saskatchewan Summer School of the Arts where Jack Hodgins was, because Turnstone wanted a manuscript by the end of September, and I didn't have about four or five stories. So I set them out on the floor in some kind of order, and I could see the gaps in between. I figured out what stories I should put in, and sat down and wrote them. And that's why so few of the stories were published before they were in book form: because I tend to write collections of stories. I just go straight through them. The same with *Ladies of the House* (1984); I had some of them started by the time *Night Travellers* was finished, but they weren't ready. *Night Travellers* was really rushed to the press, or perhaps they would have all gone together as my first publication. *Ladies of the House* was a continuation of *Night Travellers,* although thematically those stories are probably not as connected ... nor as physically or chronologically linked. I just got a notebook and said, I want to write a story about this, and about this, and I'm going to write a story a month, and finish a manuscript in twelve months. Well, I did.

Kruk: So you had a sense that each story was contributing to the whole collection.

Birdsell: Right. In fact, I couldn't send them out because I needed them there, to remind me of the other ones. Even if they weren't as connected [in *Ladies of the House*], it was still important that they be together.

Kruk: When you were writing your short stories, were you reading a lot of short story writers?

Birdsell: I liked the early short story anthology, *Short Story Masterpieces,* edited by Robert Penn Warren and Albert Erskine. I think that was one of my favourites, because you got short stories from people all over the world, and each one was so different: Katherine Mansfield, Flannery O'Connor, Eudora Welty and Sherwood Anderson....

Flannery O'Connor is another writer who convinced me that it was important and legitimate to write out of my experience. Her stories could have been set in Southern Manitoba. But, you see, in Canadian literature at that time [the 70s], that kind of story didn't exist—except for Laurence, of course. They were mainly stories of middle-class women.

Kruk: You felt there was a lack of accurate portrayals of working-class people?

Birdsell: Well—I couldn't find myself, I guess. When I was writing *Night Travellers,* I was reading Income Tax forms down at the Taxation Data Centre, and that place was just filled with women who were working for microwave ovens, or groceries. It was such a mind-numbing sort of job; I just realized that they could never go home and write about what they were doing or thinking ... or that it was impossible, even if they were inclined to; they'd be too tired.

Kruk: Were you aware of the tradition of linked short story collections while you were writing *Night Travellers?*

Birdsell: No, I wasn't actually aware of the tradition of connected stories when I was writing them....The man I worked with when I finished *Night Travellers* was as ignorant as I was regarding the form, and he said, "Well, I don't know what people are going to think about this....We'll just have to wait and see."

And I'm always asked about influences, and I have to say that when I started to write, obviously I wanted to know who was writing what around me, and I think I read just about everything that was published in Canada (which is impossible to do right now) but I never found a model among all those writers. For example, with Gabrielle Roy: *The Road Past Altamont,* not all her work, but that one book. I couldn't say I was influenced by Laurence, though the first creative writing class I went to, Kroetsch said, "Whose work does this woman's remind you of?" and somebody said "Margaret Laurence." And I have to confess that I had to go and get some of her books and read her, because I hadn't read her before.... Joyce's *Dubliners* is a book that really intrigued me and the book I read constantly when I was writing *Night Travellers* was Maxim Gorky's *My Childhood.* And when I was writing my novel, *Waiting for the Barbarians* was extremely important to me, so it's just—all over.

You see, I don't have a tradition of reading, like a lot of writers do. We didn't have books (except for The Bible) and we weren't encouraged to read fiction or non-fiction. So I had to discover, as a writer, "What do I like to read?" And there's so much, and it comes from very surprising places.

Kruk: Were your parents the models for Maurice and Mika of *Night Travellers?*

Birdsell: Not at all Maurice. If he is, he's a caricature of my father. My father had all those good-natured, soft qualities, but he was much more loving.

Kruk: Did you make him that way in order to emphasize the suffering of Mika and women of her generation?

Birdsell: Not really.... I think when I started to write, the sister stories just ran away with me. They were the most important stories for me to tell, and then I went back and looked at the father ... and the very last story written was "Night Travellers" because I had felt, after reading all the stories, that I didn't understand the mother at all. She came across, through the eyes of the sisters, as being a very mean bitch. And this perplexed me, because I thought "There's a reason *why* this happened." And so I explored that character, and I wrote "Night Travellers"... and that's *not* my mother.

Actually, I wanted them [*Night Travellers* and *Ladies of the House*] to go on to a third collection. Sort of like a triptych, you know: the three books would have made one whole picture.

Kruk: Yes. Why didn't you write it?

Birdsell: Because I was growing tired of the characters, and I felt that if I was, then other people were sure to grow tired of them as well.

Kruk: Do you think it was a good idea to put the two collections together in one book as *Agassiz Stories* (1987)?

Birdsell: Oh sure, I think they belong together.

Kruk: But yet there are real differences between *Night Travellers* and *Ladies,* aren't there?

Birdsell: How, do you think?

Kruk: *Night Travellers* seems to be a much more tightly-linked collection than *Ladies,* with its focus on one family. Since *Ladies* is more loosely connected, it doesn't quite create the satisfaction of *Night Travellers*, where each story refers to, or occasionally even answers, another one.

Birdsell: And there's the Bobbie story ["Dreaming of Jeannie"]: it was sort of a voice story. That is a big change from the first collection. I mean, if you look at the narrative line of the Truda stories—"Toronto Street" for instance—and compare it with the narrative line, even the sentence structure, of the Bobbie story, they're totally different. It comes out of that character's perception. If you just read the Bobbie story separately in a magazine, you might wonder about the writer, in a sense: how talented she was. Even the sentence structure is more simple. And the Truda story, of course, is more evocative, more textured: that's a conscious choice.

Kruk: So in these subtler stylistic ways, you were being bolder, more exploratory, in form *and* content in *Ladies.* Is that accurate?

Birdsell: Sure; that's bang on, actually. I prefer the second collection, the first one is naive in places. I think that it's overwritten in places. There always is a naivety though, in an author's first work....You don't want to lose your innocence as a writer, but you do, in the end. I found that in some of Alice Munro's earlier works, which I read when I was a young writer; I preferred them, because the writer was more visible. Maybe you get more cautious as you grow older as a writer and you learn to hide yourself. I prefer to be invisible. I think in my new novel, I'm not, as much. I'm projecting the future for a character, and the voice—outside of the other voices—is there. Whereas in the earlier works, I used to direct in the narrative line and through dialogue.

Kruk: What do you think you gain by being invisible?

Birdsell: The sense that these are not fabricated kinds of people, that these things are possible.... I'll tell you what I really tried to do, especially with *The Missing Child:* create a fictional place and people that the reader falls into, into the page. I think I have learned the most important things about myself through fiction, and these lessons have always come from being able to crawl into that world, and live and breathe and walk around in the world the author has created for me.

I think, for instance, of when I read Milan Kundera's *The Joke.* It's so totally different from his latest novels in the way that it's written and structured, but the characterization of the central character was so overwhelmingly good: I mean, I *knew* this man. That book was very important to me; much more important than his other books, which engage you on a more intellectual level.

It's a pleasure for me when different readers or critics read the works, and they speak to me, or write to me, about it, and they have found something remarkable for themselves in it. They knew I wasn't thinking about them when I was writing it, but I'm happy and glad that it's there.

Kruk: You said in one interview that you didn't like to use conventional punctuation. I wasn't quite clear which variations you were using ... perhaps because your editors have cleaned it up—?

Birdsell: They certainly have.

Kruk: So, how *would* you have written things?

Birdsell: Well, some paragraphs wouldn't have had periods at the ends of them, because of the play on words in the first word coming up in the next. I had similar little skirmishes with *The Missing Child* too, in that I let the rhythms pattern the syntax, so that the music of this paragraph had to be that way, but in terms of conventional sentence structure, it shouldn't have been that way.

I guess language has to work differently in the novel than in poetry. But, you know, just looking at the short list for the 1990 [W H Smith/] *Books in Canada* Award, three of those novels were written by poets.[2] And the poets, I think, are changing our idea of what a novel is. When I was writing the novel, I wanted to write a film. And I thought: you and I have gone to enough movies for me not to have to do the traditional, transitional breaks, lead-ups....You know that films occur in scenes. And so I don't know whether people may perceive that the novel is lacking in a certain kind of structure, because of the ineptness of a first novelist, but I want to say it was deliberate.

Kruk: You've written film scripts, haven't you?

Birdsell: Yes, I've done about a half dozen of them now. I'm more intrigued with the whole process of film-making, than the actual script-writing. What bothered me in the end about film script-writing is that it's too easy; it's like you give them an outline, and they fill in all the blanks, with all the colours.

When I started [*The Chrome Suite* (1992)], I made a promise to myself that I was going to keep it lean and mean, but I don't know if I can.... I wanted to try and explore something smaller in scope: instead of doing this whole symphonic movement, just to narrow in on one family, taken through a time span of thirty years. And yet—magic has occurred.

Kruk: Do you mean what we call magic realism?

Birdsell: Right. I think with *The Missing Child,* what was in the back of my mind, was the fact that mysticism and religion doesn't play a large part in any of the books that I've read in Canadian literature.... Everyone's going to the United Church or to the Roman Catholic Church, or one of the more established Protestant churches. And what appealed to me about South American literature was the fact that their religion is an integral part of every day—and so the belief in the miraculous is taken for granted.

I mean, I come from a place and from people where that is the same: they might be a group of Christian cult people, who are charismatically giving gifts in spirit and things like that, but their beliefs are just as integral to their everyday experiences. And miracles are possible.

I think I wanted to put a lot of magic in *Night Travellers,* especially where it concerned the father, and his ancestors. In fact, I had written some stories, part of a story of Maurice as a young man, and also a little boy abandoned by his parent ... and whenever Maurice popped up, a lot of ghosts appeared. And I was encouraged to take them out.

Kruk: The editor thought it was too confusing?

Birdsell: He was uneasy as to why they might be there ... and I couldn't really say why. So I did take them out, because I felt that until I was absolutely sure why I wanted the world to be this way, I wouldn't write it. But in *The Missing Child* I decided to just do exactly what I wanted to, because eventually I would discover why I wanted to....You see, the person I worked with for a while on my [first] short story collection, I think was a lapsed Christian. He said he couldn't believe in miracles, or magic, because he didn't believe in the Resurrection, and I think that's part of the reason why I said, "Well, forget it," and I just took all this out. I certainly wasn't encouraged to think about it further.

Kruk: So, because you yourself have a spiritual or religious belief in the miraculous, you see no problem including that in your naturalistic portrayal of the world?

Birdsell: Right. What do you think of *The Missing Child* in that sense? I mean, Hendrick Shultz has got this memorized scripture; he has a lot of information that he doesn't understand.... I think only the minister, Jacob Friesen, possesses a genuine faith, and he isn't even aware of it. Somebody plants a seed of doubt in his mind about his motives for caring for this woman, and he's immediately filled with recrimination and guilt ... and actually, his faithfulness is rewarded in a sense, and he doesn't even recognize that his church, even for a short time, is renewed. So I think the only one who really possesses any kind of happy spirituality is Minnie, and it's her own creation; it comes out in the memory of a life before birth.

Kruk: How do you feel about being a woman writer? Pros and cons—?

Birdsell: I certainly haven't been labelled a feminist writer. I think there were some early attempts—not because the material I was working with was particularly political in any way, but because I was a woman—where people said "Come and join this movement" and "Come and talk to this strictly feminist kind of meeting of artists," etc. And I strenuously resisted that. I think, as a woman, I have important things to say about being a woman, but I want it to be treated as mainstream literature. I want people to fall into the text, and get angry and experience the brutality, without you telling them to....What is gratifying, though, is that I got a response from a well-known poet (male), who said that through my work in *Night Travellers,* he finally met and understood the kinds of young girls that he used to screw when he was a young man.

Kruk: Do you see yourself as having certain skills, or interests, that male writers don't have?

Birdsell: I don't know; I think that to some extent, male writers are still writing adventure stories. Maybe as women writers, we're able to turn inward more. Maybe the way we're socialized is an advantage: I'm talking about the whole idea of empathy. It may work against me in the sense of my idea of plot and drama—I haven't gone out and travelled the world, and had those kinds of adventures.

Kruk: But I think what you're saying is that women's "stay-at-home" adventures are just as important....

Birdsell: Well, of course they are! People like Laurence, like Gabrielle Roy, for instance (more so for me than Laurence), taught us that those experiences, a child's imaginings and awareness of people around them, are important things to write about.

Kruk: Are you aware of writing for a particular audience, or do you simply write for yourself?

Birdsell: I write with a sense of an invisible reader; I don't know who that reader is, but it's just a reader who keeps me honest in terms of ambiguities in the text. I'm not aiming at a certain type of reader. I know that my work isn't aimed at Safeway bookracks....

Kruk: How do you feel about the "Canadian writer" label?

Birdsell: That's all right. Canada is a big country.

Kruk: And the "Western writer" label?

Birdsell: Well, of course it's important, but you see, it's like in a family: all the things that happen in a family can happen in the world, just like all the things in a small town happen in the world. It's universality.

Kruk: Do you like to read the postmodern, experimental writers?

Birdsell: I find them immensely clever—and I think I always admire what I can't do, you know.

Kruk: So you'd say that this is something you *can't* do—or something you don't *want* to do?

Birdsell: It's something I couldn't do if I wanted to.... It isn't work that I find particularly engaging. Clever, humourous, witty — but not my favourite reading.

Kruk: Do you have a sense of yourself as possessing a particular voice?

Birdsell: I think the tone of the stories is different from that of the novel, but the world view, say, or "Where I'm coming from," is there in both of them. The style though, is pretty set: although I'm taking more chances with structure and things, I still have this really packed, dense style that I'm so conscious of, and keep wanting to make work better for me, but that's the way it comes out. I was talking to a woman who is translating *Ladies of the House* into French, and she's been doing it for two years now. She said, "It's very difficult to translate your work." And I said

"Why?" She said, "Because it's so definite, your word choice is so definite that it's hard to translate it."[3]

I think that being published three times is some measure of success. And that gives me the freedom to relax and to enjoy the process. I live in the work, and when it's over, it's not mine anymore. The pleasure is gone, and becomes somebody else's, and then the joy is going back and finding another story to work on.[4]

Winnipeg, Manitoba: April 1990

Notes

1 This increasingly influential national award was created by *Books in Canada,* the long-running literary review, in 1976. The magazine provided the prize money ($1000) and a short list, drawn up from the year's "First Novels" reviews. A jury of experienced Canadian fiction writers selected a winner from this list. Ten years later, Smith Books became a partner in the Award, contributing the prize money (now increased to $5000), though the selection process remained the same. Then in early 1995, Coles and Smith Books amalgamated into Chapters, a large Canadian-owned chain that regularly sponsors readings, talks and workshops. The Chapter/*Books in Canada* Award ceremony has been hosted by Chapters, at its Toronto flagship store, each spring since 1995.

2 The other nominees for the 1990 W H Smith/*Books in Canada* Award were: Marilyn Bowering's *To All Appearances a Lady* (Random House), Jacqueline Dumas's *Madeleine and the Angel* (5th House), Kenneth Radu's *Distant Relations* (Oberon), Barry Callaghan's *The Way the Angel Spreads Her Wings* (Lester and

Orpen Dennys), Kristjana Gunnars's *The Prowler* (Red Deer College Press).

3 *Ladies* has been translated into French as *Agassiz: nouvelles*, traduit de l'anglais par Maryse Trudeau (Montreal: Calliope du Roseau, 1990). Critic Dallas Harrison notes, "Although *Ladies of the House* won no award for Birdsell, it has the distinction of being an initial candidate for translation into French as part of *La Collection Calliope*, a series designed to provide for the first time translated versions of a wide variety of English-Canadian fiction to francophone readers...." Dallas Harrison, "Sandra Birdsell (1942-   )," *Canadian Writers and Their Works,* eds. Robert Lecker, Jack David, Ellen Quigley. Introd. George Woodcock. Fiction series, vol. 12 (Toronto: ECW Press, 1995) 15-68. Quote p. 36.

4 Since our conversation, Birdsell has published *The Two-Headed Calf* (McClelland and Stewart, 1997), a third collection of short stories, which was nominated for the Governor General's Award, English-Canadian Fiction. See Author's Note for more information.

Joan Clark:

Letting it Rip

Kruk: You began your writing career with children's books, I understand—? And had real success with that, before moving on to adult fiction: your two story collections, *From a High Thin Wire* (1982) and *Swimming Toward the Light* (1990), and your novel *The Victory of Geraldine Gull* (1988).

Clark: Well, that's not quite true: I was writing adult fiction all along, and the first thing I wrote was adult poetry. And then, after I wrote my first books, *Girl of the Rockies* (1968) and *Thomasina and the Trout Tree* (1971), I started writing short stories and published a few in *The Journal of Canadian Fiction.* I wrote *The Hand of Robin Squires* (1977). And then I wrote more short stories, and I was publishing them here and there—so there was that duality in my writing almost from the start. Once I've learned how to do something, and have done it a certain way, I have to move onto something entirely different, or move back and forth.

Kruk: In other words, that kind of dichotomy—between your children's fiction and your adult fiction—breaks down when you look at your actual writing career: you were working on the stories that came out in *From a High Thin Wire* for a long time, and that collection was published in '82, published in between your children's novels, which were published in the '80s, leading up in *Geraldine Gull.* But I guess you got a lot more attention with *Geraldine,* because of the nominations [for the Governor General's Award and the W H Smith/*Books in Canada* First Novel Award] and the CAA [Canadian Authors Association] Award—

Clark: Yes, and I also think the adult novel is where most of the attention is. I mean, if you write poetry, it's very difficult for anyone to notice; it's not mainstream, and children's writing is ... it's off to one side. And short stories are considered hard to sell, but the novel, you know, is taken seriously. I think there's a not-so-subtle pressure on writers, too, to write a novel. Publishers prefer you to write one. Because I think they're much easier to market.

Kruk: I'm interested in why you wrote a linked collection of stories like *Swimming*, as opposed to writing a novel, then.

Clark: I didn't know I was going to go on writing about this woman, that's the first thing. I just wrote the first story in *Swimming* all by itself, and that's all I was interested in at the time. So you see, I wasn't thinking about her [Madge] all the time. But she just kept intruding on me....

When my editor at Macmillan read the manuscript of *Swimming,* she said, "Joan, do you think of this as a collection of stories, or as a novel?" And I said, Oh no, I definitely did it as a collection of stories. I think of them as stories, because of the way they came to me. I didn't write them as a novel. I got in and out of them. I wrote "Luna Moths" first. It was about a young girl, eight or nine, on a beach in Nova Scotia, Somerville Beach, outside of Liverpool. It was her sensuousness, and her discovery of sexuality, that interested me, and it all came from an image: I remember coming out of the cottage one morning and seeing Luna moths (which are not indigenous to Nova Scotia) all over the roof of the cottage.

Well, then I tried to imagine what she'd be like as an adult. So then I wrote another story: "The Madonna Feast." I put her on the West Coast, and that was instinctive, I knew there was going to be movement, I guess I sensed it: there has been a lot in my life, though Madge is not me, of course. Then I wrote "Colour Wheel," which is about the colours of light and life, which uses the colour wheel, and is in the middle, exact middle. I mean, I didn't write it like a novel.

Kruk: It wasn't a continuous process....

Clark: In a way I wrote them in pairs, and then I got to about eight or nine, and because they were all about the same person, I had to decide: do I keep on going, or not? I kept fiddling around with them, and then I had written myself into a corner, as my editor pointed out, because I had all these stories which were arranged chronologically, roughly, although there's a lot of crossing over, and my editor said, "You know, you've opened up gaps, there are parts of her life you really haven't dealt with, so I think if you're going to go this route, you better think about it."

Kruk: Think about filling in those gaps?

Clark: Yes, so then I wrote two more stories. And I was finished, pretty well. With the last draft I was thinking of it, then, as a book, so I was very aware of the shape of it. So in that sense, I suppose, it became a little more novelistic. But I still think of them as short stories; they came to me as short stories, no question about that.

Time management also has a lot to do with it. Because I write something, and then I put it away in a file. After you've lived some more, more things have happened, or you've observed them, then you sort of collect stories.

Kruk: So the stories are sort of like cast-off skins....

Clark: Yes. I find short stories have a lot to do with where I am and who I am—who I've been—in a way that a novel doesn't. A novel takes....

Kruk: More invention?

Clark: No, no, not more invention. You have to be very inventive to write short stories. It's got more to do with time, I keep coming back to time and how you manage it. *Geraldine Gull* took me six years to write, seven—mind you, I wrote other things in the meantime. Meanwhile you're living, you know. Lots of things are happening to you. There's a whole dynamic there. When you sit down to write that novel, that dynamic is not, in a direct way, influencing the novel, because that novel's gone so long along its path, it's taken a life of its own. It's off in this direction here [gestures], but my life is going on over *here*.

Kruk: So how autobiographical is *Swimming*?

Clark: It is and it isn't. I'm going to be thought of as Madge by some people. There's a lot of me in Madge, make no mistake. But she certainly isn't me. There certainly are a lot of parallels, to my life: particularly places where I lived. These stories take place in Liverpool, Nova Scotia; I lived there. Sussex, New Brunswick; I lived there. I lived in Sydney Mines. All the places are named exactly what they are. I felt quite a bit freer, writing this book.

Kruk: Freer than when writing *Wire*....?

Clark: Yes. I think the style's freed up a lot. I think it's much more confident. I just sort of—"let it rip."

I didn't have the angst about not wanting to hurt somebody. And some of the people I was writing about—and when I say "writing about," I don't mean my characters *were* these people, but I'm talking about who inspired them—these people were dead. And I'd come to terms with this moral dilemma: when you've got a story to tell, do you tell it? The person I would have to think about, in this collection, would be my sister. I mean, it's not her exactly. She's not really Ardith....

Kruk: But she's going to see similarities....

Clark: Oh she's read it already. Just as I showed her the story "From a High Thin Wire"—I was very concerned about that when I first wrote it. And I was so grateful to my sister. I said, "Well, what do you think, Gail? Do you have any trouble with this?" She said, "No—that's just your point of view. If I was telling it, I'd probably tell it very differently." That's exactly right, it *is* just a point of view.

Kruk: The collection of connected short stories is almost a Canadian tradition in a way: I mean I think of Alice Munro's *Lives of Girls and Women*....

Clark: I've been very influenced by Alice, I'm very happy to say that. The thing is she's the best short story writer, bar none, that we have in the country, and if I'm going to be influenced by any writer, I'd just as soon be influenced by the best. Margaret Laurence is also an influence.

Kruk: Yes, I was thinking of *A Bird in the House*.

Clark: Yes ... and well, just her work, and her passion, her passion. I also admire Alice's toughness. She's very hard on herself as a writer. She doesn't seem to have an exaggerated view of herself. Also, I think she's aware of the debt she owes people.

Kruk: You mean, that she's responsible towards her past?

Clark: It's the ego thing again, knowing that you are just one other human being, that the kind of thing you're doing is dependent on the good nature, the good will, of people, and the fact that they will share things with you. I feel we have to continually be aware of that. I've heard one writer say, "Of course, I imagined all that"—there's almost a denial that there's any link with humanity; that this writer's greatness and talent and skill and imagination are why these stories work so well.

You see, I come from an Irish-Scottish background where you bury everything. There are things that just aren't talked about, so consequently, there have been problems with my writing. I had a grandmother on my mother's side of the family who was really interesting; she was related to William Lyon MacKenzie. She wouldn't talk about it; she believed all history had no connection with the present. And she had all *kinds* of stories. But do you think she would share them? She denied the past.

Kruk: The idea being that there's something wrong about story-telling, and story-making–

Clark: Yes. There's this terrible fear, that a writer is going to expose something that is insidious and dangerous; there's a real fear of artists in our society, there really is. This is one of the reasons why these book-banners and censors are at work: they're terrified.

I think a lot of it, though, goes back to our educational system, the fact that we weren't really taught to appreciate literature. A lot of people don't know what literature is, you see. All they can see is the exposé, they can't see the shape, they can't understand what the writer did—for instance, what Alice Munro accomplished in these stories.

Kruk: Speaking of literary educations, did you have a good one?

Clark: Well it was sure hit-and-miss. I mean, I was always a reader. My mother was always a reader. She read to me and so on.... But you see, where I grew up—in small towns, in Nova Scotia, there wasn't an awful lot to read. The local library was above the Fire Hall, and you went up and read everything that there was there. It was very eclectic. I mean, I'd read Nancy Drew in the same breath I'd read Charles Dickens. In high school, I had a marvellous English teacher. We never wrote fiction, or even poetry. But certainly in terms of an appreciation of literature, I owe her a lot.

Kruk: Who would you say was the first Canadian author you came across?

Clark: Well, I would have to say probably Earle Birney's *David;* I loved that poem.

Kruk: And in terms of fiction?

Clark: I would say Morley Callaghan; it was the only thing I was exposed to. "The Snob," I think it was.... Then Hugh MacLennan's work. I read some of Tom Raddall's stuff, and then of course, like everybody else, Margaret Laurence...

I mean, this just had a tremendous effect on me, the fact that these women were writing. Obviously I do admire the work of many men—I like Guy Vanderhaeghe, Timothy Findley and so on, I admire their work, but it was the *women*, it was the fact that women were doing this, these women who had children! That's always been there, that's had such an influence on me. Just the *doing,* even more than the work itself.

Kruk: Right: you realize it can be done.

Clark: I remember when I had two children ... at that time Margaret Laurence was writer-in-residence at the University of Toronto, and my sister at that time was working at the CBC, she was a producer. And she was producing a program in which Margaret Laurence was being interviewed. My sister told her that she had this sister who was writing away, and asked her if she had any advice. Margaret Laurence said, "Just tell her to keep on writing, not to give up." Of course she had never seen a thing I had written or anything; what else would she say! But oh I held onto that ... like it was a precious piece of glass or pottery or something.

Marian Engel was in there too....These were women too, you know, who were brought up in small towns. And years later, there was Alice Munro, doing a small town. Margaret Laurence was from a small town. I mean now "small town, main street" is a cliché, but it's really had a very significant effect on fiction writing in this country: "Small Town Canada."

Kruk: I'm very interested in this whole idea of women writing, and the big question is "Do women write differently from men?" What would your response be to that?

Clark: Well, to be honest, I haven't given that very much thought. I do know that I'm offended when I hear a comment like, "Oh, she's writing about relationships—again." Well, I intend to write about relationships, that's what I'm interested in; I'm not interested in reinventing the world. I'm too much of a realist, too much of a pragmatist, for that. Sometimes I think it's even somewhat silly.... And that has everything to do with being a woman. So, in terms of my preoccupations, they are definitely strongly female. And I think they're every bit as important, maybe more important, than a lot of male preoccupations.

I was talking to a male writer last year about *Cat's Eye*. I really liked it. The part that was all about these young girls and their relationships—I really ate that up. I asked him what he thought of it. And he said that he thought it was probably a woman's book. And I rose about six inches off the chair: "What do you mean, a woman's book!" Because I felt it was said in a pejorative way, you know?

Kruk: So it appears there's a stigma attached to "women's writing," or the concept of it....

Clark: Well I think there still is; it's still there; for example, in the term "kitchen sink realism." I think that these preoccupations are valid and important. I'm interested in them, no apologies. It's high time we *did* write about them.

     But I don't know if I've answered your question....?

Kruk: Well, you have in a way. You've suggested that women are more interested in relationships, and I think I agree. I wouldn't go so far as to say that there's something innate in men and women that explains that, but rather that women's distinctive socialization frequently affects their choice of subject matter.

Clark: But I think this is still there: male writers are more inclined to read books about men, and women about women. There's this polarity, and this whole Women's Press thing. The whole idea— which is preposterous—that only women can write in a valid way from a woman's point of view (and presumably men, from a man's point of view) is very dangerous.[1] I don't think you can territorialize the imagination.

Kruk: Would you say you are sympathetic with feminist views? Would you consider yourself in any way consciously writing as a feminist?

Clark: That's too much of a label for me. In fact, on all fronts, I try to avoid labelling or jargon. I just cannot line up with the pack in anything. Although I've always considered myself a feminist. I never doubted that I was a feminist, from the early days.

     But in terms of my writing, I never think of that consciously; I never think "Oh, I'm a feminist writer" or "I'm a political writer." I'm just interested in the story. I think when you get to the point of trying to get your message across, I think you kill your fiction. I'm more interested in the inner workings of the story, the subtlety and so on....

Kruk: That question of literary politics came up, of course, in the discussion about *Geraldine Gull* in the *Books in Canada* interview (December 1989), where the interviewer asked you about the issue of writing about native people, as a non-native, and these kinds of concerns.[2]

Clark: I didn't feel I was speaking for native people; I think native people are increasingly able to speak for themselves. I mean, I just had a story that I felt very strongly about, and so I wrote it: full stop.

I guess I feel that way about feminism; I'm sure that creeps into my stories. It's certainly evident in *Swimming Toward the Light*. But I'm not interested in black and white writing. Life is very muddy, it's contradictory, it's not straightforward. I *want* those ambiguities, those tensions, to be in my work.

Kruk: Right. So I guess the same questioning would apply to any label such as "regionalism," especially since you've moved around so much....

Clark: That's right—I mean, where do I belong?

Kruk: Though you did say you feel drawn to the Atlantic provinces.

Clark: Well, I definitely do, there's no question but I do, because that's where I was born and brought up, but you know, here I am living now in Newfoundland, and I'm a "Come-From-Away"! When I was living in Alberta, there were the prairie writers, and clearly I wasn't one of them, though I was living there—they were prairie writers, and I never felt part of that. I felt a part of the writing community, but I didn't feel a part of that regional creative writing. Yet some of our strongest writing comes out of the regions. So I'm not denying the importance of regions at all. Now I'm a part of the literary community in Newfoundland; in fact, I'm president of the Writers Union of Newfoundland and Labrador this year [1990]....

It's also bothered me that I've moved around so much: or it did. I thought I if I was any kind of writer at all, I would go back to Atlantic Canada, back to Nova Scotia, stay there and write about it. And then I realized that because I'm *not* there, I'm writing a different type of story, I'm bringing another perspective to it. I'm not sure that I *could* just write about Nova Scotia; maybe I have to be away. There were stories, that if I hadn't moved, I never would have written: *Geraldine Gull* is an example. I never would have written that story if I hadn't lived up near Hudson Bay. So then I began to see that my moving around was a strength.

I also went through a period of time when—I've always been terribly impressionable; you wonder if you ever grow out of it—when it seemed that the women writers, most of them, were separated, or divorced, and their families split up, and I wondered if this has to be done, to be a writer.

Kruk: Like, you have to leave your husband, so you can be a *real* woman writer—!

Clark: I thought "I'm too settled" or "I'm too domestic." And actually I'm *quite* domestic in lots of ways. You know, I like being home, I like having my plants to water.... And I like having my paintings around me. I'm never happier than when I'm at home, with the door closed, the phone off the hook, and I have all this place to myself to write and to read. It's just wonderful; it's heaven! Close as I can get to it. But I can remember going through that stage where that fact, my married domesticity, really bothered me.

Kruk: Then there's the *other* sixty-four dollar question: "What is a Canadian writer?" A lot of people would say that, just by virtue of our achievements, we've transcended that question....Would you?

Clark: I think John Metcalf has said this before: we're more international now as writers. Well, perhaps we are, but there still are a lot of Canadian writers who aren't international, whose work is still unknown outside Canada.

It's very interesting, my agent has been sending *Geraldine Gull* to various American publishers, and received I don't know how many wonderful letters of rejection.... The gist of it is: "Oh we really like this novel, but we don't think we could sell it in the United States. This book is too Canadian." So if anybody doubts that we have a Canadian culture....

Still, I think you have to write what you want to write; that's first and foremost. You have to keep going back to why you write. When I talked about the fact that I respect the way Alice Munro has kept her rootedness, I know it's important for me to keep coming back to why I'm writing this story ... and that I choose to do this.

Kruk: So you write largely for yourself, then?

Clark: I think I must write for myself primarily, because I'm not conscious when I'm writing of pleasing any particular person. I'm not, really. When I get to the final drafts, I hope there's a perfect reader out there who'll pick up on this, or like this....That goes for my children's work, too. In fact, I was asked that the question by an editor, and I said, "Oh when I write a children's book, I concentrate on the story, I don't worry too much about 'Will a ten-year-old like this?'" It's hard enough, you know, just to try to get it right, to pull it off, without all this other stuff to worry about.

Kruk: You're motivated by integrity to the work–

Clark: *Absolutely.* It's the only thing. When I go out to kids and speak to them, I've often said that I think of the inside of my head as filled with undiscovered countries: when I write, I visit one of them.

Kruk: How conscious are you of your craft as you're writing—do you have a kind of aesthetic? I notice your sentences are not really ornate; they're more clear.

Clark: I really work at trying to get my sentences, my prose, as clear—as clean—as I can. Uncluttered. Yet I want the writing to be evocative, too. *Swimming Toward the Light* is more lyrical, more metaphorical, than *From a High Thin Wire.*

When I'm in the early stages of a story, I spend a lot of time doing what I call "circling": writing around it. Thinking about it ... because I've got to get the right angle. So to avoid false starts, or going in and feeling it's wrong, I take my time. All the stories in *Swimming* were written this way. I'm not thinking about craft or anything like that at this point.

What I really want to do is create a story that's layered. I want to leave enough room in the story for it to breathe. But when I start writing, I think more about how I'm going to put all these things that surface together. Then I get into the craft. Of course I do endless revisions. I even revise stories when they're published. When I get up to read—and I love to read—it's very seldom I can read a story without revising it. It's like eating peanuts; you can't stop.

Kruk: The amazing thing is that there are so many wonderful women writers today writing short stories. It seems as if the floodgates have been opened....

Clark: Well, again, I think the attraction probably goes back to the question of time management: the fact that when you're bringing up children, a short story is a manageable form. It takes me about five to eight weeks to write a short story. Before I knew better, I was probably doing it in a couple of weeks. But still—you could see the light at the end of the tunnel.

Kruk: So you sort of make a virtue of necessity?

Clark: Yes—I think that has something to do with it.

Mississauga, Ontario: March 1990

Notes

1 Joan Clark is referring to a debate in the Canadian writing community which flared up in the 1990s, touched off by controversial policies about literary "appropriation of voice" at the Women's Press of Toronto. For an excellent sampling of views on this topic, see "Whose Voice Is It, Anyway? A Symposium on Who Should be Speaking for Whom," *Books in Canada* 20. 1 (Jan./ Feb. 1991) 11-17. Contributors include Sandra Birdsell, George Bowering, Marilyn Bowering, Beth Brant, George Elliott Clarke, Don Coles, Cyril Dabydeen, Beverley Daurio, Louis Dudek, Maggie Helwig, M. T. Kelly, Daniel David Moses, Marlene Nourbese Philip, H. R. Percy, James Reaney, Libby Scheier, M. G. Vassanji.

2 "Getting it Right," Interview with Joan Clark by Patrick O'Falherty, *Books in Canada* 18.9 (Dec. 1989) 15-17.

Timothy Findley:

"I Want Edge"

Kruk: I'd like to start by talking a bit about the short stories—a relatively neglected part of your canon. What draws you to the short story form? Do you know when you begin that you're working on a short story, as opposed to a novel?

Findley: I guess I'm drawn to the short story by the fact that it was the first thing I ever read. Children's stories, very often, come in that short form, where you encounter the whole story in one sitting. And then of course, when you begin to read yourself, it's the most accessible form. There's something about the self-contained entity, that is taken at one dose....

Kruk: Which is satisfying....?

Findley: Yes. And the first things I wrote were short stories. Maybe I should say: the first things I wrote with any sense that I was sitting down deliberately, to do something other than merely entertain myself. And they were the first things, too, that got published.

In terms of form, the thing is what it is. And I know what it is I'm writing fairly quickly. Once or twice I've been appallingly wrong, of course—thinking I was writing a short story and then discovering I was writing a novel, and *then* not being able to finish the novel. Or vice versa: thinking I was writing a novel, and discovering it was a short story. Mostly I gave the project up where that mistake had been made, whether it was made in one direction or the other. Thornton Wilder—seemingly one of the most succinct and articulate writers of his time—told me that he had been forced to abandon voices when he was already five hundred hand-written pages into them. He said: "The waste paper basket is the writer's best friend." You have to learn to be ruthless when a piece doesn't work out.

Basically, the stories in *Stones* (1988) and the stories in *Dinner Along the Amazon* (1984)—and stories I'm writing now for a book called *Dust*[1]--were stories from the start, with one exception that I can think of immediately. One, two, maybe three— are novellas, or *extremely* long short fiction, and one is lifted *holus bolus* from a novel.... "Lemonade" *(Dinner)* is almost a novella. Another is "Hello Cheeverland, Goodbye" (*Dinner*), which is an extremely long piece of short fiction. And the other is "Dinner along the Amazon" itself, which is a portion from a novel—the novel that ended up being *Headhunter* (1993). The first version of *Headhunter* got written in the early 1970s and two of its leading characters appear in "Dinner Along the Amazon": Olivia, who carries the talking fetus, and Fabiana, the gallery owner. The first attempt, in the 70's, didn't work because I simply wasn't ready to write it. I didn't know enough.

Kruk: What really strikes me, when you talk about the different ways stories develop, are the *Dinner Along the Amazon* stories "Daybreak at Pisa" and "Out of the Silence," which you call plays-in-progress, or ideas for plays–

Findley: And in fact they are.

Kruk: Did they ever become plays?

Findley: Yes, they did. The really sad thing about "Out of the Silence," the T.S. Eliot piece, was that I got quite far along with it—it was originally called "Rat's Alley"—and it was about Eliot and his first wife, Vivvien. I think it was a very good piece of theatre. But just at that moment, along came a play called *Tom and Viv* and I was stopped in my tracks.[2]

The "Pisa" piece, about Ezra Pound, became a radio play. So that worked out quite well. It was published in 1995 as *The Trials of Ezra Pound* by Blizzard.

Kruk: I suggest that "Daybreak at Pisa," where you've even included the stage directions, can be read as a meta-theatrical, meta-fictional piece, in that you're dramatizing Ezra Pound's *self-dramatization*....

Findley: Yes. I'm still fascinated by that idea: that writing is a performance art. And vice versa also— you mustn't ignore the fact that the play is still the written word, and the eye can lift it into the mind, as well as the ear....

Kruk: In *Stones*, the Minna and Bragg stories ["Minna and Bragg," "A Gift of Mercy"] are, I think, quite a departure for you, because you are dealing more explicitly with homosexuality.... And also relating aspects of your relationship with Marian Engel. It's interesting that you wrote *two* stories about these characters.

Findley: Two then—and now, more. In *Dust [to Dust]*, there are two Bragg and Minna stories—and I'm sure there will ultimately be others.[3] Perhaps a whole collection. They'll come out in story form first, but I also think that, at some point, if I have the energy to do this, their lives would make a wonderful play. Glorious, gutsy roles for actors; especially Minna. With elements of all of the unwritten Bragg and Minna stories, and the four written ones, there has to be a play in these two people....

Kruk: You also have two stories about Bud and Neil in *Stones:* "The Name's the Same" and "Real Life Writes Real Bad." We get two stories, back to back, about the brothers.

Findley: Yes. And again in a story called "War," and another called "About Effie" in *Dinner Along the Amazon*. Aspects of Bud and Neil also turn up in Gilbert and Hooker—the brothers in *Last of the Crazy People*. I'd never thought of that before, but it's quite true. Those two brothers make their way —under a lot of different names—through a lot of my writing.

Kruk: So this recurring pair, the two brothers, can be classed as one of your writerly obsessions....

Findley: Yes, and it is more apt to pop up in different forms, because you could say they also appear in the title story in *Stones*. There are two brothers there who are very much in line with the other pair.

Kruk: There's a clear contrast established between your two brothers: one seems more obsessed with the traditional male role, and the other is a critic, looking on....

Findley: The sad thing is, the one who's engrossed with the male role, is also the one who is more accomplished–

Kruk: I question that–

Findley: Up to a point, I mean. In "Stones," Cy is definitely the one who takes charge. Very much in charge when the father is causing trouble. He has to do the daring thing, the difficult thing: he has to confront the father. That was interesting to me.... When I use the word "sad" about the elder brother, I mean that—in "Real Life Writes Real Bad," he loses his grip and disintegrates.

Kruk: What about influences on your short story writing?

Findley: You pass through stages; it's hard to hold on to influences as you get further along—and I don't just mean in the aging sense. As you pass through the various stages of writing, as you learn more about what you're doing.... I have passed through an *enchantment* with Du Maupassant, O. Henry, the classics—Kipling—the people who told you a story that had a surprise or trick ending. But short stories have changed since the days of those guys.... I went through a period where J. D. Salinger's book, *Nine Short Stories* was very important to me. Almost a bible. I think I read every one of those stories *eighty times* over a period of five years. The book fell to pieces in my hands! It was because *he* was my Raymond Carver; what Carver now is to young writers—and I hope that passes, by the way.... I suspect too much has been made of Carver for his own good. This over-adulation also happened to Salinger, and it stopped him from writing. Carver's death was tragic. It brought a *growing* writer too soon to the end.

Kruk: You don't approve of Carver?

Findley: Oh, it's not that I don't approve; he was a wonderful writer—although I think his writing was beginning to be self-parody just before he died. Also you get awfully sick of reading Carver imitations.... Could we leave the poor man alone to be himself, for one thing: stop the imitation, because imitation isn't getting anyone anywhere....

Kruk: But it's where you start, perhaps.

Findley: Sure it is. I don't mean that as meanly as it sounds; it's just that—I think it's very dangerous that people settle into Carver's style. Or Salinger's. Or anyone's. So far as I was concerned, I had read these nine stories over and over until they were done unto death. I don't think I ever wrote like Salinger, but I think I set out to make the attempt.

Kruk: Would you say you were trying to take the best from him—what he did in the short story form?

Findley: Yes, but ... I think I was ashamed of *stealing*.... Lest this sound noble, I mean I was afraid of being *found out;* I only mean it in that sense. Just—"Oh God, what if it sounds so much like Salinger they'll say 'Well, who the Hell is this Findley—why pay attention to him, he's only imitating Salinger.'" I wanted my own voice—but I hadn't found it. Finding your own voice is a writer's first duty.

Kruk: Were there any Canadian writers you were imitating?

Findley: Not then; not in my late teens and early twenties—and not in my late twenties, either....

Kruk: Although we have so many great short story writers....

Findley: Well, there were but I didn't know it, if you know what I mean. It's funny, I've just written a review for *Harrowsmith* of a book called *Wild Animals I have Known* ... short stories by Ernest Thompson Seton. I read them when I was a kid and loved them. And, of course, there was Morley Callaghan. He was the first writer I read—aside from Seton—who set his stories in my own world—and his—which was Toronto. You suddenly thought "My God, he's talking about Elm Street, and I know where Elm Street is." And he also wrote—*wonderfully* well. Interesting, classically structured—all kinds of good things can be said about Callaghan's novels, but the man was a short story writer, first and foremost. And I think he was a great one.

Also, don't forget how old I am. I'm sixty-five—one of a generation that includes the very best of our story writers—Alice Munro, Norman Levine, Margaret Atwood. Atwood is ten years younger but her first publication coincided with mine. So I have their example now, but not when I began.

Kruk: Okay I'm going to shift the focus, to the theme of gender. Here's a quote from critic Harry Brod: "While women have been obscured from our vision by being too much in the background, men have been obscured from our vision by being too much in the foreground."[4] Do you agree?

Findley: I'd have to take it as a jumping-off point ... but it's very interesting. I think there is a lot of truth to it, but you can spread that truth further than "men." The truth is, there are things in the foreground that are so subtle, that they are totally missed—and I think, unfortunately, a lot of men who don't like women—and there's a huge difference between men who don't "like" women, and men who are violent towards women—I think they miss *themselves*. So it isn't just the observer, from the outside, who can't see them, it's the guy who's out there with the biceps, the manipulative hands, the gun. He could be staring in the mirror and he wouldn't see himself—he's too big! Too overwhelming.... If you translate this to the writing world, think of someone like Mailer. Yes—a fine writer—but he wouldn't recognize himself as others see him. His view of himself is entirely self-engrossed. I prefer male writers such as Cheever—Styron—Ondaatje. As men, they see and write their *true* selves.

Oddly enough, I got turned on to this aspect of men in writing—and men in life, though it came out of writing first— when I read a piece about men by Gertrude Stein. It's an absolutely incredible piece. In it, she writes about men in a bar in France, and the men she's writing about are in a bar where men gather exclusively—but only because they are all men who've just left the same factory, they've just left the same workplace and they've come in the same condition into this place. And she writes so *wonderfully* about their beauty, their tiredness—their grace, their gentleness. All those things you wouldn't expect to discover in a bunch of *guys* standing in a *bar*, doing the "guy thing!" And I thought, how does a woman write so wonderfully about this very male milieu? Stupid people will say: "Well—she was a lesbian," which has nothing to do with the price of eggs at all. She was looking totally objectively at these men, in this place, in this situation. Reading it, I was thrown back on the reality, and the memory, of when I went to work in a factory, as a very young man.... This was the 1940s and it *was* a hyper-masculine place. I thought I might be beaten to death! But having been told, "Be ready for the 'guy stuff' to happen," what you get instead is a *wonderful* gentleness, and a sense of mutual protection. No come-ons, nobody putting the make on you, nothing! Whether it is that the pressure of the presence of women is taken away, they're not strutting, they're not doing all the things you think they would be doing, and they're not ... fearsome. Laughable caricatures of manhood very quickly evaporate.... Out of Stein's writing, I got a sense of men I already knew, and it threw me back into that reality—behind the stereotypes. And I got that from a *woman's* writing.

At the same time, having said *all* of that, I obviously have to address the fact, that I have also met extremely violent men. Killers. I had a man try to kill me, and in the same way that he would try to kill a woman, because it was during a sexual encounter, and had to do with a particular use of force.

Kruk: So are you saying that you were placed in a position parallel to a woman's, in that you were being treated as the "feminine" object of his rage?

Findley: Yes, yes, but in a particularly insidious way.... I am willing to stand corrected on this, but this is what I suspect: that far more women are put in jeopardy by men whose "persuasive" powers are latent in the power of their masculine bodies. I was frightened into submission. I think there's far more of that going on than actual pounding. Psychological intimidation, but it's based on the physical possibility: "I can kill you." Yes—he can. Because I was frightened just long enough to get in this corner ... and then, of course, once you're in the corner, how do you get out? This is when you acquiesce in order to survive.

Kruk: Obviously, we're talking about gender here, but we're also talking about how that intersects with your "otherness" as a homosexual writer. That places you in a position, some of your writing suggests, analogous to a woman's position—without necessarily creating homosexual stereotypes, or using effeminate language. So many of your characters in *Dinner* are women, for instance, and they seem to be associated with a certain type of perception, or perspective, that you identify with. Would you draw that parallel yourself?

Findley: Yes, but I'm very glad to hear you say that it is not— necessarily—a parody of femininity, and that I am not speaking in an effeminate voice as a consequence of that identification. I am, after all, a man. And just as "male" as any other man.

Kruk: True. But as a writer, as a creator of characters, you do seem to ally yourself with women as "other"—

Findley: Yes. But I've never, equally, felt that I wanted to be identified only as a feminist-sympathetic, or as a gay, writer.... Labels are confining. I refuse them. But I'm not turning my back on homosexuality. I'm perfectly happy to have it said, "He is a homosexual." I just don't think I want to be collected exclusively in gay anthologies.... I want my world to be wider than my sexuality. And it is. I say that emphatically.

Kruk: I attended your Duthie lecture in Vancouver [October 1993]. In it, you made a very impassioned plea for resisting the "word wardens." I thought, "How interesting," because you have this ability to be double in your presentation. You were speaking as someone who has been stigmatized as a gay person, but you were also appealing to the larger, literary tradition. So you were speaking both from the margins *and* from the centre.... Do you ever feel as though you might be part of a "gay" tradition of writers?

Findley: No, although there are voices in that tradition that I look at with particular respect. I will never recover from Tennessee Williams.... But I think it has to have something to do with the fact that he was there in my moment: as I was emerging into the world of sexuality, he was emerging into the world of writing, as a man of promise. When I turned sixteen was when I started having my whole life. A "sexually explicit" life—an actor's life— etcetera—and that was the moment of *The Glass Menagerie* and subsequently, of *A Streetcar Named Desire.* And of course, immediately I recognized the kinship between Blanche Dubois's situation and what it was to be a homosexual, *in that moment.* It would be, I hope, different now. In that moment, Williams's was the voice that defined my dilemma....

Kruk: So there was an autobiographical element for Williams with Blanche DubBois....?

Findley: Oh, there can't be any question, there can't be! Though I think he denied it.... What I'm saying is, when people say, about Blanche, that she's really just a guy in drag: it's not so. That is, as a character, she remains absolutely, totally female. And it's *not* a good idea to go off into–

Kruk: —translating the sexes, or sexualities, of characters to fit their author's—?

Findley: —because that ain't what's happening. But at the same time, there is this kinship in situations where women and homosexual men encounter violent attitudes in men.

Kruk: Maybe it's more accurate to say that there is a submerged tradition of gay male writers, writers who are mainstream, but also gay, whether openly or not. Such as Tennessee Williams ... Somerset Maugham ... Proust ... and Oscar Wilde.

Findley: Or William Burroughs—another interesting figure. And, of course, John Cheever.

Kruk: So, does that description fit your sense of your work more accurately?

Findley: Yes, it does.... Wilde and Cheever have been great heroes of mine.

Kruk: Michael Kaufman says, "Masculinity is power. It is also exclusive heterosexuality, for the maintenance of masculinity requires the repression of homosexuality."[5] How do you feel about that formulation?

Findley: I think he's wrong. It depends on how you define masculinity.... I would never define masculinity merely as *power*.... All the masculine qualities are not negative. I think there are wonderfully masculine men—and that's what I was saying before, about working in the factory, when I was in the position to be extremely vulnerable, and felt so: and I was wrong! Masculinity, when it is secure in itself, doesn't need to beat up on the world. And it doesn't. Not in the best of men.

I think another important aspect of the question we just finished before starting this one is: there's something that has to be said, too, about the fact that both a Blanche Dubois and a

Timothy Findley and a George and Martha [from Albee's *Who's Afraid of Virginia Woolf?*] and their homosexual counterparts, when they come in contact with men—either as women, or as homosexuals—they stand the chance of meeting every kind of men. But in the sensational sense, there is an acceptance of the stereotype and this is how the general subject of homosexuality is subsumed into the mass media. The stereotype becomes a part of the storyline, for the mass of people. Brute/fairy, brute/female [mimes simpering expression]; you know, Blanche Dubois languishing, falling backwards ... fainting in the presence of the "brute." What Michael Kaufman [who founded the White Ribbon Campaign, which Findley has joined] described feeds a certain prejudice. I'm a great admirer of his, but I think in this he is wrong.

Kruk: "Maybe we have to get rid of the word 'manhood.' It's done a lot of damage to both men and women." That's what you told Alan Twigg.[6] You still agree?

Findley: Yes. I still think that, because we load the words *manhood* and *manly* and *masculinity* with meanings that are ... killers. In themselves.

Kruk: In your interview with Alan Twigg, you also mentioned "Men's terrible loneliness. Women also have loneliness, but it's not the same kind."[7]

Findley: I don't think men have ever learned how to benefit from one another's company in the way that women have learned to benefit from one another's company ... with no sexual connotations whatsoever. I'm always fascinated to see that, in so many photographs of men, if they are photographed together in any context, you always see the hand placed over the shoulder, with the fingers curled against it. [demonstrates] The fingers aren't allowed to grip the other person; you aren't allowed to *hold* the other person.

Kruk: This is a result of the restriction, or taboo, on demonstrations of affection between men, isn't it?

Findley: But there has to be built into that attitude the fact that men have a different physical reaction to holding, and being held, which is *purely* biological.... I think this whole subject of gender and sexuality, both as it touches social issues and moral issues, and the issues of writing and of art, has been muddied by a misinterpretation—sometimes deliberate—of the role biology plays in our behaviour as men and women.

Let me tell you a quick anecdote, because it has to do with the way I think about men, and it has to do partly with what Gertrude Stein said about the gentleness of men. This gentleness is sometimes generated by the bewilderment men feel in the "traitorous" aspect of their bodies. It also answers something about Michael Kaufman's statement—and the question of why men can't have casual contact....

This is some years ago, because I'm now sixty-five, so we're talking around 1970. A friend and I were on a beach together, and we were talking about having reached this age: we both had achieved forty and were passing into a new area of our lives. We had been at one time lovers, and we were still extremely close, very good friends. And we talked about the burst of sexual energy that had happened in our lives—and he said, "You know, you mustn't be afraid of it"—because I had laughed about an increased daily masturbation count and the increased daily "lust" count—"A lot of it is pure biology," he said. "Don't forget, you and I have now come to an age where our bodies are saying 'It's nearly over,' and from a purely biological standpoint—go straight to the science and nothing else—the thing is to broadcast as many seeds as far afield as possible."

Well, it's time we accepted that there is a biological factor in some of this behaviour. And because men get erections, they find that they can't press in close against another warm body with *quite* the same freedom that women can. And that's part of why the fingers are closed, which I think is sad. Because I have immense sympathy for men. Immense. And I cringe when I see what men go through sometimes, and think how sad it is that women only think of men as fumbling bastards who have nothing on their minds but sex ... when often what they are trying to achieve is grace in the face of biology.

There's an amusing side to this in the theatre that I noticed when I was a young actor and watching other young actors. When you embrace in the theatre, your bum always sticks out! And directors are always having to say to the actors, "Come on, bring the bum in." But of course there's a reason your bum is sticking out: you're *terrified* of making pelvic contact. Well, I hope we come to the moment when we can say, "Hey guys—women—everybody—this poses a problem for males that we can solve so simply by saying—'It's a fact.'" Maybe if men stopped being afraid of the embarrassment factor of "inappropriate" erections, "inappropriate" erections would stop being a problem.

Kruk: So, you're saying: we shouldn't make more of our sexual and physical differences than they are—but we should acknowledge their existence, also.

Findley: You have to acknowledge it, and it is as true of women as it is of men.

Kruk: In her interview with you, Barbara Gabriel suggested that the homosexual is in a privileged position for understanding the myths of gender a society promotes.[8]

Findley: Yes, I do think there are places where—probably because one is a homosexual—I do have the opportunity of seeing what it is women *are* enduring, that other men have failed to see; failed to see because there isn't the combination of close friend, lover, *plus* the homosexual.

And I think now that situation is being acknowledged, although in a very strange way, because people talk about this [1993] as being the year of lesbians and gay men. And about how there's been a lot of gender-bending, as they say, in the movies and plays recently.... A lot of to-do has been made of k. d. lang, and Boy George's comeback, and so on. I just think that a lot of that is superficial.... What I mean is, the perception is that we've solved a problem, or that it's over, or that we don't need to worry about the problems of homophobia and discrimination anymore. I think the problem basically still exists. Because we all seem to be willing to accept what k. d. lang is about doesn't mean there is any less masking of reaction to lesbians. It's a commercialized acceptance, not a true one.

Kruk: I would like to tie this issue of commercialization in, if I can, with your discussion—in interviews with Barbara Gabriel and Terry Goldie[9]—of cultural icons, especially with regard to *Famous Last Words* (1981). What do you mean by cultural icon? Is a cultural icon simply a celebrity?

Findley: No, because I think increasingly, and this is sad, everyone, and everything, will become iconic, in the Andy Warhol "fifteen minutes of fame" sense. But not necessarily in a bid—not right off the top—to be iconic, but simply in a bid to rule, in a bid to be the King or the Queen of the moment.

What I'm saying is, that people like Lana Turner, Ava Gardner, Elizabeth Taylor—people of that era—were thought of as public whores. Well, today, someone like Madonna touts herself as a public whore.

Kruk: But she's her own whore....

Findley: She's her own whore ... but she's more than that. No matter what one discovers about her, the damage I perceive her as doing—and this is the danger of the icons of this time—is that it is pure iconography with no substance. Nobody deserves six million dollars a year: *no one.*

Kruk: Would you describe yourself as a postmodernist writer?

Findley: I honestly don't know what that means.... With all due respect to Linda Hutcheon[10] and people like that, who have delved greatly in that whole world, I have to find it in other books and discover what it means....

Kruk: Does "realist writer" seem a more apt label to you?

Findley: No, and I hope not.... Taken with its literary face, I would hope I'm not a realist, because a realist is probably the dullest thing you can be.

Kruk: Could you elaborate on that?

Findley: Yes, but only to a degree. As we came out of the 1950s into the 1960s, there was this extraordinary revolution which took place. We entered this revolution through the medium of writers who started being known as Angry Young Men, and then the "kitchen-sink" school and so forth. And you got this "realist" aspect of writing which invaded the world of fiction and of theatre and films and everything became very grungy and very dark and very gritty and we explored a lot of so-called real lives. It was just like saying, "Of course, up until now we have *not* been exploring real life" [sarcastic chuckle]. Just because it was theatrical or satirical, it wasn't real.

So I'm saying all of this to get to my point: if by realist you actually mean an anchor in the *real* heart, the *real* spirit and the *real* turmoil of *real* life: then, yes. Alice Munro is a realist in that sense, but ... a great artist in the writerly sense ... and artist is a word she would absolutely loathe, I suspect, but it has to be used because that's what she is. There is art and there isn't, the touch is there or it isn't, and that's what catches you.... I guess it's those who write in the world of Alice Munro and Margaret Laurence but who fail to do it with their artistry, who are left—stranded—in mere reality. That's what I mean by realism, and that would worry me–

Kruk: You wouldn't want to be considered in that category–

Findley: Not only that, but it doesn't interest me as reading material, it doesn't interest me as an exploration of life. I want edge. And I'm delighted by the theatricality of what's happening in fiction now—and in the largeness of, for instance, Atwood's last book *The Robber Bride,* which I have not yet completed. The bigness of those people, and the bigness of the gestures. It gives both comic edge and tragic dimensions.

Kruk: So you see a certain theatricality coming out in recent literature–

Findley: Yes—theatricality being a very positive thing. The story has to hit you, and it can only do that with its theatricality—and so does a book when you open it—"All happy families are alike..."—or whatever it is that grabs you. Or what about John Irving's *The World According to Garp,* that marvellous opening line, walking with Garp's mother into the movie theatre and taking out a razor and doing terrible things to a man who molested her in the theatre—God!! [screams] Wonderful—it's time it happened! But ... you don't stop reading. Because it's theatrical.

Kruk: Maybe "theatrical realism" is a good way to describe what you're doing, then....

Findley: It's an *interpretation* of reality. That's what fiction *is--* that's what novels and stories and plays *are* ... and that's what *art* is. It is the articulation of the ordinary in a way that makes the ordinary seem cohesive, when in fact it's not. It *clarifies* the messed-up lack of cohesiveness in real life.

Have you ever read *Camille, La Dame aux Camellias,* the novel? It begins with Armand coming back, from Egypt, where his father has sent him to get rid of him. Marguerite—or Camille—has died and the boy comes back, that's where it begins. And do you know what he does? He digs up her body ... to prove that she is dead. And that's how it opens.

Kruk: Quite hair-raising.

Findley: It is hair-raising. *Now* when they do *Camille....* [he mimes a delicate cough]. I mean, when people think that someone dying of tuberculosis, has a slight cough—"We wouldn't want to over-do it, dear, catch their attention." Well, Marguerite Gauthier caught a lot of people's attention, and she's stayed in the imagination ever since she was created. For a reason: she has *edge.*

I've just stolen one of Dumas's images. There's a little girl in my most recent novel [*The Piano Man's Daughter,* 1995], who, when she's eleven, has her first period. And when she goes to school the next day, she wears a red ribbon in her hair, which is a signal to her friends ... that it's started. She's menstruating. Well, Marguerite Gauthier—and this is back in the 1840s—was a courtesan. And Dumas wrote this wonderful thing: when she appeared at the opera, she always carried camellias, and the camellias were usually white. But when she was having her period, they were red, and that meant men were to stay away now. And I thought, God, that's very daring, for that period in time, to write that.... And I stole the signal. But it isn't just that detail.... It's the fact that Dumas got so close to her.

Kruk: You drew on some aspects of your own growing up in your writing, and you have said that some family members saw it as a kind of invasion of privacy. How does the writer navigate that dilemma?

Findley: Well, the stories about Bud and Neil are fairly close to the stories about me and my brother. And "Real Life Writes Real Bad" is my attempt to articulate my reaction to what happened to my brother. That is to say, to lay it to rest to some degree ... to lay the *un*rest in a place where I could look at it objectively and say, "That's what happened. He died." And if you write about it, there are different ways of writing about it. You write about it in your journal, and that can be cathartic. But I don't think that there are aspects of making fiction that are cathartic. Fiction mustn't be written for that reason; there are rules. Somebody said—I think it may have been Thornton Wilder—"The worst reason to write of all is vengeance." Don't ever use your writing simply to get back at someone who did you wrong, or at life for being difficult. Don't cheapen what you're making by founding it on motives such as "I'm going to seek revenge." When Thomas Wolfe wrote *You Can't Go Home Again* and *Look Homeward, Angel*, he was trying to exorcise the past. Trying to exorcise the process of growing up in this very difficult family situation, with very sad circumstances. But what happens in those books, even when he tried to get back at his mother, and wanted to expose his mother as being destructive: he writes this incredible character! She becomes one of the great figures of modern American literature. So the creative impulse overrides the spirit of revenge. If you really are an artist, as Thomas Wolfe was, vengeance loses its face.

For instance, in my most recent novel, I have taken a physical aspect from someone I know ... this woman, a favourite aunt, has passed through all of my fiction. She'd had a stroke when she was in her thirties, so one side of her face was frozen and she spoke out of the other side [imitating], in this kind of 1930s "tough guy" way, so everything she said had this kind of....

Kruk: Edge?

Findley: Edge to it.... She was a theatrical being, whether she wanted to be or not, because it was part of her physical makeup. Well, my aunt turns into all kinds of people: she's Rosetta in *The Last of the Crazy People,* other characters. And she responded with great wisdom to the canon of Findley writing. She said to me, "You know, dear"—holding one of my books—"I've never read any of your books." She said "I don't think I know any of those people and I'm not sure I really care to. And I don't know what a homosexual is ... and I don't really care." Then her eyes sort of wandered over toward the window, and she said, "I really am proud of you." I think she was saying, "I know what you're doing.... This is what you *make* of us, but it isn't us." She had read it, and she was saying "You don't have to worry about what I know, about what aspects of this of are true. This is fiction." Whereas my mother and my brother and my father were always saying "What are you revealing about us now?" Well ... "NOTHING! [laughs] How can you think that all these people are you?" But on the other hand, the base is there, and why shouldn't it be? That's where the reality is....

Kruk: One last quote: you said to Graeme Gibson some time ago, "I've often sat down and tried to write a love scene between a completely normal man and a completely normal woman. And there's no way I'm going to do that without it turning out to be the biggest laugh of all time."[11] Can you explain what you mean by this provocative statement?

Findley: I think so. Basically all it means is, that as soon as sex becomes "literature," it starts taking on this other aspect. The sexiest thing is sex itself, but how do you describe it without falling back on synonyms and all this imagery of other stuff, like waves crashing on the shore ... and the iconery of sexual pleasure. It all starts turning into "Her skin was like...", "His mouth was like...."

Kruk: There's such a stock of clichés–

Findley: Yes, but as you fight your way through this jungle of clichés, trying to get to two people actually *doing* something together in bed—and be honest about it—then you very quickly come up against all kinds of barriers. Particularly back then, in 1971, when that comment was made. Which was when we were all trying to be more honest about the sexual revolution that had begun. Which meant people had to actually acknowledge who they were ... you couldn't hide behind all that imagery—it wasn't going to help you anymore. Either in real life, or in books.... So I just used to collapse—literally—across the table screaming with laughter and frustration: "There's no way I can describe this!" It was like those wonderful monologues that Bob Newhart used to do. You know the marvellous one about tobacco? "You roll it up in a piece of paper and then you put it in your mouth, and then—what?! You set it on fire? Oh, sure, Bob!"

So, if you think, now I'm going to write about sex—male-female, male-male, female-female, dog-dog or whatever, whatever!—it's only going to be Bob Newhart funny. Then, unfortunately, it took on a hideous look, because all the sex you got, in novels, short stories and in movies, was violent sex, because it was the only excuse to have sex ... grab the reader by the short hairs and say "I've gotcha, and you're in here until this is over."

So then sex took on an ugly face. First it had this romantic face, then it had this chaste face of poetry, then it got this ugly face.

Now, I think sex is beginning to emerge as what it is, which is to say it is something real you can write about. I think I've come closest to succeeding in *Headhunter*, where it has both the horrifying edge of the clinically pornographic—and also the much sparser, sparer description of passionate sex. The best book for depictions of *real* sex between men and women, since about 1986, is Michael Ondaatje's *In the Skin of a Lion*. It's erotic and it's never denigrating and yet it never *lingers* over the thing. It does what writing should do about all aspects of life: it puts it in front of you to the degree *only* that the story requires it ... and that's where the artistry comes in.

Toronto, Ontario: December 1993

Notes

1 Published as *Dust to Dust: Stories* (Toronto: HarperCollins, 1997).

2 *Tom and Viv,* written by British author Michael Hastings, was produced in London at Royal Court Theatre in 1984, produced off-Broadway in 1985 and made into a New Era/Miramax film in 1991.

3 The stories are "A Bag of Bones" and "Come as You Are" *(Dust to Dust)*.

4 Harry Brod, "The Case for Men's Studies," *The Making of Masculinities: The New Men's Studies* ed. Harry Brod, (Boston:

Allen and Unwin, 1987) 39-62. Quote pp. 40-41. An abridged and revised version of this essay appears as "New Perspectives on Masculinity: A Case for Men's Studies," in *Changing Men: New Directions in Research on Men and Masculinity,* ed. Michael Kimmel (Beverly Hills, Calif: Sage, 1987).

5 Michael Kaufman, "The Construction of Masculinity and the Triad of Men's Violence," in *Beyond Patriarchy: Essays by Men on Pleasure, Power and Change,* ed. Michael Kaufman (Toronto: Oxford UP, 1987) 1-29. Quotes pp. 13, 19.

6 From *Strong Voices: Conversations with 50 Canadian Authors* (Madeira Park, B.C.: Harbour, 1988). Quotes pp. 86-86.

7 See previous note.

8 "Would you agree that the homosexual is in a privileged position for understanding the myths of gender a society promotes?" From "Masks and Icons: An Interview with Timothy Findley," by Barbara Gabriel, *The Canadian Forum* (February 1986) 31-36. Quote p. 33.

9 Interview with Timothy Findley, by Terry Goldie, *Kunapipi* 6.1 (1984) 56-67.

10 Author of *The Canadian Postmodern: A Study of Contemporary English-Canadian Fiction* (Toronto: Oxford UP, 1988), plus other books treating postmodernism in literature.

11 From *Eleven Canadian Novelists: Interviewed by Graeme Gibson* (Toronto: Anansi, 1973) 119-49. Quote pp. 122-23.

Elisabeth Harvor:

"A Humiliation a Day"[1]

Kruk: Reviewers have talked about your second book, *If Only We Could Drive Like This Forever* (1988), as a "comeback" book—it received very good reviews. How do you feel about the differences between *If Only* and your first collection of short stories, *Women and Children* (1973)?

Harvor: In some ways I feel that *If Only* is the more emotional book, in the sense that it goes more deeply into emotions and tries to take them apart more, but I also feel that *Women and Children* (which I prefer to call by its new title, *Our Lady of All the Distances*) is the more reckless book.[2] The thing that bothers me about *Our Lady* now, though, is that it's a bit hectoring ... in a way the voice is cavalierly political, and I don't think I was ever really that kind of woman—I just sort of *fancied* myself as that kind of woman.

I feel there's more quietness in the second book, and it's less ... maybe less dazzling, in a way. Maybe you can't have both. Sometimes you have to make a choice and say, "No, I have to let this go, I have to hold this humour off, or this image off, to protect the emotional feeling of the moment." That I can't do something very clever here, even though I'm dying to do it. Whereas with *Our Lady*, if I thought of a great joke or image, I just tossed it in.

Also, when I was writing *Our Lady* I still had a lot of illusions about ... about what? Not about love so much, I don't think.... But I think I felt, when my children were young, that they would be better than anyone else's children. And that when they were adolescents, they would be better adolescents. And of course, they weren't. I think by then [writing *If Only*], some of my most cherished illusions had been stamped on, all over, and I was more humble. Also, most of the stories in *Our Lady* are fairly linear. Either that or they're flamboyant vignettes. But in the second book, the stories are much less vignette-ish. The one story that looked as if it was in danger of becoming an extended vignette was "The Students' Soiree" (*If Only*). But I made a sort of symbolic save of that story by playing around with the idea that love is blind. I had some material that I wanted to use, which was about a French teacher I once had who was blind. And I invented a lot of characters for it. But I think some people may have read it as a romance, and I really wanted it to be an *anti*-romance. At the end, when the two protagonists are waiting for Gaetan, the blind teacher—as if for his blessing—it's as if *he* is love, and love is blind. I don't feel that the relationship between Bridget and Rory, such as it is, is going to work out. And yet people might read it quite the other way....

Kruk: I thought it was more romantic than some of the other stories....

Harvor: Yes, well I'm not sure that I quite pulled it off. But maybe I wanted it both ways; maybe I wanted it to be romantic and *anti*-romantic at the same time.

Kruk: Maybe. That looked like a bit of a happy ending— a rare thing, in your stories!

Harvor: Yes, it did, didn't it? Maybe I wanted to finally give a character something, let her have something. But there are elements of the anti-romantic, also, in that ending. A kind of ironic foreshadowing.

Kruk: It sounds like imagery is really important to your stories; you almost build your stories through images rather than plot.

Harvor: Yes, I do. Much as I admire Jane Austen, I could never write the way she writes. I don't think much in terms of character, even, when I'm beginning. I always begin with an image. And when I teach, I tell students, "Don't ever choose a symbol consciously; don't ever deliberately decide you're going to write *about* anything: begin by creating strong visceral images and your symbols will come as a surprise to you, and to the reader."

Kruk: The mother appears in both books; obviously, the mother figure is also really important to you—

Harvor: Yes, what Edna O'Brien has called "that all-important, hovering creature, the Mother." But really, there are two kinds of mothers in my stories—older mothers who tend to be an odd mix of the fey and the domineering, and much younger mothers who actually *are* hovering, because they fear life and its menace, not only for themselves but for their children. But then my own mother was a great influence on my life. And so was my more motherly father. They were Danish immigrants and artisans—potters—and they built themselves a life and a huge artistic following in handicraft circles down on the East coast. My father was a very tolerant and tender man (or so he seemed to his children); also at times a fairly depressed man—while my sister and I were still living at home, he was hospitalized for depression. I believe if that had happened in the 1990s—his depression, I mean—instead of the 1950's, he would have been able to work out his anguish with a therapist, but those were medieval times and the family was living in a rural community far from any city and the logistics of getting down to Saint John several times in a week to see a psychoanalyst (if there were any psychoanalysts at that time in New Brunswick) would have been pretty insurmountable. As for my mother, there is so much to say that it's difficult to know where to begin. She has been a great, bewildering, blaming, scintillating presence in my life, although I should also say that she has mellowed amazingly with age and illness.

Kruk: So the writing about her is pretty autobiographical, I guess.

Harvor: Well, it is and it isn't. Because I did tone her down quite a bit to make her believable as a fictional character. I was incredibly afraid of her when I was a child. And very fascinated. She was, after all, very charismatic. I think it would be accurate to say that she worshipped strangers, she loved to bask in the public eye. But that's the other side of charisma, isn't it? The worship of strangers—? Her family was her other audience, her second-choice audience, her less impressed audience. And the audience she was forever feeling wasn't helping her out enough—to impress the audience that really mattered. When I think of the fierceness of my mother's struggle to create and keep up the wholesome Trapp Family persona, it feels like my childhood—and of course also the childhood of my brother and sister—was a carnival on quicksand.

But then a stranger might very well ask: but don't you, as a writer, *also* hunger for the worship of strangers? And the answer will be, I think I hunger for the love and understanding of strangers. But I hope I don't hunger for worship. Because it leads to the seductive and dangerous burdens of celebrity, and celebrity almost always sooner or later (usually sooner) taints the work. But I also think that one of the main, and possibly not very honourable, reasons I want to write, is that I need to throw some version of what I think of as "my story" down before the World Court of Readers. And to be acquitted.

Kruk: Just to follow up on that, another reviewer noted that most of the women in your stories are at odds with their mothers and wary of other women. Yet they inhabit a world of almost "claustrophobic femaleness."

Harvor: I think that's partly true. I think the first book was describing a very close, and in some ways, very happily claustrophobic, domestic world. The second collection (*If Only*) is much more about women alone, divorced women, women without men, although the book also includes a few young-women-and-men stories ("A Sweetheart," "The Age of Unreason"). And the novel I'm just doing what I hope are my final revisions to (tentatively titled *The Lowest Place on Earth)* is about women in relation to men. But it's also very much about women in relation to older children. As for women friends, my closest friendships were with women in their thirties, when I was in my thirties. A lot of the marriages of my friends were breaking up, or seemed to be breaking up, and there was a kind of — how can I put it–

Kruk: Sisterhood?

Harvor: Yes–a desperate kind of sisterhood, between us. I think we were women who were looking for good mothers, in various ways, and then we were constantly reproaching each other because *this* woman wasn't being the good mother either.

Kruk: Here's an intriguing quote from a review: "Perhaps the immaturity of Harvor's women and the complexity and difficulties of their relationships with men stem from their being mothers and daughters all their lives, but only rarely or briefly wives or lovers."[3] I guess it is debatable whether your characters are mature or not, but I thought that was a really interesting point: the women are sort of trapped in mother and daughter roles.

Harvor: The women in the early stories are often wives, and often wives for a very long time, but I think it's partly true that there's an inability ... to break free of the mother. The mother herself, and the mother *within* the self. My female protagonists may actually be more mother-haunted than most women in Canadian fiction.

Kruk: Another critic made an interesting observation about the shape of the stories in *If Only*. She said they lack beginnings and endings: "Whole histories exist, of which the stories are only segments"[4]–as if you just plunk us right into the middle of it. Do you think that's accurate?

Harvor: No, I don't think it's even a tiny bit accurate. Both beginnings and endings are terribly important to me, and I tend to be prouder of some of my beginnings and endings than I am of what lies between them. Of course, if this reviewer meant that my stories are not formulaic or agenda-driven, then I'd be only too happy to agree. Could it have been that she felt they didn't have endings because she wanted them to go on and on? But I feel you can love the ending of a story and *still* want it to go on and on. A number of readers have told me that, about my work. That they felt that the stories were really little novels. I take this as a compliment, mainly. It seems to suggest that they believe in the stories' fictional worlds so much that they just can't bear to see them come to an end.

Kruk: What I see in a lot of stories by Canadian women writers— yours, and others— is a kind of role-reversal, where children become parents, and parents become children, and people get confused by this. This seems to occur in "A Sweetheart" (*If Only*) where you see the boyfriend treating the heroine as a child, and you can tell this is going to be bad news ... because you know she's going to resent this, her anger is going to come out later....

Harvor: Yes, you're right. That's exactly what will happen. And in fact, in "The Teller's Cage" (*If Only*), the follow-up story on these two characters, I arranged for the wife—in hospital by this time, having a baby—to have a tender memory of the husband from the time of the birth of the earlier baby. In this way I hoped to remedy all the uproar a bit. I thought otherwise it would be just too....

Kruk: Too grim?

Harvor: Too grim, yes, exactly. And I thought that the sense of loss that you have, and the damage that has been done by these people to each other, and the damage done by the mother and by life, would be felt much more intensely if you saw that they had also once had something tender. And so I tacked that on to the end of it, and I really do think that it redeems the lives in the story, gives them a kind of extra complexity, which is what I wanted.

Writing the story, I remembered being a student nurse—this was in Saint John, in the mid-fifties—and setting bunches of flowers outside the patients' doors at night, in marbled pink and maroon plastic vases, and I think when I got that final image I thought there was something sweet about it, and grand at the same time, but also, it was plastic. In a way, Kathryn's memory of seeing the student nurses performing that evening ritual of nursehood acknowledges that things weren't all that wonderful, but in some ways there was tenderness.

Kruk: For the record, which Canadian authors were you first exposed to? Can you remember?

Harvor: My parents owned a copy of a little book called *A Pocketful of Canada,* which I liked to read. I remember a poem called "The Wreck of the Julie Plante" that I was nuts about. I also liked Watson Kirkonnell. Probably because he had elements of Ogden Nash in him. And I remember being about twelve and lying in bed listening to the radio and hearing a story by Morley Callaghan being read on the CBC and being enthralled by it. But I don't remember doing much Canadian stuff in high school. A bit of Bliss Carmen and Pauline Johnson. A bit of E. J. Pratt.

Kruk: So you came upon the major women writers—Atwood, Laurence, Munro—later in life?

Harvor: Yes. The winter I was a young married woman and living in Denmark, I used to go to the American Embassy library in Copenhagen and read American novelists. I read Carson McCullers--*Reflections in a Golden Eye*—and in fact, Maria Kaminski, the protagonist of my novel *The Loneliest Place on Earth,* also reads *Reflections*, in the "Herr Madman" chapter of the novel. And I read Dreiser's *Sister Carrie,* and some Thomas Wolfe, and the stories of Hemingway, people I'd never read before. And when we came back to Canada in 1960, I started reading a lot of European women writers—the British writer Elizabeth Taylor, and also Doris Lessing and Penelope Mortimer and Edna O'Brien. And I was also reading de Beauvoir—I still think the third novella in *The Woman Destroyed* is an astoundingly intelligent and perfect piece of work. And I read a lot of Colette– especially the later Colette. When did I start reading Canadian writers? Probably not till 1968, when Laurence's *The Stone Angel* came out.

Kruk: So was there anybody who really ... set you on fire, and made you want to start writing?

Harvor: Yes, Laurence did—with *The Stone Angel*—more than anyone. I was just incredibly affected by that book. More than any other book written by a Canadian writer, more than anything by Munro or Engel or Atwood, who were all writers I was beginning to read and admire. It made my scalp crawl; I was absolutely taken by it. But I haven't liked anything else of hers nearly as much since. Maybe I related to the sexual repression: the strong sexuality and the strong sexual repression. Whereas with Munro's characters, I have sometimes found all the adultery hard to relate to, mainly because it's so full of deceit and vengeful delight, rather than passionate and private. The irony in Munro, much as I admire her work, holds me at a distance a bit more. But with Laurence, I didn't feel that kind of witty ironic overview. Her book did seem to have more emotional power, although there are certainly stories by Munro that I find very affecting, especially the stories from her best period— or what I consider her best period—the mid-seventies. And some of the very early stories too. "The Peace of Utrecht" still seems to me to be a wonderful story. And I'm also a great admirer of "The Beggar Maid" and "Simon's Luck." I'm very fond of "Dulse," too—it builds to such a quiet and emotional ending, both matter-of-fact and amazing.

But to elaborate a bit more on adultery as a theme for fiction, I think what I want to say is that I find it one of the best themes, both honourable and electric. But I would rather read about illicit love in Bernard Malamud's *A New Life* or *Dubin's Lives*, where the relationships are entered into out of despair and a hungry need for connection. And for my own beginning to write, upheaval in my personal life drove me to it. My father died unexpectedly when he was still relatively young, my husband had an affair (and I can't resist the temptation to say here that my husband's affair didn't feel all that honourable and electric to *me*, the outsider) and very soon after this I discovered that I was pregnant with our second child ... all of this happened in one very compressed period—the year I was twenty-six—and this drove me to write. I think I thought, *Now I have the right! Now I know something about life!* I also became less afraid of hurting people. After all, I had been hurt, and I had survived. I could even see that there was something energizing about being hurt. It was almost like receiving a kind of gift. This is a masochist speaking. A masochist and a writer. But I think most writers would probably feel that humiliation is useful. It has certainly always kept me from being paralysed in my work.

In fact, my working motto has always been: "A humiliation a day / keeps writer's block away."

Not that I have always been able to *finish* things. I spent eight years in psychoanalysis in the nineteen-seventies and during all that time, I didn't bring out a book. I wrote a lot, but I felt as if I had lost my way. I couldn't finish most of what I wrote and when I could finish things, I tended to despise them. The only really successful story that I wrote in the late seventies was "Heart Trouble" (*If Only*), which to my absolute amazement, I sold to the *New Yorker*: I didn't even have an agent back then, and I'd always heard that they wouldn't even look at stuff if you didn't have an agent, but that turned out not to be true. "Heart Trouble" is a story about a woman with psoriasis who goes from doctor to holistic healer to herbalist, trying to find a cure. She's the same woman, essentially, who's the protagonist of *The Lowest Place on Earth*. As for the stories I wrote during the watershed year I was twenty-six, I sent them off to Kent Thompson at *The Fiddlehead* and he bought them both. They were "The Hudson River" (*Our Lady*), a story about a woman named Mrs. Hudson who refers to the menstrual blood of her climacteric as "The Hudson River," and "A Day at the Front, A Day at the Border" (*Our Lady*), a story about a women's consciousness-raising group, set in suburban Ottawa in the late sixties. And the first story I sold in the States was about an American woman with breast cancer who comes to visit some American friends who summer in Canada (in Southern New Brunswick) at a time when the daughter in the family is just beginning to *get* breasts. It's called "Pain Was My Portion" (*Our Lady*) and it first appeared in *The Hudson Review*.

Kruk: People have drawn the comparison between you and Munro a lot. Obviously, you know her work very well.

Harvor: Yes, I do. I think I've read everything.

Kruk: So how do you feel now about that comparison: do you think it's overplayed? Is this in proportion to her influence on you, or her importance to you?

Harvor: Early in my writing life, I was most influenced by Laurence and Atwood and Engel. I was very taken by *Surfacing* and also by Engel's *No Clouds of Glory*. But over the long haul, I would have to say that Munro has been the greatest influence. I find her work extremely intelligent ... and the best of it is very good. I find that it's a bit expository at times, for me ... the way she goes off and makes a little lecture, and explains things to the reader. She takes the reader by the hand, or the collar, and says, "This is the way it is, and this is what it means..." She likes to define things—in a way that I don't think I do. But maybe I do it too, and I'm just not aware of it in my own work. Also, she's much more fascinated by rural eccentrics than I am. And I'm more fascinated by imagery than she is.

My reservations about her most recent work come with a certain amount of guilt; she wrote me a wonderful and admiring letter about the first book, and some of the quotes from that letter appear on the back of *If Only*. And yet I do feel it's important not to let personal considerations cloud literary judgments. Which brings me back to Munro's latest work. The stories, the recent stories, don't hold me as her stories once did. I find I start to read them and then the phone rings and I forget to pick them up again. They feel too panoramic, too grandly historical, too distantly and ghoulishly gleeful. There are so many characters now, too, in a Munro story. And yet, if you persevere, there are almost always amazing things in them. But then she suffers, I think, from having produced a great deal of work. Some of it must inevitably lack energy, force. Atwood has the same problem, really. Much of her later work is terribly uneven. Take a story like the title story in *Wilderness Tips*. It has a brilliant ending, really powerful. Such a brilliant ending that I wished very much that most of the story that preceded it hadn't been so superficial and glib. Not that there weren't some good bits. But they just were no match for that marvellous end.

Marian Engel's *Bear* is another book that had a great effect on me. I'm really crazy about that book—its hokey tenderness, and the way she wrote about the northern landscape. I thought it was terrific.

Kruk: Do you relate to the idea of writing within a Canadian tradition, or do you just write and not worry about that kind of category?

Harvor: No, no; I hardly think in those terms at all. I get very confused because of the Danishness of my family–

Kruk: You still feel that's a pretty strong influence on your writing?

Harvor: It wasn't that we felt so terribly Danish as children—after all, we knew very little about Denmark or its history or traditions. I think it was rather that we felt *afflicted* by Danishness. But at the same time, we didn't feel very Canadian either.

Kruk: You didn't identify with your rural community, then.

Harvor: My mother was on the School Board, and both my parents were great admirers of some of the old timers. But they drew a line between the young people and the old people. Probably I would have done the same myself, as a parent in a situation like that, where the young people were heavily into hard drinking and fast cars, or fast trucks, and there was lots of sex. Gladdie, the American mother who summers in New Brunswick in "Pain Was My Portion," makes the same distinction; she sees the old timers as salty, as people with "character." And the young people she sees as drunks and sluts.

One of the difficulties for my parents, apart from the almost insurmountable difficulty of making a living for themselves in such an unlikely profession practised in such an unlikely place, was that I think they had a real problem handling money. Sometimes we would go through periods of several weeks—always in the wintertime—when we wouldn't have any money at all, and we would be in debt to our farmer neighbours and wouldn't be able to pay them what we owed them till summer, and the tourists, came. My mother was extremely impulsive with money, and my father probably wasn't very accustomed to either making it or making it last, since he had been raised in a privileged and wealthy Danish family. Which is not to suggest he was an undisciplined or lazy person—far from it; he worked constantly.

Kruk: So your parents were quite sophisticated, compared to your neighbours.

Harvor: Yes, they were. Although I wouldn't call them intellectuals. In fact, my father was romantically *anti*-intellectual. And my mother, although she was quick-witted and energetic, feared introspection. Still, we had lots of books in the house, and singers and painters and dancers and writers came to visit. At least in the summers, when tourists would take the ferry boats from either Millidgeville or Gondola Point and drive up or down the peninsula to see us. We were relied on to work in the pottery—not to make pots or glaze or fire them, but to sell them and to lead visitors on little tours of the place, to do a little spiel, to serve tea, to exude charm with the goal of selling the pots. We got lots of positive attention from the tourists for all of this, and so along with feeling deprived and embittered, I also remember feeling spectacular and adored. But one of the advantages of growing up in a family of artisans was that I learned at an early age, how much *process* there is in bringing something to completion.

In the winters, though, we were totally isolated. And totally at each other's mercy.

Kruk: Your writing powerfully captures complex states of emotion, including sexual feelings. Do you think women will write more—or more openly—about sex, as they come to feel more fully equal in our society? And is this of special interest to you—celebrating women's unique sensuality and sexuality?

Harvor: Well, it seems to me that right now there is practically a stampede on the part of women to write openly about sex, and some of this writing is celebratory. And if this celebration doesn't involve the rattling of sexual credentials or other kinds of sexual boasting, but rather concerns itself more complexly with the intimacies that attend sexual events—including all the hesitations and doubts, and moments of shyness and awful regret—then I am all for it.

Kruk: Several critics have noted that, despite your interest in exploring sexual shyness, there is an honesty about the physical details of women's lives, that we often don't acknowledge. One of the reviewers of *Women and Children* [revised as *Our Lady*] said, "Her perspective is undeniably feminine and very physical."[5]

Harvor: Yes, but I wonder if this isn't just part of being Scandinavian too—that there's just an incredible naturalness about the body. Scandinavians may be deeply hung up, but on the surface at least, there's a tremendous acceptance of nudity, and you talk to small children about sex and so on....

Kruk: I thought that maybe this use of physical details (sweat, menstruation, etc.) was an attempt to be more open, to liberate the reader.

Harvor: Probably I was only trying to liberate myself.

Kruk: You also commented once that no serious writer wants to be too beloved of any group and that the women writers who have tried to impose feminist theory on their fiction, have usually failed as artists. Do you still feel that way?

Harvor: Yes, I do.

Kruk: So I guess that brings up the question of being a woman writer, and if you can be a feminist too. How do you feel about that?

Harvor: I do consider myself a feminist in my private life, and the way I live it. It's not something I think about when I write, though— or I try not to think about it, although I'm sure on some level I do think about it. But I would hate to think that I would make an artistic decision while looking out of the corner of my eye at any political belief, feminist or otherwise. I would like to think that I could ... just ignore all that. I'm not sure that it's all that easy, and I'm not sure that I can, always. I would like to be able to create a character, and say, "This is how this character is, and it doesn't matter whether this suits the current—"

Kruk: –"whether this is politically correct or not...."

Harvor: Exactly.

Kruk: So you would agree with Joyce Carol Oates that the woman writer shouldn't be trying to write as a woman, but simply as a writer....?

Harvor: I would agree with that.

Kruk: But then that makes you think: is it possible to write as a feminist *and* as an artist? Are they mutually exclusive?

Harvor: Well, if I think of someone like Doris Lessing, she's often managed very well. But then feminists have often been very critical of Lessing, too. She is—or certainly at the time she wrote *The Golden Notebook* was—very feminist. On the whole, I felt I believed her—I felt that her stance in relation to her characters was a pure one.

Kruk: That she wasn't cowed by some agenda....

Harvor: Yes, I feel that on the whole she wasn't.

Kruk: Do you feel there's a qualitative difference between writing a short story and writing a novel? Or between a short story and a novella, like "The Age of Unreason" in *If Only*?

Harvor: In theory, I agree with those who say that there's a closer relationship between the story and the poem than there is between the story and the novel, and yet sometimes ... and in fact this has happened a number of times ... I'll start something thinking it will be a story and then that story will turn into a novella. And that novella can turn into a novel. This is what happened with *The Lowest Place on Earth,* which began as a story called "Going to Russia." And eventually "Going to Russia" became "Herr Madman," the first chapter of *The Lowest Place on Earth.*

But I've also been very involved with writing poetry lately—making the final changes to *Fortress of Chairs* [published by Signal Editions, Vehicule Press, in 1992]—and this has made me more detached from the business of writing a novel. In fact, the more I write poetry, the more my prose sentences don't satisfy me. So there are real problems with working in a number of genres.

Kruk: So, poetry-writing and novel-writing are somewhat at odds?

Harvor: Yes. And the odd thing about writing poetry is that although it seems that you're more revealing, in a way—in the sense in which you can go more economically and incriminatingly into emotions—there's something very protective about the form as well. If I read one of my published stories, and it's a very revealing story, I may feel quite embarrassed, reading it. I feel more vulnerable in my fiction, for some reason, which is interesting, and which was a surprise to me.

Kruk: Your fiction is pretty autobiographical, isn't it?

Harvor: In fidelity to feelings, it's pretty autobiographical, but in the recording of actual events, not so very. I've never written about growing up in a potter's family, for instance. At least I've never written about it in fiction.... It's just a whole huge area that I have yet to work with. And I've just begun to write about the fact that I spent part of my childhood living with a doctor and his family in Saint John, on the grounds of the TB sanatorium there. This was for a year or a year and a half when I was around two or three, and again, when I was going to high school. There's a little group of poems that I've written in the last year or so, about the high school time.

Kruk: Carol Shields was the one who pointed out that you did start writing poetry fairly late, which is kind of unusual. Why do you think it happened this way?

Harvor: The way it happened was strange. I went to university very late, in my mid-forties, a year after my youngest son had left home to go off to college to study visual arts. I ended up doing a qualifying year instead of a B.A., and then was given a fellowship to go to graduate school at Concordia University. And I taught with the writing program there the first year following graduation. I moved to Toronto in the fall of 1987 to teach in the program at York. I was hired to teach one of the two senior fiction workshops, and was at that time very worried about my financial situation, because although York provided much more generous salaries for sessional lecturers than Concordia ever did, I still didn't feel I'd be able to survive on the eight thousand a year that I'd be paid to teach the fourth-year fiction workshop.

I arrived in Toronto somewhere between five and six on the morning of September first, and took a cab from the bus station to the address where my Toronto son was living in a shared house. The key was waiting for me in the mailbox, and a bed was made up for me in the upstairs living room. I slept until my son came in to tell me that the Director of York's Creative Writing Program had phoned, and that it was urgent that he speak to me at once. I remember being very frightened. I thought, "What if I don't have the job after all?" But when I returned his call, he wanted to know if I could possibly teach another workshop—Introductory Prose and Poetry. I'd only had two poems published at that point—years before, in *Saturday Night* and *The Canadian Forum*—and I felt I knew nothing at all about writing poetry. Still, I wasn't at all tempted to turn the extra job down. And during the next several months, I read a great deal of student poetry, and a lot of published work as well, along with bits and pieces of several books on the craft of writing poetry. I also started exchanging poems-in-progress with some of the poets I was meeting, and then I discovered that I shared several students with the poet Don Coles, and so I sent along a couple of my poems to Don, with a student-emissary. And Don very quickly sent an enthusiastic note back, and that was the beginning of an incredibly helpful work relationship. I also started exchanging poems with Barbara Carey, and this has also been an extraordinary help. Later, other poets were very supportive—Rhea Tregebov, among others.

Kruk: What about writers who are considered postmodern? Are you interested in their work?

Harvor: It seems to me that a writer's work is either serious or not serious, and whether it's postmodern, experimental, realist, minimalist or fabulist doesn't matter a great deal. A lot of dull but pushily high-decibel types are called experimental when they are, in fact, cutesy or superficial. When I think of the writers I admire, I can't think of anyone who's *irritatingly* experimental—by which I mean, experimental with the aim of being considered experimental. On the other hand, I do very much admire writers who are able to create the surreal within the real.

As for postmodernism, in the wrong hands, postmodern beliefs can be elitist and tiresome. In the right, inspired hands, they can create euphoria and excitement. I'm thinking of some of Philip Roth's earlier work, and in particular of *The Breast* and *The Ghost Writer*. Also Nicholson Baker's *Room Temperature,* a thrillingly postmodern work—at least, it seems postmodern to me, being demandingly self-referential (rather than self-indulgently self-referential) as well as captivatingly inventive. But the playful and free-wheeling off-the-cuffness that I associate with the best of postmodernism was already wonderfully well understood by the earliest modernists—think of the beginning of E. M. Forster's *Howard's End* or Thomas Mann's "Disorder and Early Sorrow;" they read as if they were written ten minutes ago. What I feel I'm always looking for in any sort of "new" playing around with techniques is not some technically dazzling and innovative way of saying, "I'm alright, Jack," but rather a using of new techniques to say, "I'm not particularly alright Jack—in fact, I don't believe I'm any more alright than you are, and I may even be a good deal *less* alright..." But too often postmodern techniques are used in the service of a mind-set completely opposed to this kind of useful—and, yes, at times strategic—humility, and so we are instead exposed to a really awful species of extra or sub-literary boastfulness. Something that comes across as pathetic and embarrassing.

Kruk: Is there something essential that's violated by the idea that "this is just a fiction" or "this is just a game we're playing...?"

Harvor: Well, yes, there can be. Having the rug pulled out from under you, as a reader. Whether this is a thrilling experience or simply an irritating one will depend on my mood ...when I am the reader. And whether I'll abandon emotion to make some sort of extra-literary commentary on the story's progress or process when I am the writer will also depend on my mood. I feel there was really a whole lot more playing around with postmodern techniques in *Our Lady,* and most of the stories in that book were written over twenty years ago.

Kruk: Perhaps so, because there was that story—the ending of "Lies in Search of the Truth" (*Our Lady*) where the protagonist is saying "This is a story" and making some kind of extra-literary comment to the reader.

Harvor: Yes, and at the end of "A Day at the Front, A Day at the Border" too: "Cinderella is home again, People!".... That bothers me now. In some ways, it almost seems to be a cop-out from real feeling. That there were real feelings there, when she came home, and instead of writing about those feelings, I superimposed a rather fetching and fashionable statement, which seems to me now to have been poised halfway between fable and manifesto. And yet there are some readers who would, I imagine, feel bereft if I changed that ending. If it's a polemic, they might say, it's a reckless polemic. They might say it has panache. And it does, in its way.

Kruk: Do you have a sense of who you're writing a story for, or are you only writing for yourself? Carol Shields says that she writes for herself, that she writes books she'd like to read.

Harvor: Yes, I do too. Now and then when I'm working on a story or only thinking of writing it, I imagine telling it to a friend, someone I'd feel safe enough with to tell the whole truth to.

Kruk: So what do you like to read for pleasure?

Harvor: I love Saul Bellow's *Seize the Day* and have read it many times, although the fey self-consciousness of much of his later work isn't so appealing. I'm a big fan of Malcolm Lowry— especially of "Ghostkeeper" and "The Forest Path to the Spring." And although much of Updike verges on irritating, I am a great admirer of some of the earlier stories. I very much like his quietest novel, *Of the Farm.* William Carlos Williams, especially "The Ivy Crown" and "La Danse Russe." Nabokov and Woolf. Lots and lots of Canadian and American poets and storywriters. Some of the early electrifying stories of Norman Rush too, although his recent novel *Mating* was a great disappointment. I also go back again and again to Bernard Malamud's *Dubin's Lives,* for his vivid way of describing landscape and daily life, and also for his original and earthy way of writing about the weather. No other writer I can think of loves weather the way Malamud loves weather. He's very shrewd, too, at catching the verbal violence of married life. And astounding at evoking loneliness. His "Rembrandt's Hat" is a story that left me trembling all over. I'd say the same of Mary Lavin's "In the Middle of the Fields." And I'm occasionally very taken by the work of Edna O'Brien too. Sometimes she overdoes, I know, but sometimes her excessiveness really works, especially when she gets Irishly all revved-up and writes about despair, and particularly when she writes about the despair of a middle-aged woman whose relationships with men, or a man, are crumbling all around her. And I've recently been very impressed by parts of Carole Corbeil's *Voice-Over,* because in spite of the fact that it suffers from certain first-novel flaws—in particular a weak beginning and a too self-consciously symbolic ending—Corbeil has a really remarkable gift for writing in the most economical and emotional way about both very early childhood and very early adolescence.

I've also recently read Mary Gaitskill's *Bad Behaviour* and especially liked a nervous story about sado-masochism called "A Romantic Weekend." What else? Mary McCarthy's "The Man in the Brooks Brothers' Shirt" is a story I read again a little while ago, after not having read it for ten or fifteen years. And I was even more impressed this time. The decorousness of the time in which it was written (in the early forties, I think; I think the book it appears in came out in '42) forced McCarthy into a situation that made her circumvent its strictures by analyzing in incredible psycho-social depth what was, on the surface of it, a one-night stand, and so you feel, all the way through the story, her natural candour at war with the time's discretion, and this added subtextual tension makes the story quiver, at least for me.

Another writer I read fairly often is the American poet Sharon Olds. She has a way of jumping right into a poem, a way of dispensing with—no, actually outright disdaining—any lyrical lead-in or fanfare, that it's hard not to admire. I do have lots of reservations about her, though—her egomania bothers me, and so does her sexual boasting (especially the poems about her sexual relationship with her husband), and sometimes I find her just too attention-seeking and luridly clinical. And I'm bothered by the all-American cheerleader persona of the woman who so often narrates her poems. All this reminds me of the critical remarks another American poet recently made about Olds—he called her "the tabloid poet." And she is. But in her best poems, the quieter ones, the ones I think will last, her ability to call up emotion is eerie. I'm thinking in particular of a poem called "May, 1968," which first appeared in *Poetry*. The line-breaks in this poem feel so emotion-driven. For instance, the ways Olds pushes the pronoun "I" out to the end of so many lines to work against what I suspect *she* suspects are her poems' tendency toward egomania.

But I seem to spend my life reading, so I should probably stop naming names. I also wander about with words from many writers going around in my head: Dayv James French writing about a boy on his way home from swimming lessons at a school pool in the dead of winter ("sometimes his wet hair would freeze into a sharp bear claw against the back of his neck as he waited for the bus home...."); Nadine McInnis writing about her mother "dragging the vacuum like a branch / over a snowy carpet...."; Roo Borson's "Into a few of the rooms go a few of the men, bringing their mushroomy smell...." (I think I've got this right). Atwood's memory of the tartan dresses of her childhood: "...many of them are in plaid, the authentic, sombre, blood-lit colours...." Or Munro talking about a dishpan with "a rag plug in it." The first line of Philip Roth's *When She Was Good,* which I think begins like this: "Not to be rich, not to be famous, not even to be happy, but to be civilized, that was the dream of his life...." Lots of other writers. Many many poets. Don Coles's *K in Love* seems to me to be an extraordinarily intelligent, pure piece of work. A terrific poem about adolescent shyness by Barb Carey called "Wire Kiss." Cynthia Ozick's "Rosa." A short story by Nadine Gordimer called "La Vie Boheme." Also her stunning short novel, *The Late Bourgeois World.* Rhea Tregebov's breathtaking, breath-hungry poems to her little boy in *The Proving Grounds.* And also these incredible lines that I read in a review—in *Arc,* I think—of the work of Phil Hall, a poet who was at that time new to me. The poem is about male violence and is called "Clothes-line," and these are the lines that—appropriately enough, in a poem which begins with clothes blowing on a line—blew me away:
Wrung out and shaken
into the sunlight
slide men's briefs
wolf heads
pinned between the flowered bedding
and the towels....

Kruk: So you like to read men just as much as you like to read women....

Harvor: Well, I do read a lot of women writers. But I don't ever think, "Oh, I would only read women writers." The qualities that attract me to a writer are emotional intensity, imagery, intellectual invention—not for its own sake, but rather intellectual invention that works to create metaphors that reflect large and humane destinations. I also admire work that has an emotional afterlife so that it stays and stays with you. I like to be haunted by the quietness at the heart of a work.

Kruk: All the reviews of *If Only* that I've read seem very positive; I would think you'd feel very confident going into the novel–

Harvor: Yes, but I've been in this novel, or had this novel in me, for a very long time. I finished what I thought was the first draft of it in 1982, and by that time I'd been working on it for at least two years. I'm talking now about *The Land of Dizziness.* The part of the book that later became *The Lowest Place on Earth* has gone through so many changes and revisions that I can't even remember how long it's been. At least seven years. And none of this has been helped by the fact that I have a habit of working on several things at once. There's the poetry book, *Fortress of Chairs,* due out in a couple of weeks. And there's another novel called *Despair and the Critic* that I've been working on for a little over a year, in its most recent version. I'm also halfway through a children's book. And I have another book and a half of poems. Then there's what's left over from *The Land of Dizziness.* And there are piles and piles of stories that are still needing a whole lot of attention and revision.[6]

But then revision seems to me to be the metaphor for the writer's life. You revise and re-think and invent and re-invent your life by telling stories. And then, one way or another, you revise the revision. The parts of my earlier work that now feel flawed to me but are already out there, out in the world, are like a perpetual notebook. A notebook-at-large, a notebook-on-the-loose. But it's still *my* notebook, I can still plunder and use it.

Toronto, Ontario: May 1990

Notes

1 This interview is unique among the ten, for it went through an additional revision process. In each case, I presented the author with a full transcript of our earlier taped conversation, which they corrected or edited, both for style and substance. They could also remove comments they did not wish, upon reflection, to see "in print." I went on to shape the raw material, selecting the most pertinent points made by both interviewer and interviewee, and re-organizing topics in the most logical and readable fashion. Each interview is thus somewhere between a recorded conversation, with its fits and starts, and a perfectly polished, formal essay. In Harvor's case, she added additional material to the revised interview, reluctant to leave it in its "white-hot" state of ideas caught in their formation. Her quest for perfection is a hallmark of her career, and her (relatively) slow output of books. As she herself says, "[T]he fact is I'm a very critical person. I'm very critical of a lot of stuff I read, and I imagine these standards being applied to me, and I can't let something out of my hands until it's much, much better" (Philip Marchand, "She Can't Let Go till Story's 'Much, Much Better'" *Toronto Star* 21 Dec. 1996: G13.) In March 1999, Harvor made a few more, small deletions.

2 *Our Lady of All the Distances* is a "slightly revised version of the first story collection, issued under the imprint of the Oberon Library by HarperCollins, Toronto, 1991" (author CV).

3 Susan Perren, rev. of *If Only We Could Drive Like This Forever*, by Elisabeth Harvor, *Quill and Quire* 54.3 (March 1988) 76.

4 Rita Donovan, rev. of *If Only....* and *A Basket of Apples and Other Stories,* by Shirley Faessler, *The Fiddlehead* 159 (Spring 1989) 116-20. Quote p. 117.

5 Phyllis Bruce, rev. of *Women and Children*, by Elisabeth Harvor, *The Canadian Forum* (January 1975) 44.

6 Since our conversation, a third collection of stories, *Let Me Be the One* (HarperCollins, 1996) has appeared. It received a Governor General's nomination for English-Canadian Fiction. See Author's Note for more information.

Jack Hodgins:

"The Voice is the Story"

Kruk: Tell me about the new novel, *Broken Ground* (1998). You've written about the Fire of 1922 in other places, haven't you? It's part of your community's memory....

Hodgins: I have mentioned it in other places, and have always known that some day I would have to sneak up on it. I wanted to deal with it by putting it together with the First World War. You see, people talked about the Fire all the time but they never talked about the War, which had happened just four years before it. I was interested in knowing why one and not the other. And what had happened in between.

Broken Ground goes back to the community where I grew up. I'm interested in the returned soldiers after the First World War. The government of Canada gave these soldiers, as a reward, pieces of property where the obligation was to turn them into farms. When they got to that corner of the Comox Valley, they discovered that it was impossible to farm because it was timberland. The land had been logged but it was still populated by gigantic stumps. My father was a small child at the time and remembers that, in 1922, they had just got their houses built, when a forest fire came down out of the mountains and more or less wiped them out. It fascinates me that these people had been through the War, and then gone to all this trouble fighting with the landscape to create farms where there was no business *being* farms, and then, after being wiped out, turned around and created a very cohesive community.

So I'm exploring the people who were, in a way, betrayed by their country. Not deliberately, but they were sent there to do an impossible task, and most of them ended up having to work in the logging camps at an incredibly dangerous job that they didn't come there to do, or want to do, just so they could feed their families ... because the farms never became anything more than hobby farms. And the Fire of '22 becomes just another story these people tell. I've superimposed a contemporary point of view on it. I don't want to talk too much about this, but ... part of the scheme of the novel is that a movie has been made based on the narrations that you read first, so we get the story from still one more point of view.

Kruk: And the movie-making really brings it into our visual culture.

Hodgins: Yes, because I'm not interested in writing only an historical novel. I'm interested in understanding these people and what these people have got to do *with us*. So, one of the narrators in the first part is an eleven-year-old boy, the age my dad was then. But looking back, he's got nearly the whole century that he's experienced, and he can see the Fire slightly different now. And the War....

About the title: "broken" and "ground"..."breaking ground" is what pioneers do, but also, you have "broken hearts." It is about people's hearts being broken, plus the idea of the battlefield, as well as the torn-up landscape of Vancouver Island when they were blasting stumps. One of the central characters is an explosives expert from the First World War who becomes the most valuable man there, because he can blow up all their stumps for them. One of the main characters has to learn that they had approached the land-clearing as if it were a battle ... while the man who is most successful, treated the landscape with respect. Even though he was blasting the stumps, he was treating the landscape not as an enemy, but as an accomplice or a friendly resource.

Kruk: Well, that's certainly a big theme in Canadian Literature— the struggle to relate to our unique environment....

Hodgins: (laughing) I guess it is. These people loved their land and loved the animals and loved the timber and loved the forest. But they had begun with this horrible battle that had to be fought.

Kruk: It's easy to forget, surrounded by the cosmopolitan culture of Victoria, that not so long ago a lot of this area was frontier.

Hodgins: And not so far *away*. Victoria was kind of an island of its own, a settled "cosmopolitan" centre long before the rest of the Island was settled. If you go over the Malahat Mountain, you get into a different world, one I've written about often before. This time I'm dealing with people who came from all over the country, but I have written so much about Vancouver Island before, that I realized at some point I had forgotten to show the landscape from their eyes; how overwhelming it must have been to them, or frightening, or beautiful, or whatever. And so that was a new layer. I had to find new ways of showing my old landscape as it appeared to these people ... to whom it was unfamiliar.

Kruk: I think of Joseph Conrad's dictum here: "above all, to make the reader *see.*"

Hodgins: To make the reader see it, yes. You can't very well have a footnote saying, "Read *Spit Delaney's Island* (1976) if you want to know what this place is like..." I thought it was going to be a simple, short little novel when I started, and it's turned out to be very complex, much more complicated, I think, than anything I've done before.

I've been doing the odd short story as well, but they tend to just come and go.

Kruk: So, you don't *plan* to write stories?

Hodgins: Well, novels tend to grow and accumulate and get me excited. I see them as books from the very beginning: "I'm writing a BOOK." Whereas short stories will come out of left field and hit me between the eyes and I'll realize that this little feeling I have, or image I have, or character I want to write about, needs to be captured in something short, and I'll try that first. I think the older I get the more difficult it is for me to imagine how something as complex as life can be captured in a short story. But occasionally it can, and when it does—it's a wonderful feeling.

I've incredible admiration for good short story writers. More so knowing that it's not easy to come up with a short story that hasn't been done before. I guess I have pretty high standards for a short story. With a novel, you've got the opportunity to be complex, rich, varied. There's a zillion ways that a novel can accumulate to become, quote, a "success," whatever that means. Or in other words, you're satisfied with it. With a short story, I feel it has to have some spark of brilliance—which is a scary word to use—from the very beginning, to have even a *hope* of working. So that's why I say it has to sort of jump out and hit me over the head or between the eyes or something, so that I think, "Wow, maybe this will be a good short story."

Kruk: It has to have a certain gem-like shine to it?

Hodgins: Yes, I think so, because it doesn't last very long on the page. Therefore it has to have something that lasts longer in the reader's mind. Mind you, you want your novels to do that too, but the novels will do that, maybe, in an overall feeling, or a sense of the whole world of the book. A short story will often be a moment, or a discovery, or an image that will just be so original or exciting, that it will stick with the reader.

One of the rewards of the short story is a more immediate discovery of what you've done, and easier—no, I'm not going to use the term "easier"—a more *direct* relationship with the whole, so that you can experiment with something and tell almost immediately if you've changed the overall pattern. Whereas with a novel, if you add a chapter in the middle, it may take you an awful long time to discover what that chapter has done to the reading of the whole novel.

Kruk: You mentioned to me a year ago that you were working on a third collection of stories...?

Hodgins: I'm close. I have, I think nine, no eight, stories that I'm proud of, that have been published in periodicals or are going to be published in periodicals. And I have a couple of ideas and sketches that I haven't got down to. So I suspect, that as a change, after this novel is out of my house [the final manuscript of *Broken Ground* was sent to its publisher during our interview], I may work on some short stories instead of the two novels that I interrupted in order to write *this* one.

Kruk: And when you put them together in a book, that brings up the question of form: what makes it into a collection? Or even, a linked collection? People have talked about your two story volumes, *Spit Delaney's Island* and *The Barclay Family Theatre* (1981), as being put together with a certain amount of artfulness to create *different* kinds of linked collections.

Hodgins: Well, it's interesting, because one collection happened by accident—not by accident, but without my being aware of it—and the other one happened deliberately. *Spit Delaney's Island* was simply a selection from about twenty short stories I had published at that time. I sent Macmillan twenty stories, and they said "We will do a story collection of yours, and these are the ones we like." It took them so long to publish that I was writing new short stories, and I would send one to my editor and say put this one in, take "X" out. Eventually we ended up with ten stories, but it was only at the last minute that I realized I had a second short story about Spit. We decided to put these two stories at the beginning ["Separating"] and the end ["Spit Delaney's Island"] and it created the illusion of it being a unit. It was only after I read the reviews of *Spit Delaney's Island* that I saw there were advantages in collections of stories that had a sense of being a unit.

Kruk: An advantage for the writer?

Hodgins: An advantage for the book, in the sense that it gives reviewers something to get their hands on. If a story collection really is a collection of disparate stories, completely unrelated to one another, then maybe it's harder to talk about.

Kruk: I think we all look for unity, and so we'll probably find it.

Hodgins: We do, and in Canada there is a strong tradition for the story sequence, or the cycle. In fact, there was a time when if you asked somebody what they were working on they didn't say "short story," they'd always say "I'm working on a book of short stories." Which always struck me as strange. I never thought of myself as working on a book of short stories until I realized that I had a collection of stories that *needed* to be in a book.

Reviewers and scholars have seen all kinds of things that tie the collection together but I wasn't conscious of that at all. To me—you see, this was the beginning for me—every short story was so different from every other one ... I thought that there would be a wide range. But readers then start to see themes being repeated and, of course, to readers off Vancouver Island, it all seems like Vancouver Island, whereas to me a story set in Courtenay is in a very different location then a story set in Qualicum or Victoria.

Kruk: Well, that may be a function of Canadian readers' Ontario-centric perspective....

Hodgins: An Ontario-centric perspective creates our audience in this country partly because of *The Globe and Mail* book pages, and such things. My publisher presented me as a new voice from a new region. The suggestion was that nobody had heard anything from this place before. In fact, there had been *plenty* of writers writing here before me.

At first, the Canadian literary world was sort of happy to welcome a voice from Vancouver Island as a Canadian writer. And then I moved to Ottawa for a couple of years, during which time the Toronto magazines were phoning me for quotations and asking me to write articles on writing and living in Ottawa, and treating me like a real Canadian writer. The minute I came home to Victoria, there was a feeling that I had become merely a West Coast writer again. So that when *The Globe and Mail* lists the Canadian writers who were at such-and-such a festival in Europe, they will list all of the people who live in Toronto, etc. and at the very end, if they include me at all, they'll say, "and West Coast writer Jack Hodgins."

Kruk: Tell me how you put *The Barclay Family Theatre* together.

Hodgins: *The Barclay Family Theatre* was a more deliberate attempt to create a unit. In fact, my editor questioned whether we should call it a novel. I don't know what it is. It's a collection of stories about people who all happen to be in the same family. I had written about half of them before I realized this was the case.

I grew up in a small rural community within two miles of both grandparent families. My mother and father had grown up two miles apart and there I was surrounded by grandparents and cousins and aunts and uncles and more aunts! My mother was one of six daughters, the second-oldest, so they were all adolescents, or in their early twenties, when I was born. In fact, one was only four years older then I was. While I was growing up, they were a huge presence, a dynamic, noisy, talkative, dramatic, eccentric and extravagant bunch and they fascinated me right from the beginning. I grew up surrounded by all these women's voices. I then discovered somewhere in the writing of *The Barclay Family Theatre* that I was borrowing—I wasn't modelling these people on specific aunts, but I was borrowing from the experience of having grown up amongst them. So the opening and closing stories of that collection ["The Concert Stages of Europe," "Ladies and Gentlemen, the Fabulous Barclay Sisters!"] are about as close as I've ever come to autobiography. They both deal with the pre-adolescent boy, and his relationship with his aunts. The others are about what happened to the other fictional aunts in later years.

Kruk: But if it were a novel, it would certainly be seen as a very discontinuous novel, whereas as a collection of stories, with each story you're opening a new door, as Edna Alford puts it, and meeting a new aunt, and your reader's prepared for that—

Hodgins: Not every English-speaking country has a tradition of the story cycle, or the sequence of stories, and it's like we have so many success stories with the Alice Munro collections and Margaret Laurence's *Bird in the House*, that people tend to think that short stories eventually equal a short story unit. So to get back to the original question, this next book of stories, whenever it should happen, at the moment looks very much like a collection of stories that just happen to be between covers. I think that's still legitimate; it's just that it's not as easy for the publisher to market them.

For a while I thought they were going to be all stories that came out of living in Ontario, and then I discovered that the *next* story didn't work that way. There are similarities that somebody can find, I can see, but there won't be anything linking them.

Unless I wake up some morning with some revelation that causes me to rewrite them all!

Generally, my instincts tend to lead me towards the novel rather than the story collection. Just by the very way I described the short story earlier, discourages the notion of the story collection as a unit of similar stories, because I wait for that very individual story to come along. I don't go looking for it because I'm obsessed with a certain theme at the moment. If I'm obsessed with something, I may think I'm starting with a short story, but it may very well end up as a novel ... because the whole world wants to get in on it.

Kruk: So the size of the obsession implies a sizable commitment and an interest to match. Big scope— which needs that big canvas—?

Hodgins: Big canvas, and sometimes a big cast. If I find myself working into what is obviously going to be a novel, I discover that my characters are giving themselves permission to have more to say, or more to do, than I would allow them if I were working with a short story.

Kruk: Would you say that this "bigness" comes out of your interest in community? Because that's something that's evident in almost everything I've read of yours.

Hodgins: Almost undoubtedly. One of the things I'm interested in, in fiction and in life, is the way different people form communities, and the importance of communities and the different ways that community can be defined. It's a little harder to do that in a short story, but if I'm writing a novel, sooner or later, the notion's going to come up. At least it has so far. What is the world in which these people live? What do their neighbours mean to them? How do they get along? How do they *not* get along? Whereas in the short story, I tend to think of these people as living in bubbles. I mean the bubble includes the landscape, and it includes other people who are important in the story, but it doesn't necessarily include the whole world.

Kruk: Interesting.... In my conversation with Jane Rule, she talked about recognizing the value of community based on caring for other people—all sorts of people. Obviously, like Jane, you're not interested in an homogenous, or an artificial or made-to-order, kind of world, but one in which people are free to be themselves. Can you expand on your understanding of community?

Hodgins: In the communities that I have either observed or lived in or invented, the sense of community comes out, quite often, through a sharing of a story. One of the things that I've noticed growing in the writing of this new book *[Broken Ground]* is that these people came from all over Canada; in fact many of them had come from other countries before the War; they were Canadians but they had other backgrounds. So they had come from all these countries to a new country, then they came from all over the different landscapes to this one little spot on Vancouver Island with almost nothing in common except some version of the English language. It was very difficult for them to create a community at first, at least in my imagination, but as soon as they had experienced that Fire, they had stories to tell each other about themselves and about one another. That common history, if you wish, was the beginning of a sense of community.

By the time I came along all those years later, there was a very, very, very strong sense of people—people of Finnish, and Swedish, and German, and French, and English, and Irish, and Scottish backgrounds and everything else under the sun—who all identified very strongly with the place. The relationship with the landscape was very important.... Many of them worked at the same kind of work, with the common experiences of raising families, with shared joys and disasters. The Fire was just one disaster they all went through, but other things followed, of course, good things and bad things.

People begin to be part of the community when they start talking about what they have shared. It isn't the sharing, necessarily, that's the important thing; everybody goes through the Fire separately. But afterwards, when they've got a little distance from it and they start talking about it, then it's everybody talking at the same time and putting in their two bits worth. "And how I felt and how you felt" and "You looked like this and, etc." That to me began the community. It's, "Here we are together having survived something in the same place." I think being in the same place is important. Well, it isn't if we're talking about real life here. It's more convenient in fiction to have people in the same place, but I can imagine that it's possible to get that sense of people living in different places if they've been through something together ... like a war. If they're going to *talk* about the war. I don't think a war creates a sense of community if people don't want to talk about it.

Kruk: If it's suppressed....

Hodgins: If it's a suppressed memory, then they are all experiencing it separately. But if somebody says "Do you remember the time such and such happened?" and somebody laughs because there's a story to be told about that, and does—then somebody else laughs—that's the community at work.

Kruk: For this kind of communal story we could substitute "myth," in a way, because myth underlies communities, though often it's given down by someone else. By someone with more power, like the priest, or the teacher.

Hodgins: Yes, often there will be the keeper of the myth, and in a small community, it might be the teacher. Yet there doesn't have to be a lesson that's learned from it. It contains an instinctual and an inspired and an emotional truth that it would take somebody else to come along and give a name to, or create a lesson out of. To the people living it, it's just a sense of being part of something.

The need is there in most of us, there is a need for that community or the symbol of a community. Whether it be a building, or a statue, or a whatever. So you steal a church, as in *Broken Ground*. When somebody brings up the idea of stealing a church, somebody else objects, "We never wanted a church here." Somebody else says, "A town hall with a statue in front of it would do just as well but you don't have the legal right to that. We're just a crossroads community, but we could have a church." But when they had moved the church—which was a bit of fun to write—and they had put it in place, it was just a dinky little chicken shed of a church, there was no steeple on it. The Douglas firs soared above it. I couldn't resist writing that anybody driving through could miss the church altogether, because their eyes would be going up to the Douglas firs.

Kruk: Another aspect of story-writing I'm interested in, without— I hope—being either simplistic or dogmatic, is gender. The ways in which men and women might write differently. Have you got any thoughts on that, from your experience?

Hodgins: I'm not sure, because it's something I didn't think very much about until recently. It's something that I've just blindly gone sailing ahead into, making assumptions about [male and female experience], because often characters will come alive for me or not come alive for me, depending on some kind of emotional connection I will make with them. If I don't make the emotional connection, then the character just lies flat on the page. But if I find something I have in common with that character, or if I can somehow feel myself in that character's bones, then it doesn't matter to me whether it's a man, a woman, a child, an old person, whatever—then they will come to life. Then I will at least believe that I know what that person's feeling and thinking.

Kruk: So the imagination transcends gender for you....

Hodgins: Yes. But partly I'm also relying upon the fact that, as I mentioned earlier, I grew up surrounded by voices, and a good number of those voices were women's voices. But I was also in the wonderful position of being able to listen in on women's conversations and men's conversations separately. You could go from one to another and notice how different they were. The topics were very different. The sentence patterns were very different. Since then, I have spoken to one linguist who went to great lengths to explain how women use more subordinate clauses then men and all kinds of things like this and I thought, "Well, I guess." I mean, that's great, but if I start analyzing it, I'll lose it. I'd rather rely on my ears, and my instincts, and my memory.

Plus, the assumptions that were made about audience in these conversations were very different, and because I was comfortable hanging around in any kind of situation, whether it was in the kitchen where women were having coffee and talking, or whether it was in the garage where men were hanging over the open hood of the car talking about what was the problem, it was all fascinating to me. I also think in that rural society, the narrative form was probably used more often by women than men. Women at the kitchen table, with a cup of coffee, they're telling tales about what they did or what happened to so-and-so last week. When I go out to the garage and I listen to the men looking into the motor, they're talking about solutions or they're talking about, if you do this, this will happen or if you do that, that will happen and sometimes Corky So-and-So did this and it worked. I don't remember narratives going on for any length of time. They got told fast. So it was information-sharing rather than storytelling.

I wasn't thinking at the time that I was learning anything about voices, or about men and women, or writing, or anything else. It's when I started to write that I would discover that I could start a sentence and know how it was going to be finished because I would hear a certain rhythm coming from a certain kind of voice, and it just didn't occur to me for a long, long time to even question whether I was right, because I was operating on instinct, which is what I think I'm probably doing most of the time when I'm writing. Mind you, the voices of the women of my childhood were rural, were of the forties and fifties. Now whether I have the right to project beyond that I don't know, except that I continue to live amongst the voices of many strong and independent women. When I stumbled upon Maggie Kyle [of *The Invention of the World* (1977)], this was so exciting for me I could hardly bear it. I just knew Maggie Kyle inside and out and just *had* to write her story. Never stopped to ask questions about her at all. She was living in my head all my life, I think. And the same thing is true of some of the male characters.

Kruk: It's good to escape that crippling self-consciousness that I suppose a lot of writers are prone to now, where they think, "Should I or shouldn't I, do I know enough to speak in this voice—"

Hodgins: That kind of scares me. We need to think about these questions, but I think we need to be careful not to be intimidated by them, because after all, fiction writing by its very nature is projecting into other people's worlds. Which means, freedom to write about anybody who excites our interest. You shouldn't be judged on whether you do it or don't do it, or are presumptuous or not presumptuous, but whether or not you succeed at it.

Kruk: A critic named Harry Brod has written about "the case for men's studies," looking at things from the *other* side. He says, "While women have been obscured from our vision by being too much in the background," (that's the feminist political position, of course) "men have been obscured by being too much in the foreground." Does that resonate with you at all?

Hodgins: I guess he must mean that *individual* men are obscured by being lumped together as men, in a world where men have had more attention and more power than women. So what it would suggest to me is that people will make assumptions about men. We're living in a very sensitive time where a lot of things have to be adjusted, and are being adjusted, especially in the university. So with somebody like me, who is strongly encouraged to be part of a group on sexual harassment in the university, part of me is saying, "I don't need this, I was taught this stuff as a kid. Why am I having to listen to this?" And then I have to remind myself this is because men in general need to be learning some of these things. I think it's a stage we have to go through to get somewhere better, but also I think it is a symptom of a current tendency towards black and white thinking. There are good guys, there are bad guys....

At the same time, there is a strong impulse towards blame and revenge in our society, including gender issues. I think until we reach a stage where people are comfortable enough with themselves to see all other people as individuals rather than as part of labels or groups ... this is just something we may have to wait out. I don't know.

So I think of myself as a male who happens to be a writer, or a writer who happens to be a male, whatever. Again, I guess it goes back to the kind of thing I said before, the kind of balance there's been in my life of women and men and the voices and the strengths of both. Certainly I've been aware of the packaging; you grow up in a rural community in northern Vancouver Island,

and you are made very aware of the line between men's and women's roles. If you elect to stay there, you are electing to adopt the role, or you wouldn't survive.

In a way, I had to turn my back on some of that background, but at the same time, I've dedicated my life to celebrating it. I didn't turn my back on it out of despising it. I admire it, to a certain extent and even envy some of it. But I turn my back on it in the sense that there wouldn't be a place for me within it. I grew up in an Alistair MacLeod world of traditional family roles, but I grew up in a family so filled with variety that I never bought the either/or's, or the "must's," or the "you have to's," or any of that.

Kruk: Because your parents were sceptical about the "have to's"?

Hodgins: I would never call them sceptical. To a certain extent, they accepted their gender roles but the roles were one of the least important aspects of their lives. My dad worked in the logging camps because that was what work there was and he has many of the aspects that you'd expect to come out of that. He is, and always has been, a really rounded character whose attitude towards women I now see was way ahead of his time. My mother, who had the traditional role of raising children and staying home and being a wonderful cook and all those other things that women had to do then, was also a dynamic personality who influenced lives all around her. She never had a profession or anything but she was always somehow a force in the community, somehow affecting other peoples' lives for the better.

Kruk: Today, we often talk about women who didn't get to be artists or didn't get to be writers because they were denied the opportunity. You spoke about the theatrical Barclay sisters ... maybe "performing," as themselves, is their kind of creative outlet—?

Hodgins: My mother was also an incredible storyteller. I didn't know for a long, long time or didn't notice, that our visits often included bringing me up to date on stories—local gossip. When *The Barclay Family Theatre* was published I was living in Ottawa, and crossed the country doing promotion. I met up with my folks in Nanaimo; they came down for a booksigning. I said to my mother, "If you've been sort of secretly a little uncomfortable about these stories I've been doing recently, you can relax because I'm not going to do anymore like that. I'm leaving the Barclay family alone." And her face dropped with disappointment. She said, "Oh, well why were you asking us all those questions about our trip to Reno? I could hardly wait to see what you were going to do with that one." And then I realized that she had been feeding me little titbits and then gone home and waited to see what I did with them.

Kruk: She's part of the process....

Hodgins: She's always been part of the process. So you see what I mean? My parents are very strong independent, but inter-dependent, characters. Because they lived where they lived, they accepted the outward roles that were given them. But somehow they were larger than their roles ... at least in my perceptions.

Kruk: I notice that the mother/son relationship seems to pop up in a number of stories. For example, *The Barclay Family Theatre* stories "Invasions '79," "The Concert Stages of Europe," and "Three Women of the Country," "The Religion of the Country," "Other People's Troubles" in *Spit Delaney's Island.* There's a son who's often in intense conflict, or connection, with his mother. To me that says something about the maternal influence on you, coming through in your characters.

Hodgins: I'm not surprised.

Kruk: In interview with Jeanne Delbaere, you describe your life as "a parade of strong, energetic, tough, enthusiastic, accomplished women from my grandmother to my own daughter."[1] It seems to me there has to be an instinctive gender balance and feminist sympathy in your life, as a result.

Hodgins: I think I would even use a stronger word than "sympathy." I think it's "identification," temporary identification, mind you and a limited identification, but those relationships have allowed me to at least *imagine* identifying—because none of these people have ever felt foreign to me. I'm always surprised when I see people writing about women and men as if they were foreign to one another.

Kruk: Me too. Also, the mother's often the storyteller or the one who keeps the family stories. She often keeps the family history too, so that the son learns it from his mother—perhaps, to write about it.

Hodgins: I rather guess that in North American society, especially outside the big cities, the males who become artists, have often had strong mothers. In fact I read somewhere, and I wish I could remember who had said this—perhaps with a grain of salt—that a predominant number of North American male writers write with the voice of their mothers. And we have no way of proving that, of course, but I'm not surprised to hear it. I mean, I can hear my mother's voice in some of my narrative passages. There were male figures in my childhood who were, and still are, great storytellers, but they tend to stand out, whereas I guess I've just always taken it for granted that all women are great storytellers.

Kruk: Or that, as you say, they would find the material of their lives something to spin out in stories. Sociologists have talked about this too, that men often want to look for solutions, fix a problem, "let me tell you how to solve that," as opposed to women's frequent attitude of just, "let me share it with you."

Hodgins: I suspect that, fifty years from now, because of our acute consciousness of these things, a lot of this will have disappeared or blended so that it will seem absurd to talk about women as storytellers and men as solution-givers, because I just think it will change....

Kruk: I wanted to come back to something else that critics have talked about in your work: the borderline, the drawing of the line. Spit Delaney wonders, "Where is the dividing line?" That's come up a lot as a kind of motif in your work. And yet, interestingly enough, the experience of "overlapping borders" appears as a *good* thing. Then there's the idea of "invasions." Invasions which are going across borders you're not supposed to cross. Am I on the right track?

Hodgins: I haven't thought about all three together at the same time, so you're pushing me into thinking about them. When I think about "overlapping," I'm thinking about those areas where one person can find a way of empathizing with another person. That shared experience....

Kruk: So when Phemie Porter ("Spit Delaney's Island") says "we touched, we overlapped"...?

Hodgins: That means, in some way, "we identify with each other." Invasion would be to assume power over others. It's colonization. So I guess it's "invasion" *vs.* "overlapping."

When I speak of "dividing lines," I'm speaking of the line that has more to do with perceptions. The line between the things that last and the things that are temporary, or the things that are solid and the things that are *not* solid. Sort of a lasting reality and an ephemeral temporality.

Kruk: I'm really intrigued by this idea of borders and lines and boundaries, because it seems to me that's what our culture is all about—making them up, right?

Hodgins: And then having to live with them. It makes us feel more comfortable if we know where things belong. The problem is that this leads to pigeon-holing, to stereotyping, to invasions of privacy and space.

Kruk: So, there's a temptation for humans to create order, but that can become very rigid and hierarchical. Even when we talk about men and women writers, and their differences.... If we're not careful we can say, "Well, she's just a woman writer; I'm not going to read her," or vice versa. Drawing lines becomes a way of excluding or silencing.

Hodgins: On the one hand I abhor the misuse of borders, and I dislike the idea of dividing everything up into pigeon-holes. As soon as somebody wants to call me a certain kind of writer, then everything in me wants to write exactly the opposite, next time. On the other hand, I majored in Mathematics, along with English, at university; taught Math for several years. I especially loved geometry. I loved structures.

I still do. To me a novel is an architecture and a novel feels like a novel when it has its own structure and shape. It doesn't have to look like anything else that's ever existed in the world, but it has to have all the pieces in place. When I wrote *The Invention of the World,* I had no reason to believe that anybody else would say this was a novel because it didn't look like any other novels I'd read—except for maybe a couple. Yet I knew it was a novel because I knew exactly how it was held together.

What the foundation was, what the shape of it was, what the structure was and why it had an integral whole. What delights me is that *The Invention of the World* has enough variety and surprise in it, even now, when there have been so many more unconventional novels written since then, that people can still get excited talking about what I've done. That keeps the book alive for me.

In other words, even though I wouldn't want to build a house like this myself, a house that is, let's say, a Victorian three-storey house that suddenly has a round brick turret in the air ... it would look absurd, but it would be a complete structure, because there would be some function for that turret. I've read lopsided novels that feel still like completed novels. They catch me by surprise; I think, "How can you get away with this?" Until I get to the end and I realize, of course, this was necessary to do whatever it is doing.

Structurally, things have to be related for me. They don't have to be traditional; they don't have to be recognizable instantly; they don't have to be beautifully symmetrical. But they have to have integrity They have to have their own sense of wholeness.

Kruk: Okay, so the disorientation, if it's intended, is part of the meaning of the thing. It's valuable. That's what postmodernism, as a cultural movement, has done. It's allowed us to say the effect can be to disable or disorient the reader, and that it doesn't have to, in one way, cohere. But I guess what you're saying is, there should be some coherence at a philosophical or intellectual level...?

Hodgins: Yes. There's a reason for it, even if it is an instinctual rather than a totally intellectually thought-out reason. It somehow reinforces the impression that the novel as a whole was intended to give.

Kruk: I'm interested in the title of your second book of stories, *The Barclay Family Theatre*. I notice the "family" stuck in there and wonder if you're suggesting that family is the origin of theatre, and of performance—?

Hodgins: In a family, you are "on stage," so to speak, especially if it's a large family. You go to the grandparents' place, where all the uncles and aunts and cousins are gathered, then you're "on stage," being "YOU," whoever you have decided you are, or *they* have decided you are—more often the latter is the case. And I think especially in large families, if the children not only go through adolescence within the family, but stay on, and live their adulthood within the family circle, then the roles are even more strongly reinforced. And it's an ambivalent thing. You must get away; on the other hand, you're sacrificing an awful lot, to get away. Because there's such pleasure, and joy, and fun, in being part of the family theatre. And you've stepped outside it ... you've become another creature. At least in the eyes of those people ... you have to create yourself, anew.

In my experience, members of a family have always been the best audience for one another. My own extended family has never seemed to need an audience beyond themselves. A group of six of them will start telling each other stories that they all already know. But they will be telling them and overlapping and butting in on one another. Laughing till the tears are coming down their faces. So family, I guess, is like a ready-made audience, a built-in audience, a sense of a *safe* audience.

Kruk: They can be very harsh critics, too.

Hodgins: They can be harsh critics, but stepping out onto the stage in front of the public is another matter.

Kruk: I was also thinking that in a family you're introduced to the idea of identities, like the oldest child, the middle child, the father, the mother.... Family is where you first try on roles: the rebel, the pleaser....

Hodgins: That's right, and labels. This is why I felt I had to write *The Macken Charm* (1995) as a sort of balance to *The Barclay Family Theatre.* The Macken family, which is also huge, predominantly male, is also its own theatre, but the audience in that case presumes to create labels that are actually crippling. All the family members are given specific labels and expectations are made. So the main character has to get away from this, even though the attraction of this ready-made theatre, and audience, is huge. To escape the pigeon-holing borders that we were talking about earlier, it's necessary to get out of the family.

But I've been very fortunate in the family's response to my work. Either that, or I've been protected from what people might be really thinking! And even though I often will tread on family toes, so to speak, in my material, if I've been uncomfortable about it, I've checked it out, ahead of time, to see what the reaction will be.

Kruk: Well, it sounds to me as though *your* "family theatre" is a pretty good-natured one, and that comedy is much more evident than tragedy.

Hodgins: I grew up among people who laughed *a lot.*

Kruk: There's a lot of comedy in your writing, both in the structural sense of showing people coming together to build a community, and in its humour. And talking about humour ... I was teaching Leacock this year, and I notice you've written an "Afterword" to *Sunshine Sketches of a Little Town* (McClelland and Stewart, 1990) which tries to get at the secret of Leacock's humour. Do you think about a Canadian humour tradition, including Leacock, W.O. Mitchell, Robertson Davies, Mordecai Richler, that you are a part of?

Hodgins: There probably have been times when I've thought of one or another of those writers.... I've often thought that I've appreciated Stephen Leacock's humour more than a lot of other humorist writers, and I've never known why—except that maybe his people remind me of people I know. My official position is that I'm not trying to be a comic writer, ever; that people do laugh, people who enjoy life laugh, people make each other laugh, and if I'm doing a good job of creating the people that I'm writing about, then the humour in them will be an integral part of who they are.

I wouldn't make a very good serious satirist. To be a certain kind of satirist, you have to hate, you have to be really absolutely sure you're right and everybody else is wrong. And to me, almost everything has so many ways of looking at it, that the minute I wrote a serious piece of biting satire, I would be able to sit down and write one from the opposite point of view, and be just as sincere.

Kruk: That makes me think of a comment by Carol Shields, that either *everybody's* life is extraordinary or *nobody's* is. Everybody's life is worthy of attention. I think that notion creates the good-humoured humour in her work, too.

Hodgins: I identify with that. In fact, it's something that I struggle with, for the tradition of the novel, and especially the tradition of the short story, implies selecting one person whose story is, for the moment, more important than anybody else's story. And I just don't believe that anybody is worth more in this world than somebody else. How do you reflect that in fiction? It's a little more natural to do it in a novel, I suppose, because you've got more room, you can have ten main characters if you want, but even as soon as you do that, you're implying that the *other* people's stories aren't as important as *these* people's stories. So it's a tough one; I don't know if it's solvable, except maybe this is a partial explanation for the fact that people wander in and out of my books ... that somebody who's a minor character in one, will show up as a major character in another. I didn't plan that, but it seems a perfectly natural thing to do....

And I do tend to have more group scenes than a lot of writers, because I find that interesting things happen when you throw a bunch of people together, on the page. If you put a lot of people together, and they all have their say, in a way, we're treating them all as equals.

The novelist's territory is to be able to see from many points of view, so it seems a contradiction to set yourself up with a point of view that's superior to others. Except perhaps in the ability to see many points of view; that may be the only superiority that is possible. But to have many points of view is not to erase yourself! It's like voice: don't bother worrying about it too much, because it'll be there whether you want it or not.

Kruk: But for those of us who've read a lot—you've talked elsewhere about your love of Faulkner hindering your creative voice, as you began writing—it's not that simple—?

Hodgins: Oh no, it was never simple. But it was deciding not to worry about my own voice, to cut myself free from creating a voice, that made it possible for me to find the voices of my characters. I have no doubt that I have a voice. This is your voice, combined with your point of view, your world view ... and your place. Where you are in the world, and in time. I've overlaid invented voice on top of that, the voices of the characters. My natural voice probably includes Faulkner's voice, because I read so much of him. I probably even speak some sentences that I couldn't have spoken if I hadn't read him.

Kruk: I'd like to come back to the question of empathy or "overlapping." In "The Sumo Revisions" (*Barclay Family Theatre*), for example, you've got the character of Conrad, who seems to be the butt of the joke. Jacob Weins keeps thinking, "What a jerk, what a loser," but Conrad has this wonderful speech, which I thought was very funny—it made me laugh out loud—about manhood. [reading] He says, "They should send you out on the mountains for a month in the dead of winter, stark naked, and when you come back with a cougar's eyeball between your teeth, they should give you a certificate to hang on the wall that says, *you are a man now, so stop torturing yourself."*

I thought it was great, because it does seem to bring up the new self-consciousness about gender and masculinity ... and in the context of Jacob's own crisis of self.

Hodgins: And that is a subject that people don't laugh about very much. It might as well be made fun of; how do we know what our masculine or feminine identity is, anyway?

Kruk: It's too simplistic to call it a "mid-life crisis," but that's sort of what many of your male characters are going through ... like Spit Delaney, like Des Macken in "The Plague Children" (*Barclay Family Theatre*) when he's confronted by this strange youth, and he feels old and confused ... and Jacob as well, and his suicide attempt: he says he has to get "reborn," that's his expression. Again, coming back to gender for a moment, I wonder if this is more of a masculine plight. Perhaps men have more rigid identities for themselves?

Hodgins: Well again, it's not something I've thought about, but it's certainly consistent with my observations. I mean, you don't get very far into this life as a male before you start hearing about mid-life crisis. I had mine at thirty, and got it over with! And it's always interesting for the fiction writer to catch people at moments of crisis, of course, and those built-in moments of crisis that society foists on us. They don't have to be middle-age crises at all, but it's nice to have something to attach the crisis to, so that readers can identify it more easily.

Kruk: But the repetition of men's crises, suggests a certain empathy—only natural in a male writer, after all. Alistair MacLeod talks about how he feels great empathy for these men who risk their lives in their jobs, yet can never really articulate it, so in a way, it's as if he's speaking for them ... or better, they are speaking *through* him.

Hodgins: Yes. I think the first time it surfaced for me was with Spit himself. And it caught me off guard; I hadn't planned to identify with this character who's about as different from me as you can get. And yet what he went through is something I can easily imagine ninety per cent of males going through in this society: the sense of having identified yourself so strongly with a thing, or with a role, that to lose it would be to lose all sense of who you are, and what you're going to do with your life. This was one of the big surprises: feedback! It never occurred to me that I was going to get letters from readers, but I did: "I know Spit," or "I was Spit," or "Spit lives next door to me."

But only part of me—a huge part of me, of course—created Spit out of empathy. There was also the sense of wanting to challenge that attachment in the first place.

Kruk: But you're not satirizing Spit....

Hodgins: Oh no, I felt bad for him. I must have; that's why that other story ["Spit Delaney's Island"] came six months later. I could not stand leaving Spit the way I had left him.

Kruk: Coming back to "The Sumo Revisions".... I notice an obvious fascination with surfaces, in the gender-bending of Kabuki theatre (a male playing a female), the Sumo wrestlers themselves, who offer an elaborate performance of masculinity. Jacob wants to dress up in costumes. It comes back to theatre, to performance. So I wonder if we can link up these different concerns by asking: is community based upon performance?

Hodgins: I think that performance facilitates community, if that makes any sense; performance certainly is something that makes community easier to happen. Taking on roles, telling stories, identifying with one another, working together to make something happen ... artificially-created reasons to get together, like Community Hall stuff, shared disasters, shared joys ... all of these things that get rehearsed are theatre or performance of one kind or another.

And you have no way of knowing this, of course—again, in *Broken Ground*, performance and costume came in and became a through-line in the novel. The novel begins with the appearance of a figure who looks like he's been through a fire; his clothes are all burnt and shredded and he's a clownish-looking figure. His name was Wyatt Taylor. By the end of the novel, of course, everyone has been through a fire, and at the Dominion Day Festival, the tradition becomes to wear this garb. Even though he's gone, they wear their Wyatt Taylors! There's even a Wyatt Taylor look-a-like contest....

Kruk: Their shared experience of the Fire becomes ritualized....

Hodgins: It becomes ritualized, and I was a little nervous about this, until somebody sent me a package, saying "We heard from a mutual friend that you are writing a novel about the Great Merville Fire of 1922. I just thought you might be interested in some of the enclosed clippings." In there was a transcript of a talk given by one of the pioneer women I remember. And she talked about the earliest parties, which were in the schoolroom. I had already written about a party in the schoolroom. She said, "So-and-So used to always come dressed up in funny costumes to make us laugh, and one day he came in dragging this person"—who is now a distinguished grandfather in the district—"wearing a bearskin rug, bare feet, logging chains and his hair all greased up ... and this guy came in saying, 'I have just captured the Spirit of Merville. When I was blasting out my stumps, I found his cave underneath!'" And I thought—here it is, costume! I had already created a mythical figure, the Portuguese who used to live in a cave in the side of the creek, but I felt "How am I going to use him now? Do I write him out, do I get rid of him?" And I thought, no, I don't; better still, I have somebody dress up as the Portuguese and bring him into the party. And by the end of the novel, that's one of the costumes that people wear, every July, from then on.

Kruk: So you're intuitively guessing what was already there....

Hodgins: This is always happening! I think I've invented something, and I find out it was there all along. Makes you feel humble....

People have always given me more credit for imagination than I deserve. I remember the time that David Staines from the University of Ottawa came here; he was teaching one of my novels. I drove him all over the Island and introduced him to my relatives and friends, and when I took him to the ferry to go back to Vancouver to catch his plane home, he said "I used to think you had the best imagination in Canada. I now know you haven't got any at all!"

Kruk: The art of the imagination is not so much inventing things, perhaps, because bizarre things are always happening, but in making that link between people—"overlapping"—

Hodgins: In fact, the imagination is the ability to "know" what it feels like to be somebody else, to put yourself in somebody else's shoes. But it takes a certain authority...."What right have you to tell me a story, why should I listen to you?" You have to earn that right, and I think that's where voice comes in. Wright Morris, an American writer, has said, "In every novel"—and I would say it would be the same thing for a short story, but maybe in a shorter space—"there's an invisible contract in the first few pages, and by the time the potential reader has read these pages, they know whether they're going to sign the contract or not." There's a point beyond which if your reader goes, you have the right to assume they're going to stick with you to the end.

Kruk: Do you think there's a prescribed limit to this contract; say, the first five pages of a novel?

Hodgins: Well, I wouldn't want to put a number on it, but probably there is. One of the reasons I read novels is for that wonderful sense of being drawn into a complete world where I'm gong to stay for a while. I'm not going to be thrown out quickly, so if the beginning is slow, it better be awfully good writing about fascinating people, because then I'll say, "Okay, I'm going to settle down for a long time, a long slow time, but I already know I'm interested."

Kruk: Glad you raised the idea of creating voice again. You say you've done a lot of listening; this is evident in your characters, whose personalities come out through their voices, their speech rhythms and patterns. And even the narrator, in your work, has a kind of storyteller quality; it's not usually the neutral omniscient narrator.

Hodgins: I don't think I've ever written anything that has the traditional omniscient narrator voice; at least, if I've tried to, I'm sure it didn't come out that way, because the voice I write with is very close to a spoken voice, and that automatically evokes a personality. Not necessarily my personality, or what is dominant in my personality, but some aspect of it, or somebody I know or have heard.

Kruk: That's right: so "The Plague Children" opens, "Maybe this youth is dangerous and maybe he isn't, nobody knows for sure."

Hodgins: Right: who's saying that?

Kruk: It could be the voice of the community, the gossip, the speculation, but the way it opens, in this very human way, gives it a warmer, communal feeling. Very different from saying, "There was a youth seen running up the island today."

Hodgins: Yes. I wouldn't be able to write that story. In fact, a lot of stories start out with me trying to write an ordinary sentence to get me into it. And I think, "No, I don't want to write this story; I wouldn't want to read it." I have to wait until there's a sentence.

Kruk: So the voice is really important to the creation of story—?

Hodgins: The voice *is* the story. I know, that sounds so ... dogmatic. But there's no story until there's a voice to tell it, for me.

Kruk: You need a storyteller.

Hodgins: Yes, I guess I do. Even though, to me, it's a different storyteller for every book or story. Until I can find the voice that's going to tell this story, whoever that person is, whichever part of me that is, I can't tell it. But if I write down a sentence that has some personality to it, that makes me want to write the next sentence, and that will get me into the story.

Kruk: I see. To find the voice of the story itself; not just the voice of the character.

Hodgins: I remember when I tried to get started on *The Resurrection of Joseph Bourne* (1979).... I wrote the first page about a hundred times, because this was going to be a strange story, compared to what I'd done before. And I knew I had to create a feeling and an image, and I knew I had to do something to create a narrator who was so noticeable that we realized the storyteller was an important part of this story. Because that narrator's voice is going to be superimposed upon everybody else's voice. So I rewrote the first page, until I got a sentence or two that leapt to life, and I heard the voice of the person who was going to tell this story. Sitting in this room, I wouldn't be able to tell the story of the novel *The Resurrection of Joseph Bourne* in the voice I'm using to have a conversation with you. I would have to go out in the hall, and think a bit and come back in, with a different posture and maybe even change my shirt, to be able to do it. Somebody told me it's the village voice, the voice of whole community. At the time, I was thinking "I need a voice to tell this story that is more powerful than the story itself even." Because everything in this novel is going to depend upon the reader falling under the spell of a storyteller who's going to tell some pretty far-fetched things.

And to go back to what I said earlier about short stories, there has to be that package that leaps out and hits me between the eyes, saying, "You've got to write me, as a short story, even though you're in the middle of a novel." That will be a sentence in a voice that's very distinct that will make me want to do that. The sentence that opens up the story to me. If it's strong enough, if the personality or voice is strong enough, I can just go back to it, and then I will hear the voice again. So if I write three pages one day, and I come back the next day, if it's a strong enough voice, reading it will put me back into that voice's world. Because I don't want my characters to say what they *meant,* only; I want my readers to *hear* what they meant and I want them to talk like real people.

Kruk: When you speak of capturing voices and creating empathy for a diverse range of characters, you support what Mark Abley said in a review of *The Barclay Family Theatre:* "imagination, the process of reaching out, has in [your] work a moral force."[2] Crossing borders in the positive sense of "overlapping." Or, in other words, imagination in the service of empathy....

Hodgins: Yes, I like that. If I don't do anything else in this world, I think that's worth doing.

Victoria, British Columbia: December 1997

Notes

1   Delbaere, Jeanne, "Jack Hodgins: Interview," *Kunapipi* 9.2 (1987) 84-89. Quote p. 87.

2   Abley, Mark, "In Place," rev. of *The Barclay Family Theatre, Canadian Literature* 93 (Summer 1982) 120-22. Quote p. 121.

Alistair MacLeod:

"The World is Full of Exiles"

Kruk: I had planned to ask you about the appeal of the short story, and if you think you'll want to write in any other form, but I believe you *are* starting to do so....?

MacLeod: That's what I'm doing right now: trying to write a novel. It's called *No Great Mischief If They Fall* [published as *No Great Mischief*, 1999].

Kruk: Do you find writing it more difficult than writing short stories?

MacLeod: I find it different in that you've got to sustain a storyline for a long time, and history shifts as you're working on a novel. I think one of the advantages of the short story is, it's something like a hundred-yard-dash.... When you're dealing with a novel, you have to balance everything, you have to wonder if what you were saying two years ago is as relevant, in the present moment, as it was when you began. It's sort of like a long walk—like walking to Montreal, that's how I think of it. I've been working on it now for about five years.

Kruk: What does the title mean?

MacLeod: It's the statement that General James Wolfe, he who gave us Canada, made concerning Highland soldiers, at the siege of Quebec. And the idea was, you put them in the front lines because they would be big and strong, and they would get up there first—

Kruk: And take a lot of bullets....

MacLeod: Yes. And if they didn't get up, it would be "no great mischief if they fell."

Kruk: So, what *is* the appeal, for you, of the short story form?

MacLeod: I think it's sort of an intense moment, and I don't know if I would compare it to the lyric poem, but it allows you to write a letter to the world. And I think it's constrained, and I think you can deal with two or three characters in a given situation, briefly, and succinctly, and I think it's a good thing to do. I don't know about comparing various forms of literature.... There are obviously splendid poems that are worth more than bad novels, although one may be longer than the other, so I think that whatever you do in a literary manner, you should do to the best of your ability and probably just leave it at that.

One might argue that one may get more literary precision, perhaps, in some of those short stories that one finds in Joyce's *Dubliners,* as opposed to *Finnegans Wake.* And some of the D. H. Lawrence short stories are splendid as well. The point is that a "good" short story may, in the end, have as much "value" as a "long" novel. Length is not as important as quality, precision, accessibility, etcetera. Better to be "good" than merely "long."

Kruk: And what you're writing now—the novel—just demands a bigger canvas?

MacLeod: I think so. There are some things that you can accomplish in thirty pages, and some things you *cannot* accomplish in thirty pages. Actually, my short stories are generally fairly long short stories. If I have something to say, I just keep on until I've said it, and then that's the end. Length suits the "statement." Then

I try to get a string to put the beads on, so that I will have a necklace at the end, rather than beads rattling round in a box.

Very often, when I write stories, I write the concluding paragraph or line when I'm about half way through. And I find that this more or less helps me, because I think: "This is the last thing I'm going to say to the reader—the last paragraph or the last sentence." And this gives me a destination, and I think that you function better when you know whether you're going to Toronto or Toledo or Miami or whatever....

Kruk: Other writers have told me that short stories are not as well-received as novels—if not by critics, then perhaps by publishers. And yet you say you haven't come across this attitude yourself. You had no difficulty getting your two collections published—?

MacLeod: I think that *The Lost Salt Gift of Blood* (1976) was the first collection of short stories that McClelland and Stewart put out that was not from someone who was also writing novels. Jack McClelland told me that at one time.

In the case of someone like myself, I make most of my income from teaching. So my response to that problem of marketing is, why don't I just make my work as strong as it can possibly be? But I think if you're trying to live by your pen, or by your word processor, or by whatever tool you're using, you are under different kinds of pressures. And in that case, if somebody said to you, "You should write a novel, because we can sell it easier," you may say, "Okay, even though I don't like writing novels, I'll do this." I think that maybe in my situation—I teach Creative Writing at the University of Windsor—I may have kind of an advantage. I'm allowed to do—within reason—whatever I want, in a literary way.

Kruk: Who are the practitioners of the short story that you admire?

MacLeod: I admire a lot of people; I don't think I ever have anybody who's a model....

I think that what you try to do as a writer is try to develop a distinctive voice. And I think that one of the kind of wondrous things about literature is that no two voices are the same ... you can't have clone writing, or why do it?

Kruk: In one interview, you singled out William Faulkner and Flannery O'Connor–

MacLeod: Those are splendid writers. Flannery O'Connor was a splendid writer. And I think it's nice to think of Flannery O'Connor as a writer who didn't write an awful *lot*, in terms of weighing the pages, or measuring them in a longitudinal manner, and who didn't *have* to write novels, but wrote splendid splendid stories.

Kruk: And now, the obligatory question: which Canadian writers do you admire?

MacLeod: [pause] Oh, I hate doing this, because people are always going to phone up afterwards and say, "How come you didn't mention me?" [laughs] Well, Alice Munro is a very good writer.... And W. D. Valgardson ... a story like "Bloodflowers," I think is almost the best short story ever written in Canada. And Guy Vanderhaeghe has some very very good short stories–

Kruk: Do you think the short story is of particular interest to Canadian writers?

MacLeod: Well, it seems that very very good writing—some of the very best writing—is done by short story writers in Canada. But I don't know why that is so. The country's so tremendously huge—four thousand miles across—and the short story anthologies reflect that hugeness, I think: from Jack Hodgins to ... perhaps to people like myself, from one coast to the other. And I think it must be almost accidental.... I mean the Canada Council didn't put us all in a room and say, "Now we want short stories from you people." I think our excellence in short story writing evolved in the mysterious way that things do.

Kruk: I was wondering if you were especially interested in Scottish writers, given your Celtic roots?

MacLeod: Well, my work is very very popular in Scotland; I had a letter the other day from a man who wants to translate the stories into Gaelic, because he said they were the most Gaelic stories he knew....

Kruk: That's fascinating ... and you said "Fine, go ahead"?

MacLeod: Oh sure. I think that once you write these pieces, there's no need being precious about them. And they've been widely translated ... they've been translated into Urdu [the second language in Pakistan] and they've been translated into French, and they've been translated into Russian, and they've been translated into Norwegian, and so on. So I think it's nice to realize that well-crafted work can travel, you know, and that people can appreciate the work in Russia or Norway. It's very popular in Scandinavia, perhaps because Scandinavians inhabit the same kind of cold landscape, surrounded by water.

Kruk: I'm quoting now from an interview you did with Andrew Garrod. You said, "I'm interested in the idea of mistaking silence for lack of feeling or stupidity or something like that."[1] What do you mean, here, by silence? And is this related in any way to *men's* silence?

MacLeod: In that interview with Garrod, we were talking at one point about professional athletes ... people who are tremendously articulate, shall we say, with their bodies, but who, when they're interviewed, cannot describe what they do, although they can really *do* it. And that was what interested me when I was doing "The Closing Down of Summer" (*As Birds Bring Forth the Sun and Other Stories,* 1986). If you're supposed to get up on a podium and talk articulately about being a basketball player—it seems to me that has nothing to do with being a basketball player, it's a whole other skill. And one of the things I was interested in was: if you're in a completely verbal situation—like interviews and so on—and you're not a verbal person, the fact that you're not a verbal person may be mistaken for lack of intelligence or lack of feeling. The reverse would be true if interviewers were put on a baseball field or a hockey rink; they may not do very well there. So what I was interested in, was just kind of exploring what it means to not be articulate—in the acceptable way.

I don't know if you know the Newfoundland novelist Percy Janes. He's got a novel called *West Mall.* And there's a scene in it in which the Newfoundlanders are getting ready to go to Toronto to look for work. And when they go for the interview, they start to perspire.... Because they've the wrong kind of accent. And it's like people who come from Poland, or whatever, and have the wrong kind of accent ... these people are nearly all silent, unless they're speaking their own language.

Kruk: So you're getting at that kind of silencing which results from being colonized ... from being told too many times, "If you're not like us, you're wrong"—?

MacLeod: Yes ... or you may be *perceived* to be that way.

Kruk: Your stories return our attention to the physical life, to the life of the body. And this life of the body is as longed for as the landscapes, and the cultural communities, the protagonists leave behind. In "The Closing Down of Summer," as you pointed out, there's a kind of longing.... I mean the narrator is still living this existence, but the mood the story creates is almost one of regret at the fact that this is a passing way of life–

MacLeod: I'm not sure if that's true. It's a passing way of life; I'm not sure if he really regrets it, he's just thoughtful about it. The situation you've got here is a whole lot of people who encourage their children not to do what they do ... and the children do not rebel against this advice, they accept it! What happens, as I say in the story, is that when children take that advice, they become alienated—from the men, in this case, who give the advice. And there may be a kind of sadness in that.

Also, I think what I was interested in is that people—be they male or female—people who lay their bodies on the line everyday, have a different risk factor than do I, as a university professor. These people who work in that way, ticking in the back of their minds, is the possibility that they may lose their lives, just doing what they do. Not because they're stupid, or not because they're careless or anything like that, but because this is what they do. And that adds a different dimension to their working lives. They are people who are risking their physical lives in their day-to-day occupations. I mean I may flop over from a heart attack at my desk, but they may flop over from a heart attack too.... So I was just kind of interested in that idea.

Kruk: Yet it seemed in "The Closing Down of Summer" as if the protagonist were elevating the dangerous work he was doing, over what his sons were doing: jobs in law, dentistry, and so on.

MacLeod: No, I don't think so; I didn't mean that at all: I meant that their work would be different. They will go into different lives. "And what we're doing here"—the narrator says—"we're just using our bodies all the time, all the time, and our bodies are falling apart." These people—who are going to go into law or dentistry—they're going to pay to join the squash club because they're going to want to use their bodies, in another way.... I guess I was kind of interested in the idea that maybe you have to use your body some way or the other. As the narrator says, "They will join expensive clubs for the pleasures of perspiration; I'm not going to do that." Nobody who works with their body ever jogs.

Kruk: But what's interesting about the narrator of "The Closing Down of Summer" is that he does use his mind ... he starts university, and then drops out.

MacLeod: Yes. Well, I see these people as big people, you know? Physically big people. That's what they're given. Like the colour of your eyes ... the colour of your skin. And because they're big people, they can do these things, because mines don't hire people who weigh ninety pounds.... I think what happens to the narrator, is that he feels university is not enough for him. You hear this from big people–

Kruk: They're not comfortable in the classroom chairs–

MacLeod: No, not comfortable in the chairs, and the teacher's always looking at them because they're the first person that he/she sees, and so on.... So they kind of say, "I don't know if I'm *made* for this completely sedentary life. I can read the poems, I can write the papers, I can do this—but I just don't know if it's enough for me. So I'll go and do this instead." And of course, he's got a history of mining, because it's what his family does. And so he goes and does that. High physical risk, that's kind of what I'm interested in.

I think the bottom line is: all writers write about what they care about. And they care about very different things. A good example, in Canada, is some of the writing that comes out of Quebec which is a kind of contained place. And Quebeckers have a history that is not a melting pot history. I think in Newfoundland you get this too—although they write in English—there's a kind of fierceness that grows out of their history. And this is very different, say, than generations of people who grew up in the mall, or somewhere like that, who do not feel fiercely about anything other than their record collection....

"What do you worry about?" Here's an example: people in Canada worry about winter. There's a whole concern of big worries and little worries that run all across Canada. People trying to get their snow tires, trying to get their anti-freeze, trying to get their house winterized. Nobody worries about these things in Los Angeles. So I think your literature kind of comes out of what your concerns are—I don't mean worry as being negative—but what do you think about when you wake up at half past five in the morning? You think about whether your car will start....

Kruk: "Winter Dog" *(Birds)* opens with the worries about driving a long distance through the winter storm to see a dying relative, for instance.

MacLeod: Yes. I don't think that those worries or concerns are any better, or any worse, than the worries and concerns of people who live in the Southwest, like Arizona and New Mexico. But they are specific to a certain landscape. I think landscape just has an awful lot to do with all literature. I think *Wuthering Heights* couldn't have been written coming from any other landscape....

Kruk: Your point puts into question the whole "regionalist" label, because then *every* writer has their region ... every writer has their landscape. Even if it's an urban landscape: Morley Callaghan writing about Toronto, or Mordecai Richler writing about Montreal.

MacLeod: Oh sure. Mordecai Richler writes about a certain area of Montreal—his *region* of Montreal.

Kruk: Ken MacKinnon has said, "There is a sense in which all of MacLeod's work is more or less part of one great story with a single great theme ... the long homeward journey from exile."[2] What do you think of that description, "the long homeward journey from exile"?

MacLeod: I think what he's finding in the stories is that sometimes people do things that they don't want to, and I think this is one of the central issues of that short story "The Boat" (*The Lost Salt Gift of Blood*) ... that sometimes people choose to do what they do not want to do—perhaps out of love, or perhaps out of necessity, or whatever—and I think that's what MacKinnon is talking about. A lot of these characters are successful perhaps, but they feel exiled. They find themselves living their lives in places where they are perhaps not happy.

I think the world is full of exiles—you meet them all over the place—people who would really rather be back in Greece, back in the former Yugoslavia or wherever ... but who are unable to be where their hearts might lie.

Kruk: In both collections, you consistently adopt a male perspective. Is this conscious or unconscious?

MacLeod: Actually, in the story "Island" [published separately in a specialty edition by Thistledown Press in 1989 and then in *Island* (2000)], I have written from the female perspective. I just think about the story, and the question I ask myself is "Who gets to tell the story?" Because that changes everything.... For instance, my short story, "The Boat": if the mother were to tell that story, it would be a very very different story.

Kruk: So would you say your work is autobiographical?

MacLeod: No.

Kruk: Even though you're drawing on your Celtic roots, your regional affiliation—?

MacLeod: Oh, the regions are there for everybody, but I'm not telling the story of my life. It seems very autobiographical, but I think it seems very autobiographical because I work hard to make it seem true. Sometimes people who've only read one story of mine, will come up and say "Oh it's too bad that you've lost your father." My response to that is, "I didn't lose my father at all." And they say, "Oh but I thought it must be true." But I'm kind of glad to hear that, because I think that *is* what I'm trying to do, I'm trying to create an illusion of reality. So that when the Ancient Mariner tells his tale, it sounds pretty true. I think Alice Munro's phrase is "Not true but real, not real but true."

Kruk: But if you invent too much material, experiences that you can't get close to, that doesn't work either–?

MacLeod: That's right, absolutely. The reader will find you out. But you can know things through other ways than experience. You can read things, and you can imagine things, but it has to have— I think—the ring of authenticity. You have to keep saying to the reader "Do you believe me?" And the reader has to keep saying, "Yes, I believe you; I'll turn the page."

Kruk: This makes it clear to me why the short story is so appealing to you; you are in some way tapping into folklore, oral story-telling. In "As Birds Bring Forth the Sun," for instance, with the story of the grey dog ... and the appeal to oral tradition in the opening. Even in "Vision" (*Birds*), there are all these folkloric stories about blindness—woven together in a much more intricate story—but still it has an oral quality, because of the various narrators telling tales within it–

MacLeod: Well, I'm kind of interested in that, because I know that story has obviously existed longer than literacy has ... so there are all kinds of people who can tell stories, who can't read or write.

What I'm interested in with some of those folklore stories, and this is true in "The Lost Salt Gift of Blood" too, is that what is folklore to some people is truth to others.... So I think of people who live their lives according to folklore as being somewhat similar—I don't mean this in any derogatory way—to people who live their lives by certain strict religious principles. So if you're outside that religion, you don't understand why people want to go to Mecca, or why people have certain dietary rules or why people wear certain clothes or anything like that—you just think of them as quaint. But inside the Muslim mind, these principles are not quaint; they are *real*. They say, "*You* may think that's funny, but we'll *die* for this. This is the way we live. This is who we are." What I was dealing with in "The Lost Salt Gift of Blood" was this stupid man who goes into a culture that he doesn't understand, and runs around in it, trying to get his thesis finished. But he doesn't understand what he's collecting, because he's too dim, because he's there with his little blinders on.... I'm interested in the question, "What is it worth?" Grandma's old rocking chair may be an antique to somebody, and somebody else may throw it in the garbage, and buy a chair from K-Mart....

Kruk: Would you describe yourself as a realist writer?

MacLeod: Yes, I think so. What I think of, in terms of realistic writing, is: telling the truth as I happen to see it. I think Raymond Carver calls it "bringing the news." I don't see myself doing "romantic" writing. I'm satisfied enough with realistic writing.

I would like to think that what I do will last, will stand the test of time. I look at people around me and I say, "Now this will last." For example, the writing of David Adams Richards. What he's doing is "real" in that kind of tragic sense, somewhat similar to what Thomas Hardy did—people trying to live their lives in a certain place and a certain time. And in a hundred years, that work will just really really be standing. I think Sandra Birdsell's work will be standing. And you can say "What about the other hundred and sixty people"—

Kruk: —"that I haven't mentioned yet"—

MacLeod: —but those are two who come to mind. What I tell my writing students is, "You just do the best you can, and it will all find a home." Write from the heart.

Kruk: That's considered old-fashioned advice ... but it still works—?

MacLeod: It has always worked.

Windsor, Ontario: January 1994

Notes

1 Andrew Garrod, "Alistair MacLeod," *Speaking for Myself: Canadian Writers in Interview* (St. John's, Nfld: Breakwater Books, 1986) 154-71. Quote p. 162.

2 Ken MacKinnon, rev. of *As Birds Bring Forth the Sun and Other Stories,* by Alistair MacLeod, *Atlantic Provinces Book Review* 13.2 (May/June 1986) 3.

Jane Rule:

"I Don't Need Other People To Say What I Feel"

Kruk: What are you working on now?

Rule: I'm retired.

Kruk: From writing? I don't believe it....

Rule: It's true! I do an occasional essay or book review, but that's all.

Kruk: So, you feel you've said all you need to say in the world of fiction—?

Rule: That's right. It's done.

Kruk: It's nice to meet a writer who feels that way.

Rule: Well, I've been lucky, in being given time all through my career, to get my writing done. I haven't had to put it off, as so many people do. I taught every *other* year at UBC [University of British Columbia] rather than every year. And that gave me, really, sixteen months off for every seven or eight months I worked.

Kruk: When did you retire from UBC, and from teaching?

Rule: In 1976.

Kruk: So, since then, you've been writing full time.

Rule: That's right: from 1976 to 1989 [when *After the Fire,* her last novel, was published].

Kruk: As I said, I'm studying the Canadian short story; I feel it's a somewhat neglected genre. So I guess I'd like to start by asking you: what is the appeal, for you, of the short story form?

Rule: I rather think that *novels* can do a lot that *short stories* can't. And it seems to me that I've often used—and not always published—the short story to experiment with a point of view, or a technique: to see how it works in a small form, and to see whether or not it might fly in a novel. To pose parts of questions, rather than whole visions....

    So I've always thrown a lot of my short fiction away, because I've done it simply to find out how something works. In fact, I've never tried to sell it–

Kruk: But you have published three collections of short stories: *Theme for Diverse Instruments* (1975), *Outlander* (1981) and *Inland Passage and Other Stories* (1985). How did they come about?

Rule: Well, when I have enough that I think are interesting enough, I just—bring out a collection. And if somebody asks me for a short story, I'll send them whatever I have on file. But I really think of them much more as homework. As research.

Kruk: Written mainly for yourself—?

Rule: All of them were. And if they happen to be interesting to someone else, that's fine.

Kruk: Still, you did publish a great number of your stories in popular journals such as *Redbook,* and also in lesbian journals such as *The Ladder*. Wasn't this a way of supplementing your income?

Rule: The *Redbook* stories were, and they were written quite early on. I stopped writing them when I didn't need the money. Most of the *Redbook* stories aren't in the three published collections.

My New York agent knows nothing about the Canadian market, and so I would try to steer that office and say, "*Toronto Life* has asked for a story, *Chatelaine* has asked for a story; these are editors who are interested in my work." And one of the short stories I sent out was "Home Movie"(*Outlander*) which is a lesbian story.

First the agent sent it to *Toronto Life,* and got a very nice letter back, saying they thought it was an absolutely beautifully-written short story, they'd enjoyed it very much; unfortunately, it wasn't set in Toronto. So the agent sent it to *Chatelaine,* and *Chatelaine* said, "This is a lovely story, beautifully written; we love publishing Jane Rule's work. But most of our readers would not understand this story, and those who did would be offended." That's far more honest than the *Toronto Life* response, which is just a dodge.

All of the "Harry and Anna" (*Inland Passage)* stories are presents to my mother. My mother has a grand sense of humour and loved the "Harry and Anna" stories, but she could also recognize details of our family life.... My father, for instance, *did* in fact make my brother and me skeleton costumes for Halloween. My mother *did* say to us, "You can bring home any stray you want, as long as it's human." The characters aren't anything like my mother and father, but there's something in each of the stories that my mother can recognize as coming out of my childhood. And, of course, they were very saleable. My mother used to say, "You see, if you wrote everything for me, you'd be rich!"

Kruk: So the collected stories are the ones that you feel to be the best?

Rule: Ah ... they continue to interest me, and they seem to me to be whole in themselves, and not simply experiments. Although the experimental is very obvious in something like "Theme for Diverse Instruments" (*Theme for Diverse Instruments*) which I say is my thirty-six page novel with fifty-two characters!

Kruk: Certainly in the stories of *Outlander*, you're opening up a side of personal experience—lesbian experience—that is still unfamiliar to those of us in the "straight" "mainstream".... But other stories, the ones noted as being sold to *Redbook*, lack that focus on lesbian life. So it seems to me you span the continuum in terms of subject matter: from nuclear families to lesbian couples. Stylistically, you are also diverse, creating straight-forward realism as well as more experimental prose pieces.

But, for you, your novels are your main projects—?

Rule: Well, it has always felt to me that a novel is big enough so that you can create the climate. A short story—unless you're using a fairly conventional vision of the world—isn't. You don't have enough time to teach your reader how to read it. To perceive your character, for instance. However, I think that a *collection* of stories can do that.

I mean, a great many of my characters, left by themselves, would be people that readers would not understand, or like, or *get*. And so the novel appeals to me because what I want is psychological insight. The short story is a hard form in which to get that, unless you're working in fairly conventional terms and expectations.

Kruk: Define what you mean by "fairly conventional terms and expectations."

Rule: For instance, if I want to include homosexual characters. They are clichés for people you're supposed to hate, or feel sorry for ... and that is clearly not my attitude. If you take old people—the perception of old people is that they are problems. Not that they are *people* with problems. And it takes the time of a novel to teach your readers to fall in love with old people. And with children, too. There are so many cliché attitudes towards types of people.... People with handicaps—if you put a person with a handicap in a short story, it turns out to *be* a handicap.

Kruk: So they remain types....

Rule: Yes. And to write so that people have a new perception of a character as a unique human being ... you can do that so much better in a novel, than you can in a short story.

Kruk: But then what about the stories of *Outlander*, which is a book devoted to challenging our perception of lesbians as cliché characters—?

Rule: That is a book that I "gave" myself for my fiftieth birthday, for the lesbian community. Some of those stories were written for particular publications that were gay publications.... I collected them and asked Naiad to do it. Barbara Grier at Naiad said, "This will never sell," and I said, "I don't care." She was leery of putting essays and stories together; it didn't seem commercial. And it has sold quite well, in fact. It was only offered to the gay world. But it's out there for anybody to buy if they want to....

Kruk: Yet it hasn't been reprinted; it's still just with Naiad–

Rule: Don't say "just with Naiad." Naiad is a publisher that keeps books in print, on and on and on, and I wouldn't give a book to a big publishing house now in the States—I publish with Macmillan here in Canada. I could publish in the States—I have done—with a big press. And they're lousy. They sell books like cottage cheese!

It's out of date in six weeks, and they're terribly pleased if they sell out the first printing, within four months, and don't bother to print again. Unless they've got a huge best-seller. By the time somebody hears about the book, it's out of print.

Kruk: You mentioned something that I want to get back to, about the idea of a collection. You said, with a story itself, you can't seem to get enough out of it, but a collection is different. How do you define a "collection"? If these in *Outlander* were collected after the fact, does that make it a "collection"?

Rule: Well, I certainly write them one by one.... It's just like looking at one painting of a painter's collection: you may not know quite how to look at it, but if you go to a whole show, those paintings "speak" to each other, and you begin to see characteristic uses of metaphor, or image, or colour considerations....

Kruk: So a story collection can have the same effect?

Rule: Yes, because even though the stories may be quite diverse, I think you begin to get the tonalities and concerns.... If you read nothing but my "Harry and Anna" stories, you wouldn't really have much of a sense of me as a writer. It's much too narrow. In order to get a sense of the world I write in, a collection, I think, is necessary. And more satisfying.

Kruk: Right. But similarly, if we just read *Outlander*, and we didn't read any of the other stories, it would also be a partial vision–

Rule: Exactly.

Kruk: Looking at a *collection* of short stories, then, could you not compare it to a novel, in terms of depth and complexity?

Rule: It's different, but it has the richness of a novel, and that's why, for me, the selling of one story, or the publishing of one story, isn't as interesting as doing a collection. I feel more comfortable with that.

Kruk: Certainly *Theme for Diverse Instruments,* while "diverse," seems to me to work well as a whole. There's the recurrence of the "house" as theme or symbol: you've got four titles with "house" or "home" in them. I noticed also that you introduced and ended the collection with the more inventive or experimental stories. And most of the stories in *Inland Passage* are about relationships: raising children, marriages, marriages coming to an end. They seem accessible, written in the style of domestic realism. The story, perhaps, gives you a break from the intensity of the novel—?

Rule: Yes. "Dulce" (*Inland Passage*), for instance; I had more fun writing that story! I wanted to write about who the Muse really was. Because I think the Muse really is some poor, benighted woman who's the carrier of other people's fantasies.

Kruk: Are there any short story writers you especially admire? Any influences?

Rule: Influences, no, but I certainly admire Alice Munro enormously. I think that her short stories are wonderful.... Marian Engel's short stories I love, and they aren't well enough known. She brought out a collection called *Inside the Easter Egg,* which came out the same year her novel, *Bear,* came out, and *Bear* was such a—scandal—the book of short stories just went by the board; nobody paid any attention to it.

In fact, the writers who might have been my mentors I didn't encounter until I was old enough to have pretty well established what my own voice was. I think I was influenced more by poets than by prose writers—people like Donne, Auden and Yeats.

Phyllis Webb, here in Canada, is a poet I've admired enormously. And Adrienne Rich, of course.

Kruk: It's interesting that you mention these traditional poets—so-called "dead white males" Yeats, Auden, Donne—in the same breath with female, and feminist, poets such as Webb and Rich. But you admire their use of language equally. And that use of language influences you in your prose-writing?

Rule: Very much. As music does. I like the passion and complexity of the metaphysical writers, Shakespeare. But in contemporary stuff, I read mostly women. I don't read many contemporary men.

Kruk: Do you know for certain, when you start writing, if you're writing a short story or a novel?

Rule: Most of the time, I do know; but occasionally I've started what I thought was a novel, and realized "This is not going to be a novel, but in fact it can be shaped as a short story." And "Inland Passage" is one of them; that particular story started as possibly the beginning of a novel. And then I thought "No: I want to keep this light and not complex, and so I will simply shape it as a meeting, rather than a beginning."

Kruk: You see the short story as a form which allows you to keep things "light," emotionally?

Rule: Well, you can suggest backgrounds, but you don't have to get into all of that. I'm trying to think of the title of the one that is about a man who's just died, and the couple who are going to his funeral....

Kruk: "Blessed are the Dead" (*Inland Passage*).

Rule: Yes. That was going to be the opening of a novel.

Kruk: "'Such a satisfying death,' Martin said, shaking out the *Vancouver Sun*."[1] It's a good opening....

Rule: And then I thought, "No, this is just good fun," and I saw the shape of this, and that the tonality ... was not going to open out. It was staying so marvellously light-hearted and goofy–

Kruk: Yes. But you're not suggesting, then, that your short stories are all "light," that they're all comic vignettes?

Rule: No, but I'm saying that that tone was so strong—I wouldn't have ever written a whole book in that tone—but it's so strong it would have been hard to break into other elements of attitude. I was thinking it would be very interesting to look at a community at the loss of its first member—all being the same age—and how it affects various people. So I was playing with openings. And I just had fun with this one, and thought, "There—and that's all I need to say about that situation; I've got what I want."

I also love doing a short story that gives a sense of lots of world around it. I do that in "My Country Wrong"(*Theme for Diverse Instruments)*—create the sense that there's a lot of world around this story, that it isn't a little world in itself.

Kruk: Obviously, what you're aiming for, in a novel, is complexity. Many different voices....

Rule: Yes, but as I say, it also has to do with tone. With "Theme for Diverse Instruments," I had no idea how long it was going to be. It could have gone on forever, but it would have driven a reader *mad.*

Kruk: I don't mean to make it sound too neat, but there is a skill you've developed at writing a kind of short story that is spare and not overwritten. Do you write a lot and then cut back, or do you start out writing that way?

Rule: I have become increasingly spare as a writer. My earlier work is much more ornate.

Kruk: Do you think this is something all writers have to work through?

Rule: Well, I think we go into writing with the voices of our education. I think you don't *know* what you know. So you elaborate what you know, and call on all the help you can get! *Desert of the Heart* (1964) is filled with literary allusions.

Kruk: Do you think writers need to get rid of those voices?

Rule: For some of us, not; for some of us, they may serve forever. But I really thought: "I'm outgrowing my education; I don't need other people to say what I feel." I don't need to be backed up by Dante, or Shakespeare, or whoever.

Kruk: Talking about our shared literary education.... Do you accept the label "realist writer"?

Rule: Yes.

Kruk: Then what does "realism" mean to you?

Rule: I think, by and large, I really want my reader to feel that this is a believable world, and that the concerns in it are the concerns of the world we live in together.

Kruk: Right now, a popular critical opposition is that between "postmodernist" writing and "realist" writing. Do you have any sense of "postmodernism," or interest in it?

Rule: I think postmodernism is a hilarious term; I haven't any idea what it means. I left the academy before it was invented.
But I think that there is a danger for writers living in the academy; I think it's a very bad climate for writers ... because of the fierceness of critical fads. And those are not the things that we should be listening to; we should be listening to what it is we've got to say, and how on earth we can say it. And not be particularly influenced by what is now acceptable—either in subject matter, if you're trying to sell it, or in stylistic quirks, if you're trying to impress scholars. And I think both of those temptations—whether writers are popular for dollars, or academic for praise—are really deadly for writers.

Kruk: Okay, another huge question, huge debate: is it possible to distinguish women's writing from men's, in any way?

Rule: Umm ... I don't suppose it is. I suppose you could make generalizations but the moment you do, you think of a thousand exceptions. I think that my own choice to read more women writers than men writers is because I find women now write about things that interest me more than men do. Men are inclined to be grandiose and historical, and elaborate in their inventions, and women are ... much more domestic and humane in their concerns. And that's what interests me. The amount of violence and anger that is in a lot of men's writing ... I find hard to take.

Kruk: But in Alice Munro's stories there are fierce battles on the domestic front. All those mothers and daughters, battling–

Rule: But those seem to me to be *real* battles ... you don't get in Alice Munro the extremes you get in Timothy Findley–

Kruk: In some ways, although a male writer, he presents a feminist point of view.

Rule: Oh he does; politically he does. But as he chooses to express it, he chooses to go to the most violent, most offensive things people do, in order to analyze and to cope with evil. I enormously admire Tiff Findley and his work. But I am not comfortable with it ... I read it as a duty; I don't read it as a pleasure. *Headhunter* (1993) is devastating. And I know that temperamentally my view of the world is not nearly as bleak as his.

Kruk: We were talking earlier about the fact that you've been writing as a voice of the gay community, with the stories later collected in *Outlander,* as well as in your many essays for gay publications such as *The Body Politic* and *The Ladder.* Is it really possible to be a lesbian *without* being a feminist?

Rule: Oh yes ... alas. There are a lot of very conservative lesbians.... I think I became very much aware of that terribly conservative world when Donna Deitch was trying to raise money to make the film *Desert Hearts*.[2] And the way she did it was to ask people like Gloria Steinem to give fund-raising dinners. And they asked a number of very rich, very conservative lesbians ... and they weren't "out" in public, but they had whole worlds they lived in. And because Anita Bryant had caused so much trouble in Florida, suddenly, lesbians who had nothing to do with "causes"—they didn't believe in them—wanted films made, wanted to sponsor that sort of stuff.

Kruk: So these women helped raise money for the film?

Rule: Yes. But they were *not* feminists....

Kruk: On the flip-side of this question.... I think of Adrienne Rich's "lesbian continuum," and her suggestion that you must inevitably be "lesbian," in some sense, if you're part of feminism. That's been open to question, too. At first, lesbianism seemed to come out of feminism. But now, it's changing direction, there's gay and lesbian studies, there's "queer theory," a seemingly more politicized approach to these studies....

Rule: I was talking to a scholar from Smith College about this the other day. She said, "You don't fit in 'queer theory'," and I said, "I know I don't; it's mostly invented for gay male fiction anyway."

Kruk: This raises the question of whether, as a lesbian, you identify with the feminist movement or with the gay rights movement....

Rule: I don't identify with either of them. What's that old cliché: "I am a part of all that I have met."

Kruk: So you eschew the identity politics that force you to line up one way or the other–

Rule: You get labelled anyway.... For instance, I was very badly criticized for writing for *The Body Politic,* because it was male-identified.

Kruk: Obviously, you've seen both sides of the fence. This leads me to your thesis in *Lesbian Images* (1975), that there is a lesbian tradition of writers. Would you consider yourself part of it?

Rule: Sure. Virginia Woolf is part of that tradition ... Vita Sackville West is part of that tradition ... Willa Cather is part of that tradition. I don't mind being there, that sounds like good company.

Kruk: Barbara Gabriel has suggested in interview with Timothy Findley that the homosexual is in a privileged position to understand the myths of gender society promotes.... What do you think about that idea?

Rule: From my own experience, I think people can gain insight or be narrow, from whatever vantage point they're given. I don't think that, because you're a homosexual, you have a better insight into the clichés of gender.

Kruk: As an example, there are these very conservative lesbians you mentioned.... But it gives you the impetus, perhaps—the opportunity—?

Rule: Yes, I think so. But all of us are given all kinds of opportunities; we don't always take them.

Kruk: True. But *you've* taken the opportunity. This leads to the familiar question, and at the risk of repeating it, does your sexual orientation affect your writing in any way?

Rule: It does sometimes.... It was very interesting; June Callwood once did a stage interview with me at Harbourfront in Toronto. And she said, "I wanted to say, 'How do you see being a lesbian in relationship to your writing?' But first I thought I'd try this on myself: 'How do you see being a heterosexual having any effect on your writing?' And she looked up, and the audience was just cracking up! [laughs] Of course it affects your writing, but how would you answer that question? If you're writing about sexuality in any way, your own sexuality is relevant to it. You have a personal experience that you bring to it....

For instance, I think *being tall* affects how I write. This scholar from Smith College—she's short—said to me, "I felt discriminated against all through your fiction!" I said "Size has to do with extinction; when a species begins to get big, it's going to quit. So don't think it's a great virtue!"

Kruk: There hasn't been very much criticism of your work, but are you familiar with Marilyn Schuster's article, "Strategies for Survival: The Subtle Subversion of Jane Rule"? She writes, "In Jane Rule's fictional communities, difference is valued and jealously protected. The outcasts who form these communities evolve an unwritten social contract that protects their outcast status, rejecting blind, brutal conformity to a dominant norm. They are, in a sense, communities built on a lesbian model."[3] I'd like your comment on that.

Rule: I don't know what a "lesbian model" means.

Kruk: Perhaps, the "lesbian model" goes back to current "queer theory" debates, or earlier, feminist studies, which used the lesbian as an image of the ultimate feminist, ... the idea that because you're two women together, you're not going to get into the hierarchical power-tripping that heterosexual couples can get into, with the man generally dominating the woman–

Rule: Which is a fine fantasy....

Kruk: However you define it, though, this theme of "community" comes up so often in your novels and in your stories–

Rule: I'm fascinated by the way that people make community, because so many of us are cut loose from the communities that we would otherwise inherit as our own. People move around; we don't stay in the towns we were born in; we don't stay near the families we have. And extended family therefore gets invented out of strangers. It's fascinating to watch the different kind of responsibilities people take on ... the different kinds of needs they ask to be filled.

Kruk: Okay: how would you define *community*?

Rule: Community has all kinds of responsibilities involved. One of the reasons I like living in this one [Galiano Island, B.C.], is that the fire department is volunteer! A great deal that is done in this community is done by people who know there is a need, and respond to it. Not because they're paid for it. And so, the year before last, my swimming pool was the pool for the kids in the summer. I lifeguarded, seven days a week, two hours a day—I'm too old to do it now. But there was a *need*: the children weren't learning to swim, because the ocean was too cold and too scary to learn in. So these kids were going out in boats, and didn't know how to swim! And I thought, "We've got to do something about this": so we did. But all over the island there is a sense that you don't go some place and buy this; you have to do it for each other. We don't have people who are paid to go in and tend sick people; we organize that and do it. We don't have gravediggers; we do it ourselves. Here, it's so blatant and so obvious; it's just so clear that people need each other.

Kruk: That's obviously something that's really important to you, and to your characters—the connection with a larger group or community. I'm interested by the fact that in your fiction the younger generation is always being nurtured, in some way, but not always by biological parents.

Rule: I don't think this is a good thing or a bad thing, I just think that, given the state of the world, very few of us are in the neighbourhoods we were born in. And that if we're going to have community, it's not a given; it has to be made.

If it's your grandmother, you know you're supposed to be responsible. If it's the old lady up the road, you may or may not know. But if you don't have a grandmother, it seems to me people nearly instinctively find one.

Kruk: Like your story where the family goes out and gets one: "A Chair for George" (*Inland Passage*). You don't buy into a belief in the biological imperative, that women have to have children to truly nurture, to be fulfilled in that way–

Rule: No. But I think some women do feel that, and I don't have any quarrel with it: if that's what women want to do, they should go ahead and do it. But I think the notion that is—trapping—is not that people want to do something, but that *everybody* has to do all of the *same* things.

Kruk: The word "moral" also comes up a lot in your writing.... Here we are, at the end of the twentieth century, and I'm thinking, "That old-fashioned word 'moral' flies in the face of how society's moving, in our increasingly postmodern era ... symbolized by computers ... cyberspace ... 'virtual reality'." What does "moral" mean to you?

Rule: It is not necessarily good. Morality for me is a neutral term and a lot of people's morality, I think, is bad morality. But the moral content is part of an experience, just as taste is part of food, and texture is part of food. And I'm fascinated with the moral content of human experience. I look at Dante's *Divine Comedy* and say, "This is very bad morality; this is a very sadistic, very vicious piece of work." It's a revenge work—fascinating. People talk about the grand inspiration for writing. I think with an awful lot of very good writing, the motive for it is just—awful.

I suppose one of the interests I had in writing *Contract with the World* (1980), was to explore a bunch of people—artists—and what motivated them to do what they were doing. Partly to take away some of the silly romance about what inspires artists: grief inspires them, hate inspires them, love inspires them—it's open. My sense is that a concern for morality, a concern for good and evil, is inherent in the human condition. And it's very dangerous. It is what really motivates people, most of all, to be brutal and to be destructive. And so we really do have to understand it ... we really do have to understand the motive for being right, the motive for being righteous, and what those things mean. And they mean dying for Allah and going straight to Heaven, and sending as many infidels down to Hell as you can when you go.

Anybody who's in love with finding an absolute morality should be locked up—put some place—but not in control.

Kruk: But that doesn't mean there aren't moral choices to be made–

Rule: That's right. It's part of the human condition, and that's why it seems to me so very important to understand our morality. We, in this culture, base a lot of our moral attitudes on a teaching that starts with, "God so loved the world, he killed his only son." Now what the Hell that has to do with love, I don't know. I think it comforts "Gold Star Mothers" during wars—they've given their sons. But who the Hell are they to think they *own* them?

I think we have to look at the basic teachings that we're given, and say "What does this mean? How are we behaving?" I am amazed at people being so upset at the violence against women, when nobody ever seems to complain about the violence against *men*--which is far, far more universal. I mean, if you turn on the television, you're not often seeing women beaten up, you're seeing men bloodied, bludgeoned, decapitated—it's only when it happens to women that people start getting upset. I just think, "Wait a minute—when we talk about violence against women, we don't own up to the fact that, in practically every generation, we send our young men abroad to kill and rape other people"—rather than figure out what to do with their young sexuality and energy. The message is: "This is the way you become a man—but not here."

Kruk: Sounds like you are saying that violence against women, this issue, is part of a larger culture of violence that we live in. This is something you abhor, yet want to draw our attention to— through your fiction, its own suggested moral values....

Rule: Absolutely. I really do think that good morality is based on love, but you have to find out what you mean by "love." And I don't mean by "love" what Christians mean by "love." I don't mean killing people to show how much you love the world. Like Abraham and Isaac: "Okay, now that you've shown that you will kill your kid, you don't have to." It's ugly, ugly stuff!

I really think that the job for the world, if it's going to survive, is to dismantle all religious structure. Because historically, we look at it, and we say "There isn't very often an example of any powerful religious structure that hasn't been, on the whole, terribly terribly destructive." When you take a look at the blood in Palestine ... from the very beginning, that has been the bloodiest land in the world, and it's because three different religions are in conflict there.

Kruk: With their different, strongly held moral convictions. Maybe it's the organization, the hierarchical organization, of religious belief—?

Rule: The setting up of a community of righteousness ... is apparently a very dangerous, bad thing to do. You know, on this island [Galiano], you have to get along whether you agree with people, or like people, or not. I joked when I first came here, saying, "The one thing we agree upon is that fires do have to be put out. Beyond that...." For instance, some people want a garbage dump, some people don't. We don't agree on very much ... and that feels comfortable. Because it *does* mean that people have to learn how to live with different views ... and to know that that's possible as long as there is a respect for each other's places.

Galiano Island, British Columbia: June 1994

Notes

1 Page 237, from "Blessed Are the Dead," by Jane Rule, *Inland Passage* (Toronto: Lester and Orpen Dennys, 1985) 237-47.

2 *Desert Hearts,* a Samuel Goldwyn Production, directed by Donna Deitch, 1985.

3 Schuster, Marilyn R., "Strategies for Survival: The Subtle Subversion of Jane Rule," *Feminist Studies* 7.3 (Fall 1981) 431-50. Quote p. 443.

Carol Shields:

"Inhabiting the World"

Kruk: *Various Miracles* (1985) was the book that caused people to label you a postmodernist. And then you wrote *Swann: A Mystery* (1987), with its experiments with narrative voice and point of view. How well do you feel the postmodern label applies to those works?

Shields: Well, I certainly think the stories are more adventurous. I really thought of them as experiments when I started out; just trying out different things. So just the fact that they were experiments was a kind of liberating influence. I didn't really know if they'd ever form a book; I'd hoped, I guess, that they would. Some of them seemed more like narrative ideas than stories. And, of course, I have certainly read postmodernist fiction, and even though I have as much trouble as anyone else *defining* it, I have a sense of what it is, a feel for what it is, and I expect that some of those stories—certainly not all of them—fall into that general category.

Kruk: I think you said somewhere that you wrote those stories to help you loosen up the narrative point of view so that you could write *Swann,* which you were having trouble with.

Shields: Yes, that's absolutely true.

Kruk: So you wrote the stories for *Various Miracles* all more or less around the same time?

Shields: Yes. I had already started *Swann*, and had got stuck, so I just put it aside. I spent about a year on them. One of those stories I had written earlier, but the rest I hadn't, the rest I wrote during that one year.

Kruk: So you saw them as going together, as a book of experiments.

Shields: Yes—and of course, after a while, I saw that there was another kind of theme that seemed to be running through them. But that just happened; I didn't sit down and think, "Oh well, I'm going to be writing about language." I was just writing about a number of different things that I was thinking about. But I very consciously—in writing those stories—decided that I would let the stories have their way, in a sense, which is something I hadn't done much before.

Kruk: I just want to get at how much you're interested in the postmodern experiment—in terms of what you like to read, what you like to write....

Shields: I'm very interested in it, but I'm only interested in it when the language that underpins it has a kind of animation and felicity about it.... I'm trying to think who else's stories I've liked, in that mode.... I love William Gass; he's a writer I like very much. I've liked some of a man called Guy Davenport, he's an American too. There don't seem to be very many *women* postmodern writers, do there?

Kruk: I think you said something about wanting to combine the two literary modes: combining the postmodern language play with a realist's sense of character and story.

Shields: Yes. And I don't know why we *can't*. And this is another thing: a newly converted postmodernist is the most elitist of critics. Unwilling, really, even to consider notions of character. And I wonder why ... and I can't help thinking that we will bring the best that postmodernism offers into fiction—because it offers a lot to a writer.

Kruk: Like the freeing up, which you've noted, of your later writing....

Shields: Yes!

Kruk: About stories: I wonder if there is a kind of qualitative difference, as well as a quantitative difference, between a novel and a short story. A short story is of course much smaller, but is there a different feel to it, or can it do different things, as compared with the novel?

Shields: I have thought about that, but I haven't resolved it very well. Sometimes I think of short fiction as being more closely allied to poetry than novels. I don't think of the short story in that old Hemingway sense, of being exceedingly spare, so that every detail in it must add up to the statement of the story. I like a kind of *novelistic* density in short fiction. I like more than a lot of the stories that I read have, in fact. I suppose I resist some of those myths; like, people say, "It's harder to write a good short story than a novel." I just think that's total nonsense. It's harder to write a novel, every time, than a short story.

Kruk: Because it's just—bigger?

Shields: Yes, it's just bigger. And it's a tremendously complex balancing act.

Kruk: You told me why you started writing the stories of *Various Miracles*—it was to help you with *Swann*--but a lot of women have said that writing short stories was just a practical choice for them, because, especially when they have children, they don't have the time to write a novel. Plus, you once said you're primarily interested in novels. Is that still true?

Shields: I think so. When I finished *Swann,* I wasn't ready to start a novel again, so it made perfect sense for me to work on short stories, and I thought, "Oh, this is rather a nice rhythm, actually: not to do novel after novel."

When you write, there's the rather abstract reward of actually just finishing something; and then there's the *real* reward of placing it somewhere. Because as I was writing *Various Miracles,* I was selling them [the stories]. And I can see why people would like this. With a novel, you go two or three years without any reinforcement at all. But I don't think it makes much sense to be writing short stories, if that's not your form ... just because it happens to fit in with raising children, or whatever. I feel sometimes, when people show me their short stories, that they should be writing a novel. It's a different way of thinking, it's a larger way of thinking, they're thinking out a larger design—so that the actual writing seems out of proportion to the story that they're telling. It doesn't fit.

But I don't think of the short story as "filler" and unimportant. Writing *The Orange Fish* (1989) stories gave me a great deal of happiness. I loved writing those stories. I didn't feel I was working in an inferior form—that's what I wanted to say. Because, funnily enough, most of my favourite writers—like Mavis Gallant, and Alice Munro—are short story writers. And short stories that are memorable do have a wonderful power about them. I'm an enormous fan of Alice Munro, and her stories often have for me that novelistic feel to them. And I think she's wonderful at shaping the *ends* of her stories. I don't know anyone who writes better endings than she does.

Kruk: When you are contemplating putting out a collection of short stories, you must look at the book, and see how it works, with all the stories together. There are stories written around the same time as those included, for example, which were left out of *The Orange Fish,* so you must have had a sense of its shape.

Shields: Yes. Well, I didn't leave them out, my editor did, and so he was maybe more conscious of the shape. He also spent a lot of time with both those books [*Various Miracles* and *The Orange Fish*]; he was the editor for both–

Kruk: Who was the editor?

Shields: Ed Carson. He spent a lot of time on the arrangement of those stories; he felt they had to be arranged in a certain way. And as soon as the book came out here in Winnipeg, I ran into a friend of mine—the day after she bought the book. And she said, "Oh, I read—whatever it was, the last story in the book ["Milk Bread Beer Ice"]—first." And I said, "Oh, if you only knew how much effort this man put into organizing these!" [laughs] And then I thought, Well that's the way I do it; I always read the shortest story first. I look through the table of contents and pick the shortest one, and then I might start at the back—I certainly don't read front to back.... I heard Alice Munro say something, in a radio interview, about why she hasn't written a novel. And her belief is, that isn't the way life *is,* life is much closer to the structure of a short story ... life is anecdotal.

Kruk: I think you said you had trouble with the artificial nature of plot.

Shields: Yes, I do. I see it more and more as a set-up. The novel I'm writing now, there is some of this kind of set-up. But I hope I'm approaching it somewhat parodically; I think I am. Well, I hope so.... I sort of feel I'm using the conventions, instead of being used by them.

Kruk: You also said, in *The West Coast Review,* "I like to think that these categories of reader response are breaking down as rapidly as the boundaries between genres, and that this process has been accelerated by feminist writing."[1]

Shields: Well, I guess most of the writers I know, where I see this breaking down, have been women: starting with Susanna Moodie. And certainly with Alice Munro's *Lives of Girls and Women*—I think it crosses that boundary. *A Bird in the House,* which is my favourite Laurence book, feels very much like a novel to me. Maybe there are men who are doing this too—but why can't I think of any at the moment? And I think people like Daphne Marlatt and my friend Sandy Duncan, who's using fable and novel—women seem to be doing a lot of this. And maybe there are real reasons for it; maybe women's writing comes out of different forms—it comes out of diaries and journals and letters, and it comes from ... different places.

I suppose there's nothing about existence that interests me more than language does. I think it's what makes us human, and it embodies us in a way that physicality doesn't, for me. I guess I'm interested in the transcendent moment where people do sense something spiritual, or are somehow enabled to. I'm not talking about people who are connected to religions, or other forms of spirituality, but just sort of a human spirituality. And what creates those moments? We don't know; I mean I think it's a kind of chemistry, but I think language has to be a very large part of that, and opens up that ... kind of moment.

For example, I feel with "Today is the Day" [in *The Orange Fish*], not everyone understood what I was talking about. But I met someone who told me—we were talking about language, this was a man who knew a lot of languages, and told me some wonderful language stories—and he told me about an African language which is spoken only by women. And so of course that was the idea behind it. And also the other source I suppose, was that I was on a trip in Louisiana, driving on the highway ... they've built this big highway across the swamps, the Bayou. And it must've interfered with the wildflower life, because, while we were driving (it's a very long drive; it's about forty miles over this stuff) there were women planting wildflowers down the median. Hundreds of them! So it must have been like a big project that some community had done. It just thrilled me, for some reason, to see this very bizarre sight. So that, and then this language thing, were the trigger for that story.

Kruk: Were you thinking of the question of art when you were writing *The Orange Fish,* and its title story?

Shields: Well, I guess I'm always thinking about the question of art in a way. The making of art, and who makes it, and how it's made. Because it always seems to me that it really comes from common clay. And it's extraordinary to think of that, that people are capable of doing, making, something larger than they are. So the mystery of art is something I suppose I'm always thinking about.

But no, with "The Orange Fish" I wasn't thinking about that particularly. I was thinking about—death, of getting old. And of how one thinks of going toward death in this linear way, of simply going through birthdays, and going through years. But instead— the other way of arriving at death is through ... multiple images. Rather than linear, by multiplication. Which is what happens to the painting of the orange fish. So that death arrives ... in another direction. It's a kind of space-time thing. That was what I was going after. The orange fish isn't dying because it's getting older and older; it's dying because there are suddenly *millions* of them.

So that death simply comes on a different time line. I don't think many people *did* understand that ... but it's all there, if you read it!

I was very surprised, with that story, that people sort of thought of the characters as being real people, because I didn't think of them as "real people."

Kruk: Did you write *A Fairly Conventional Woman* (1982) with the issue of the artist in mind?

Shields: I thought of Brenda Bowman as a woman who discovers that she is an artist, and nothing in her life has prepared her for that ... acceptance. And she's someone who thinks of art in a kind of mystical sense, but of course, how can it be mystical when she herself has not thought of herself as having an entree to that world of mysticism—? I try to talk about the way the images for the quilts arrive in her head. So I suppose that was a way of demystifying the artist, too.

Kruk: You said *A Fairly Conventional Woman* was your favourite book. Why?

Shields: I loved writing it. Certainly structurally, it's the most daring of the those four early novels, the going backward and forward in time. And I loved dealing with the fifties, as a period, and just thinking about that time again, talking about it. And, you've probably noticed in all my fiction, that I love the idea of the randomly assembled group of people—for whatever reason they are assembled. And so this is why I loved this—writing about the convention. It gave me a lot of pleasure to write. And it gave me a lot of pleasure to fit it in with the other novel, *Happenstance* (1980). It was like a game, playing it, and getting everything just right. In fact, there are two chapters in each book on their [Brenda and Jack Bowman's] first meeting—because I think that is the great narrative that married people share—and they're quite different, of course.

Kruk: How they first met, and became interested in each other....

Shields: Yes. And the editor I had at the time, phoned me, when I was in the "Brenda book" [*A Fairly Conventional Woman*], to say "You forgot the cheese sandwich!" So I had to put the cheese sandwich back into their meeting scene. The other thing I wanted to do was to write a novel about an intelligent woman, who hadn't necessarily had a lot of formal education. I wanted her to be reflective. I almost never find reflective women in novels. And I think everyone has this reflective side; why doesn't it get into our novels?

Kruk: What do you think about the argument that women write differently than men?

Shields: I think there are certain things about the *tone* of ... a woman's voice that's different. It tends to be much more intimate ... more personal. It has a "present-tense" feel about it, to me.... I guess the thing that worries me when you start to talk about women's voices is that you get into this idea of a "miniaturist" voice ... which I think is diminishing to women. That precious Katherine Mansfield-ish kind of voice. So that worries me a little bit, but I certainly think that women deal very differently [than men do] with similar kinds of experiences.

Kruk: Would you say there's more interest in people's daily lives?

Shields: Yes, although I understand that men are now starting to write domestic novels, and they're thought of as being very sensitive and revolutionary. [laughter]

Kruk: It does seem that, by virtue of their socialization, women particularly emphasize personal relationships in their writing. Joan Clark told me she wasn't interested in "reinventing the world"; I believe she meant that a lot of male writers like to create a world, a large vision. Whereas it seems that a lot of women are more interested in going down deep....

Shields: Inhabiting the world, I think: that's what I would say.

Kruk: Do you feel your fiction is in any way an expression of your feminism?

Shields: I think, inevitably, it is, but it's not something I sit and think about as I write: that I'm now expressing my feminism.

I asked a friend of mine, who's Jewish—in fact, she says she's the most Jewish woman in Winnipeg! She's president of the Jewish Council—I asked her one time how much time she spends thinking about being Jewish. And she said, "About as much time as I do thinking about being a woman." Which I thought was a good response; it's absolutely *part* of her. And I feel being a feminist is part of me. And I'll always express myself as a feminist, simply because—it's the only language I know.

Kruk: You said before that you write for yourself. You don't particularly write for a female audience, or think about that?

Shields: No, I don't think about audience very much when I'm writing. I think about *making* something, that's how it feels to me. That I'm making something.

Kruk: Even in the sense of sewing ... or quilting!

Shields: Yes—very much so.

Kruk: How conscious are you of your style, when you're writing?

Shields: I'm very conscious; maybe too conscious.

Kruk: Do you still write a few pages, and then rewrite them the next day, so that you're going over the sentences "with a fine-tooth comb"?

Shields: Yes; I love sentences.

Kruk: Do you ever feel restrained by conventional punctuation?

Shields: Actually, I love punctuation, too.... I'm quite happy with conventional punctuation. I guess I do see certain changes in my sentences, and part of it comes from editorial direction. Ed Carson does not like semicolons. And I do, because I really like British novels; they use a lot of semicolons. There was a time when I didn't use many dashes, and now I'm using them more. I find that sometimes it functions like a semicolon, but it also gives—when you set something in dashes—that marvellous thought, just beneath the thought before.

I love long, complicated sentences. But they have to work. They have to come in on this wonderful landing—like airplanes. [laughter] They've got to come in right, and they've got to make absolute grammatical sense. I'm not very interested in—reading or writing—short, declarative, Hemingway sentences.

Kruk: You're another one of our *claimed* Canadian authors, though you grew up in the States. Do you think about the differences between Canadian and American literature?[2]

Shields: Well, I think the first Canadian book I ever read was Marian Engel's *The Honeyman Festival*. And I thought, "Why am I loving this so much?" because nothing much was happening.

But I loved it because I was *in* that woman's *mind*. Then I always like to say I "discovered" Alice Munro—because she hadn't published a book yet. But I was in bed one night, this must have been in the late sixties—maybe she had published *Dance of the Happy Shades,* although I hadn't read it and hadn't heard of her— and I was reading in the *Montrealer* magazine her story "The Red Dress," which is still one of my favourite stories.... And I thought, "Oh! This is amazing. And she's Canadian." So I felt I'd discovered her, this wonderful writer. And she is, I think, our best writer. I'm delighted at the acclaim she's had with this last book.[3]

Kruk: Other Canadian writers?

Shields: Well, I always read Atwood's books. And I think it's marvellous too ... what she's done for Canadian literature and for women internationally. I always read them with interest. I'm very interested in her work.

Kruk: What do you think about the change between her last book *[The Handmaid's Tale]*, and this book, *Cat's Eye?*

Shields: I love *Cat's Eye.* Much more than *Tale.* I read it on the plane, on the way to my thirty-fifth high school reunion. So I was really ready to read about memory, and how it works. I also thought it had wonderful writing in it, very careful writing—the most careful I've ever seen in a book of hers. The wonderful thing about Margaret Atwood is, she always seems to know, two or three years ahead of everyone else, what we're going to be talking about. She's prophetic. And I'm full of admiration for her.

Kruk: Do you like Mavis Gallant?

Shields: I love—*much* of Mavis Gallant, not all of it. *From the Fifteenth District* I think is my favourite book. It's full of compassion. I thought she was very close sometimes to being almost sentimental, but never, *ever* overstepped. It's a beautiful, a beautiful book.

I remember once driving in a car, and turning on the radio in the middle of a reading of a short story. And I could tell that it was a Mavis Gallant story, even though I had missed the introduction. The same thing happened to me once at the cottage, listening to the radio and I tuned in to the middle of a Marian Engel story: I just knew. And I thought, "Isn't that amazing, and wonderful, and enviable, that these people have a voice so personal that you can pick it up, like a voiceprint."

I love Margaret Laurence, too. I guess I love *The Stone Angel* the most. *The Diviners* left problems for me, but still I can remember finishing it, and being unable to sleep that night ... I was just—caught up in that narrative, that sense of it all....

Oh, and I love Beth [Elisabeth] Harvor's stories, too. I've always admired her.

Kruk: You've moved around a fair bit ... though you say you're happiest in Winnipeg....

Shields: I don't know—did I say that? [laughs] I'm quite happy to live here. But of course, I get away a lot. I might feel differently if I were in Winnipeg every day.

We go to France every summer, we have a little house in a village there. It's very modest, but it's away from Manitoba. I think if I *didn't* get away, I might find it a little isolating. But I love living here; it is an underrated city, in fact.... I feel that I have a portable sense of "home." I need certain things around me—and certain people around me—but once I've got those, I can fit in.

Kruk: Do you feel, as you're working on your new novel, that there's pressure on you to write in the ways you've written before?

Shields: No, I don't feel any pressure. And I don't think that writers should ever feel that they have to top their last book. That's a false challenge; that isn't the way the creative life works at all. We're all trying to write the best books we can. I don't think people try and write *less* than that.

I was worried just before *Swann* came out. I had pre-publication jitters because I thought it was such a different book. And that people would say, "Why doesn't she write the way she used to?" Because actually there were a couple of reviews of *Various Miracles* which said just that. I expected that. If they [readers] are on to a certain thing, they really don't want you to change too much.

This may be very arrogant of me, but this is one of the nice things about getting older: you really don't care that much—everyone is just going to have so many books that they're going to be able to write in their lifetime. You know it's a finite number. And I guess I do feel the pressure of that. I don't know how many more books I'll write. And I'm trying to do something different in this new novel, which is to get away from the set-up of the isolated character in their situation. And to get in some of the noise and confusion of the world around them. I've put in much more of that—that's the different thing—and it's made the book quite long. But I hope it's got a kind of texture that my other books haven't.[4]

Kruk: Bringing in more background, more "ground" for the "figures"?

Shields: Yes ... I really mean the noise of the world around people. I want to make it *more* realistic, in a way that realistic novels haven't done before.[5]

Winnipeg, Manitoba: April 1990

Notes

1 Harvey de Roo, "A Little Like Flying: An Interview with Carol Shields," *West Coast Review* 23.3 (Winter 1989) 38-56. Quote p. 39.

2 Shields actually has dual Canadian/American citizenship, which allowed her to win the Pulitzer Prize for *The Stone Diaries.*

3 Shields refers here to Alice Munro's seventh collection, *Friend of My Youth* (Toronto: Penguin, 1990).

4 This novel is *The Stone Diaries* (1993), the acclaimed examination of the life and times of Daisy Stone Goodwill.

5 Since our conversation, a third collection of stories, *Dressing Up for the Carnival* (Toronto: Random House, 2000) has appeared. See Author's Note for more information.

Guy Vanderhaeghe:

"A Vernacular Richness"

Kruk: Can you tell me what you're working on now?

Vanderhaeghe: I've started sketching another novel. At this point, I don't know whether it's going to work, or gel, or anything else, so I'm just fiddling with it.... And for the past year, I've been doing a treatment, a screenplay, of my latest book, *The Englishman's Boy* (1996).

Kruk: That seems an obvious choice of novel to think of translating into film ... did you have that in mind, when you wrote it?

Vanderhaeghe: No, never. It never entered my mind when I was writing the book; the only thing that I could probably say is that I made an attempt to make the book visual.

Kruk: Yet it does seem that working in film is one of the few ways a writer can make a living today--

Vanderhaeghe: Yes, there are a certain number of Canadian writers who write novels and often, screenplays of their work. Paul Quarrington ... Timothy Findley ... and a number of other people. So, financially, that's the "whipped cream" on whatever you do. But I think there is probably a great danger in consciously writing with film in mind; I think that a novel's a very different thing from a screenplay, and the first consideration, as a writer, has to be whatever medium he or she is working in—that's going to determine the choices you make as a writer.

    I teach one class of Creative Writing, and in the ten years since I started doing that, I find more and more students who are interested in writing for film, or television. But I also think that film has been influencing writing for sixty-five years. All you have to do is think of Graham Greene, and the impact film had on his writing ... the sort of scenic structure of his novels. And I think that was equally true of Evelyn Waugh. I think one of the influences film has had on writing are the narrative "gaps" that you see in books today that you wouldn't see in the nineteenth century. Film makes huge leaps in location, it is much more cryptic than literature *used* to be. And I think that the hesitancy of contemporary writers to explain, is at least partly the influence of film. I'm just reading Cormac McCarthy's *The Orchard Keeper*, and there is that kind of structure to the book: leaps in time. The sort of connective tissue that was a staple of the novel is dispensed with for ... almost a montage of incident and conversation.

Kruk: And of course, *The Englishman's Boy* deals with the early film industry of Hollywood, and the impact film has had on twentieth century culture .... our popular myths of the West, the cowboy, the Native....

Vanderhaeghe: It also owes part of its structure to D. W. Griffith's movie *Intolerance,* which is the history of "intolerance"... and jumps back and forth between ancient Babylonia, to the Huguenots, to a twentieth-century story. The attempt to tell several stories widely separated in time. In terms of film history, there's all kinds of argument about Griffiths, but I think basically he created the vocabulary of film.

Kruk: I've done some reading of earlier interviews with you, and you said several intriguing things that I'd like to draw you out on. For instance: "Basically, I don't think I am a short story writer. I may develop into a better novelist than a short story writer. Now, why I wrote short stories is that when I was working, it was easier to write short stories than to say, 'I'm going to write a novel,' because I had only so much time. Secondly, the way publishing is constituted in this country, there is an outlet for the short story in literary magazines. It's easier to get short stories ... published...."[1] Is this still true for you? Or has your attitude towards writing short stories changed?

Vanderhaeghe: Well, it's not that I don't admire the short story, and love it, but it always seemed to me that the short story owed more to a poetic sensibility than it did my own consciousness, which I think is more or less shaped around narrative. When I first began, my stories were sort of fictional essays, with summary conclusions at the end of them, and all the rest of it. And I think it was quite a struggle for me to sort of bend myself to the short story....

I don't think of myself as a "natural" short story writer ... which doesn't mean that I don't *like* writing short stories. I'm not sure that I have the finely tuned, poetic sensibility which the very *greatest* short story writers have ... like a Chekhov, or a Mansfield. And I would argue that any notion that the novel is just an extended short story is incredibly wrong-headed. I think they use entirely different muscles, and to sit down and write a short story, you really have to— switch your reflexes. And I think that the reflexes of a short story writer are more akin to those of the poet, than they are the novelist. The short story reveals itself in its meaning with a sudden burst or immediacy that novels often don't do.

Kruk: So you're not saying that the short story is simply a utilitarian way to get to something longer and perhaps "better"–?

Vanderhaeghe: I certainly don't think of it as something that you approach in your first stage of development, and then discard as you move on to higher and better things.... And many of our greatest writers are, basically, short story writers. One thinks of Alice Munro. And Mavis Gallant, though she has written a few— short—novels. I'm not abandoning the short story; I'm not renouncing it ... there's no hierarchy in my mind, it's just that I had felt, even as I was writing short stories—and I suppose to a certain extent making my reputation as a short story writer, because the first book I published was a collection of short stories *[Man Descending* (1982)]—that maybe whatever talent I had was not necessarily the talent of the *true* short story writer.

Kruk: I still think you're being too hard on yourself....

Vanderhaeghe: [laughs] I'm not saying I'm a bad short story writer, or anything like that....

Kruk: Yet I suppose it's only by working hard within the short story form that you can gain that knowledge: to see how far you've gone, and how far you want to go ... the limits of the form. I'm interested in this question of form, and literary politics, because so often it has been the case that short stories have been subordinated to the novel ... and I wonder whether writers are ever pushed in that direction?

Vanderhaeghe: Certainly they are pushed by publishers; a publisher does not leap for joy when he or she sees a collection of short stories. They may not necessarily leap for joy when they are confronted with a novel, either. But everyone who's in the business of publishing knows that the sales of novels are much stronger than the sales of short stories. I think that it's one of the oddities today that fiction has gotten compartmentalized. But I think it's also very true that the novel always was more popular than short stories, and there was a time when the short story was basically relegated to magazine reading—

Kruk: Which was popular, populist reading, though—?

Vanderhaeghe: Yes, it was popular, and there was a large American market for short stories, in *The Saturday Evening Post, The Atlantic*

Monthly and *The New Yorker*, and all the rest, in which very great story writers contributed stories. But, by and large, the novel has held sway, since the nineteenth century. I'm talking in worldwide terms; I think in Canada the position of the short story has always been stronger than it is in other countries. In Britain, for instance, you find very few collections of short stories, and I don't think the British are particularly adept in the form.

Kruk: Whereas we seem to have developed some strengths, some distinctive voices....

Vanderhaeghe: Yes. And if I think of two countries with great short story writers, Ireland and Canada come to mind. Now, Thom Jones is a very popular American short story writer, but I don't think that he carries the weight or prestige of an Alice Munro, in Canada. I would argue that even John Cheever didn't achieve a comparable celebrity....

The short story really came into its glory, in Canada, in the late sixties and early seventies, basically through the influence of CBC radio, and literary magazines. When publishing was restricted for Canadian writers, that's where they found their outlet: in literary journals and on the radio.

Kruk: And that's changing again—with cuts to arts funding, we may see online journals. Or more self-publishing, perhaps.

It's heartening to see that story is always with us, but in different ways. The novel has been the dominant form, and short stories have either been extremely popular—like pulp magazine fiction—or extremely artistic, as in the Modern short story of Joyce or Mansfield. Apparently, stories can span both ends of the spectrum.... However, I do think that in Canada we've developed a certain interest in short stories, and short story collections. We also have a bit of a tradition of the short story cycle, or linked collection, as I'm sure you are aware: Margaret Laurence, Munro....

Vanderhaeghe: Edna Alford's *Sleep Full of Dreams*....

Kruk: Yes, and Sandra Birdsell's *Night Travellers*. Even going back to *Sunshine Sketches of a Little Town*.... I wonder whether, to jump to your three collections [*The Trouble With Heroes* (1983), *Man Descending, Things As They Are?*(1992)], you see any kind of link with this trend–?

Vanderhaeghe: Well, I certainly never had that in mind. I mean, in both *Man Descending* and *The Trouble With Heroes*, the stories were written when I could find the time to write them. I certainly never had a plan to link them in any way. Now, in *Man Descending*, there are two pairs with a similar character, Ed [in "Man Descending" and "Sam, Soren and Ed"]—

Kruk: And also Billy Simpson in "Cages" and "Drummer"—

Vanderhaeghe: Yes. And then, the boy, Charlie, in "The Watcher"—

Kruk: —shows up in "Loneliness Has Its Claims" (*Things As They Are?*).

Vanderhaeghe: Right. After I had written "Man Descending," I was prompted—I don't know if it was a novelistic impulse or what you would call it—to return to that character. That was equally true of the Billy Simpson stories. And again, the boy in "The Watcher," I returned to in "Loneliness...." But I had no idea of making some kind of linked collection, and wasn't thinking of Munro's *Lives of Girls and Women,* or anything like that, when I was writing those stories. *My Present Age* (1984) followed those stories because I thought that I had fudged the outcome in "Sam, Soren and Ed" ... in some way I had cheated the inevitability of that character, I had drawn back from the inevitability of his character. The story had a kind of uplift that was dishonest and that's why I went on to write *My Present Age*. I had a character that I had at least sketched in the short story, so I had worked something out there. But I certainly hadn't worked out, or begun to work out, the structure, and the narrative thrust, of the novel.

Kruk: And that *does* seem like one of the unique advantages of the short story, that you can try something out, in a short form, such as a character, and then visit them again, without making a huge commitment—yet creating two distinct stories. Rather than making half a novel, you've got two separate stories that are also ... family members. So even though we agree that stories are not *necessarily* training-grounds for novels, you are sort of working out problems .... Perhaps then, if you have enough energy, or momentum, you move the character, or dramatic situation, into the longer form?

Vanderhaeghe: I think there's a degree of truth to that, but I wouldn't give it *too* much weight. I think that what's worked out in the short story, going back to what I said earlier, are different kinds of impulses. What I really had in the short story "Man Descending," or "Sam, Soren and Ed," was only the nugget of a character.

The structure of the novel is very, very different from the structure of the short story. I mean, Ortega Gasset said something very interesting: that great novels are always imperfect. And I don't think great short stories are imperfect, great short stories are chiselled and cut and refined and faceted in a way that makes them—and this is not a dismissive phrase—like a fine cameo. Whereas novels I think have to have a certain amount of baggy trousers to them. In fact, novels actually have to have slack stretches in them, and the pacing is very different from that of the short story. As is the structure.

Kruk: Why do novels need "slack stretches"?

Vanderhaeghe: Well, I don't think anything can be intense for three hundred and thirty pages ... with the kind of intensity that the short story often carries. Novels actually need space for the reader to chew the cud ... you almost have to have a breather to absorb what you've already read, and prepare for what you're going to encounter.

Kruk: There has to be a kind of "rest" for the reader—

Vanderhaeghe: But the "rest" is deceptive. I often wonder, aesthetically, about the arguments that are made about the "failures" of what I consider great novels. For instance, *Huckleberry Finn*–

Kruk: Obviously a favourite novel of yours—

Vanderhaeghe: Everybody makes the argument that perhaps the last thirty pages are ... too silly. But I think that the silliness at the end of *Huckleberry Finn* actually highlights the rather sombre intensity of the first two-thirds of the novel. And I think that Tolstoy's *War and Peace* is flawed in a similar way. There's an essay at the end, and it's very silly. But I think what it does is to throw into relief the truth of the fiction, as opposed to the "theorizing" Tolstoy. And this might be what Gassett is talking about, that all great novels are flawed.

Kruk: Even though these books violate some ideal of unity....?

Vanderhaeghe: I think many great novels are Manichean: they display both the author's foolishness and his or her wisdom. Even Faulkner's *Light in August,* which is a great novel, has one of the most appalling endings.... It seems to me that Gassett has a crumb of an important idea there ... that, looked at bit by bit, lots of things in a novel can be dismissed, or said to be silly ... but it's really the whole that you're looking at. And sometimes that whole has to be articulated in a very different way ... than the short story's articulated. The novel is a much looser form.

Kruk: Well, maybe we're talking about the Modern ideal of the short story as very unified ...as rewarding close reading. We've talked a bit, now, about the advantages, or opportunities, of the novel.... What about the *story's* strengths?

Vanderhaeghe: Well, again, I turn to the kind of ... luminous quality of the short story. In the hands of a master, there's a kind of explosion of understanding. I've never read James Joyce's "The Dead" without being amazed by the last half-page. Good short stories operate by subconscious associations. You'll hear this faint ring of the bell on the first page, and it may peal again and again throughout the short story ... but its real force, its real melody, the "chimes" of the short story, are always given on that last page.... Whereas most novels never conclude imagistically–they slide away with a kind of dying fall, I think.

So often the short story can't be parsed, the way a novel can. I mean who can really explain the meaning, and put it into words, of Chekhov's "Lady with a Lapdog," or Joyce's "The Dead," or Mansfield's "The Garden Party"? Often short stories are difficult to teach because they're like a joke. If you get it, you get it....

I also think that the short story is much more sensuous than the novel ... and that's why the discrete particular detail is so important to the texture of the short story. And when I was talking about why I didn't particularly think of myself as a short story writer, that was in part a reflection on the necessity of heightened language in the story.... For instance, I'm one of the few writers that I know of who didn't have a period of writing poetry. I've written five poems in my life and I got three of them published. I've never written any poems since. Though I've recently started writing song lyrics, because somebody [Canadian musician Barney Bentall] asked me to....

Kruk: I do find that strange, because in your prose, there's a *lot* of sensuousness. One critic even analyzed your prose style. He looked at alliteration, repetition, assonance, and so on, in *My Present Age.*[2] He *did* parse some of your prose for poetic techniques, so maybe it's more unconscious than you think—?

Vanderhaeghe: Let me put it this way, without sounding arrogant: I think I write pretty good prose. But there's a distinction between prose and poetry.... I think that the prose in the novel, or the short story, is the servant of the narrative. It doesn't "come forward" in the way words do in a poem. That's why I'm always very suspicious of any novel on which there's a blurb which talks about "poetic prose." What I would argue is that, in the novel, if one becomes too aware of the prose, it leads to a shift of consciousness. Now, many postmodern writers, some magic realists, in fact, would take violent exception to what I'm saying. They are perhaps more interested in creating that poetic texture in a work.

Kruk: For instance someone like Daphne Marlatt ... who is constantly slowing us down, slowing down the narrative, by throwing a spotlight on the words. And if you are at all interested in where she wants to go, it's fascinating. Obviously, what she's doing in *AnaHistoric* is quite different from what you're doing in *My Present Age* or even *The Englishman's Boy.* You're more in the realist camp, to use an old but still useful term.

Vanderhaeghe: There's certainly no doubt about that. I'm more linked to the realist tradition, which probably is *the* strongest tradition in Canadian writing. *AnaHistoric* I think is ... well, certainly it's a novel, but it's also a meditation ... and by definition, a meditation is going to be less interested in narrative thrust.... If you're writing a meditation, which is in some ways much closer to what some kinds of poetry do, the surface quality of the prose ... is going to be interested in creating internal resonances in the reader. So when Marlatt writes what she writes, she is also making the prose, I would argue, serve her purposes.

But because of the kind of writer I am, I approach prose from a different angle—and I'm not saying one's right, and the other's wrong! I'm not saying that fine writing has no place in the novel either; the distinction that Cyril Connolly came up with, between the "plain" style and the "mandarin": there are many "mandarin" writers who are great novelists. I'm not making an argument for the "plain" style. The question that I'm raising, and it's coming from the sort of angle that I inhabit, is whether in fact the prose and story, or prose and narrative, are one. And sometimes it seems to me that in so-called "poetic novels," that the surface—it skates there, it's like light hitting glass, and in a sense it almost blinds the reader to what's behind the prose. In my case, because I write narratives, I try to make the poetry *serve* the narrative. For instance, in *The Englishman's Boy*, I think that the prose is much more heightened than in many other things that I've written.

Kruk: More heightened than in *My Present Age*, I'd say. There's a definite difference.

Vanderhaeghe: And *Homesick* (1989). There's a big difference. *Homesick* is probably the ... sparest of my books.

Kruk: Did you have to work at that new prose style of *The Englishman's Boy*? Or was it a natural evolution?

Vanderhaeghe: I think my feel for what I'm doing dictates the prose.

The story, and the characters that I'm working with, and all of those sorts of things. And because *Homesick,* for instance, was kind of stripped-bare—I was dealing with lives that were stripped-bare in many ways—the prose is like that.

Kruk: Do you know when you're writing a short story, as opposed to a novel?

Vanderhaeghe: Oh yes. It's always clear for me.

Kruk: So, do you have a favourite short story, of those you've written?

Vanderhaeghe: Hmmm..... I suppose there's a difference between what I think is my *favourite* short story, and what I think might be my *best* short story. I think probably "Things As They Are?" is my best short story ... or "Going to Russia" (*Man Descending).* And they're the least anthologized.

Kruk: As for me, I'm very interested in the stories about fathers and sons, and find that whole dynamic fascinating in "Man on Horseback" from *Things,* "The Prodigal" of *Heroes,* "Cages" from *Man Descending.* I've lectured on "Cages," and despite what you said earlier about the short story's subtlety or diffuseness, that one teaches really well.

Vanderhaeghe: Especially with younger people ... the males often identify very strongly with it.

Kruk: To move to questions of gender.... I'd like to think a little more self-consciously about gender roles, identities, themes.... Women have benefited from the rise of Women's Studies, Feminist Criticism, courses on women writers, and so on. Men as men have been somewhat taken for granted, almost ignored. But men *also* have secrets, problems that haven't been addressed. As a theme for literature—do gender issues interest you? You do write about men, primarily....

Vanderhaeghe: Yes, I write about men because I'm a man, and it seems much easier to ... slip into that consciousness. It's interesting that you raise this point, because I did a reading, not too long ago, and in fact a gentlemen who was in "Male Studies" showed up, and tried to press me into making some sort of—iconic statement about maleness. And what I think isn't necessarily what other men think.

There's also a phenomenon going on now, where increasingly, men don't read fiction. Which means, in many ways, that the most important Canadian writers, and highly-regarded writers, are, in fact, women. I think that most women are naturally attracted to women writers.... As a result, there has been a great deal of focus on women writers, in Canada, in the last twenty-five years.

Kruk: True. And you don't want to be a spokesperson for your gender ... or any other group—?

Vanderhaeghe: I'm always very suspicious of movements of any kind. Quite frankly, from the little I know about "Men's Studies," I find it ridiculous. Men's Studies doesn't make converts. It attracts people who already feel this way, and act this way.

Kruk: Well, I'm not surprised to hear you say that. I'm partly raising the example of Men's Studies to be a bit provocative, but I also think it may be valuable, instructive, to take a look now at how *men* are socialized and gendered—just as women have been. If we can be conscious of the social pressures on both genders, we can come to a little common ground. Becoming aware, in another way, of the ... contingency of our identities.

Vanderhaeghe: Certainly there are great differences between men and women, but what sometimes disturbs me is, when you are searching for your commonality *within* a gender, you can easily neglect what I would call "common humanity." And I'm still a firm believer that what's held in common is much more important than what's gendered.

Kruk: You say you write about men because you are a man, and that seems perfectly commonsensical, but ... here's where I get analytical: what does that really mean, "to be a man"?

Vandcrhaeghe: Okay, the obvious thing to say is that I'm a product of the socialization of the '50s, and that socialization got shaken up by feminism in the seventies. And it led to a kind of personal re-orientation in terms of thinking. I mean, I grew up in a very macho male culture—rural, working class ... hockey, rodeo, horses, fighting ... all of those kinds of things. I remember when I was living in a sawmill camp in B.C., this kid who was two years older than me used to beat me up every day on his way home from school. And my father solved this problem by saying, "Okay I'm going to teach you to fight." My father called him in, off the street, into our house, and this kid and I duked it out—in my living room! And as a child you don't necessarily question that. When I came to university, I was thrown into a milieu of different values ... then there was feminism ... and all of these things made males of my generation and social class, either react with a kind of violence, or else, for lack of a better word, with a kind of accommodation, an attempt to think through the thing.

Anyone can write about anything they want to. But a person probably has a greater understanding and sympathy for his or her own gender, his or her own social class ... and the relationships that formed them. I've always thought of my writing as a form of questioning. And it seems to me that there are certain so-called traditional male values that have, at least, importance for me. And I might go further to argue that they have some virtue in themselves. And other ones that certainly don't make any sense in the world as we experience it today.

Oddly enough, I grew up with very strong women, almost "masculine" women, in the traditional sense of the word.

Kruk: Like Grandma Bradley in "The Watcher" and "Loneliness Has Its Claims"—

Vanderhaeghe: Or Vera in *Homesick*. None of the women that I knew backed down an inch. So, in some ways ... feminism wasn't a shock. You know, there was no June Cleaver in my house!

Kruk: Is Vera of *Homesick* based on your mother, in some sense?

Vanderhaeghe: In some ways, like my mother. My mother was never as fierce, or bitter, as Vera. Vera's not a likeable character.

Kruk: Vera's a very strong personality, though, so obviously you had some powerful female role models there, or you wouldn't have been able to create her.

Vanderhaeghe: Well, you were talking about women being socialized ... my mother was made to box with one of her brothers, because he had a brother who was three years older than he was, and that brother was too big for him. So my mother used to box with my Uncle Jack; became his sparring partner. And my mother taught *me* how to box, when I was nine.

I think I write a great deal about fathers and sons, because of failed expectations that at least I sensed on the part of my father and my uncles and all the rest of the males around me, in terms of how I should behave and what I should be. I was interested in books, I was interested in reading, I was interested in "art": these were things that none of the males who were older, and had a large part in my life, were interested in, knew anything about or cared anything about. So there are many men in my books who fail expectations—not just with their father, but with the other people around them, whether with wives, or sons, or brothers.

Now, it's interesting that I've written about *brothers*, when I'm an only child.

Kruk: And of the brothers, one is usually more extroverted, the other more introverted, so he becomes a kind of eye-witness to the action. Like in "King Walsh" *(Things)* and "Cages" and "Drummer" *(Man Descending)*.

Vanderhaeghe: And if I want to get really psychological about it, that might be my divided personality. And the one who is in some ways more traditionally male, whether it's King Walsh or Gene Simpson, is the one who, as you said, acts and displays ... and the other one, like Billy Simpson, observes.

Kruk: Yes, I see the "watcher" as the predominant image of your stories.... Speaking of characters ... we often encounter characters' voices directly in your stories. What is your attitude towards the first person voice?

Vanderhaeghe: Well, I think that the biggest advantage of the first person voice is intimacy. Because I'm interested in colloquial language, I'm drawn to the first person. The other reason is, I often like using an unreliable narrator. So that the person who is telling the story may be hiding things, may be not admitting something to himself.... I think the first person actually allows a vernacular richness that you can't achieve in third person.

Kruk: Except in dialogue....

Vanderhaeghe: Yes, but dialogue is much more difficult to handle than a simple narration. Because dialogue usually involves contending voices, so you're switching back and forth between several voices. It's more difficult to read personality and character, I think, in dialogue, than in a monologue of some kind.

Kruk: Jack Hodgins said he has to get the voice first, then he has the story.

Vanderhaeghe: Yes....

Kruk: Another aspect of your fiction people have commented on is the frequency of acts of violence.... There is often violence, whether it's physical, emotional, or even verbal. For instance, you're very good at capturing the way boys tease and mock each other, the crude slang and profanity. Do you think the experience of violence is part of being a man ... or, just part of being human?

Vanderhaeghe: I would say it's part of being human. I think that there's a great difference in how much violence males are exposed to, in terms of their social class. I think that, by and large, middle-class males probably experience less violence than working-class males, partly because their culture, to a certain extent, may discourage it more. Which doesn't mean that middle-class males don't experience violence or can't be terribly violent—

Kruk: But it's not as normalized, maybe?

Vanderhaeghe: It's probably not quite as normalized. There's probably more fighting among the working class, than among the middle class. For instance, I had to start helping with the butchering when I was quite young ... in the city, you wouldn't see a steer being hit over the head with a post maul, to kill it and have its throat cut. And I would have to help my father stitch up horses, that had been cut with barbed wire, that had flaps of skin hanging—

Kruk: Replayed in the episode in "Man On Horseback"—

Vanderhaeghe: Yes. Certainly, that's not an urban experience. I don't want to make too much of this business of violence, but what seems relatively normal to people in certain situations, strikes others as extraordinarily *ab*normal.

Kruk: Maybe it's because you're writing about your past ... and the stories are frequently being read and discussed by middle-class people, well-educated people, so that the story about killing the dog ["The King is Dead," *Heroes*], boys beating each other up, are shocking—at least they are shocking to me, a middle-class female.

Vanderhaeghe: I guess that's what I'm talking about: "situational ethics." My mother was probably even more adamant than my father about—as she would have put it—sticking up for myself. And sticking up for yourself meant if you had to "pop" someone, or felt you had to "pop" someone, then you did it. And many middle-class parents would have a horror of that.

Kruk: This is where gender socialization and class role training interacts in fascinating ways....

Vanderhaeghe: Well, I always think that class is much more important than gender....

Kruk: A lot of people would agree with that, but in Canada, we've not paid much attention to that aspect of identity until recently. In many of your stories, we see men who are very upset because of losing their income, or being unemployed: they don't have the car, the house, or the clothing that goes with their desired status. To what extent is money linked with manhood, in your opinion?

Vanderhaeghe: The traditional idea of the male as being provider still holds largely true. Women almost always refuse to marry out of their class, or their social position. That's partly ... a kind of class training that women have absorbed. Whereas men get other signals.

Kruk: You mean men aren't as affected by these social prejudices?

Vanderhaeghe: Well, traditionally, the notion is that if a man is always going to be the provider, it doesn't really matter what *she*'s doing. With a woman, it has more to do with the prestige that the husband carries.

Kruk: Your point shows that there still is lingering sexism in relationship-forming, in marital roles—But I note that you and Margaret [Vanderhaeghe's spouse], you're both artists, so—?

Vanderhaeghe: But I stayed at home and wrote while she had a job as a researcher at the Dept. of Health. Then *she* was the provider. Virtually no one overlooked that—

Kruk: It's still a woman's prerogative, it seems, to be the homemaker, to opt out of the "provider" role. So it's revealing that, in a lot of your stories, the men are in a state of crisis through their gender identity being undermined by their *economic* loss of identity and status. Like "What I Learned From Caesar" and "Reunion" *(Man Descending)*.

Vanderhaeghe: Working-class life is much more tenuous than middle-class life. I remember how my father broke his leg when I was six years old, and my mother went out to work. At that time, we were living in—a shack, it was just a kitchen and a bedroom. And there were no reserves, nothing to fall back on. So the terror of unemployment for the working class male is a difficult thing to handle.

However, in my mother's case, it actually gave her the opportunity to do what she really wanted to do, which was work. My mother had far more education than my father ... and maybe, in some ways, was more ambitious.

Kruk: So, things sort of shifted around; she gained power, he lost it—

Vanderhaeghe: Oddly enough, I think that he was more understanding than many other men of his generation would have been. He didn't like it, but he didn't complain all that much. And so my mother kept on working.

Kruk: Was your mother a big influence on you, in terms of your writing?

Vanderhaeghe: Well, I think that my mother was the influence ... my mother was a reader. Although, I must say, both of my parents, they never once said that I shouldn't be a writer. I didn't have those kinds of problems–

Kruk: I just attended a conference on "Mothers and Sons" [York University, September 1998]. I got the impression that male writers often have a strong connection to their mothers.

Vanderhaeghe: Yes. I think often females are much more likely to extend approval to artistic activity. And women are much less rigid in terms of expectations of children. I think that women are probably less prisoners of prejudice than men.... Not to say that women can't be prejudiced either, not by any stretch of the imagination. But it seems that on many issues, they allow a wider latitude.

Kruk: Women are often the ones who keep the family history. So that might be attractive for a reflective writer-child. But obviously, the father's really important, too, or you wouldn't have written so many stories about fathers! For instance, "Man on Horseback," that now seems to me more autobiographical—

Vanderhaeghe: —than usual, yes.

Kruk: The man caring for the horses, that was his way of expressing emotion—*through* the animals. A critic has noted the bear image in your fiction,[3] but horses are pretty important also ... is that a function of the prairie environment?

Vanderhaeghe: My father used to rodeo, and we always had horses. Until he became ill, I used to go home and ride with him, maybe once, twice a year....

Kruk: I'm interested by the title of your first collection—though published second—*The Trouble With Heroes:* it seems to suggest a questioning of "heroism." I notice the heroes here are all male, and wondered about that ... is it a male construct, and one that, maybe, we're starting to let go of?

Vanderhaeghe: Yes, well, one of the problems with the notion of heroism, is that it can fall too easily into conventional notions. Heroism, like situational ethics, is a matter of degree. Someone given a certain hand of cards, and who transcends those cards, in whatever way, even one that society would look on as being minor, actually exhibits an enormous amount of heroism. The "trouble" with "heroes" is really the notion of what heroism is ... what constitutes heroism. And in my mind, it has more to do with the distance you travel, than with measures of conventional accomplishment.

Kruk: Like the young man in "Things As They Are?" who's extremely disabled, and wants to be a monk. He acts as a kind of a reproach to the writer, who's perfectly physically able but who seems to be depressed, lethargic, alcoholic ... the disabled man is kind of an opposite for him, and also gets him to think about illusion, delusion and faith—and the meaning of "things as they are."

Vanderhaeghe: I suppose, in a niggling kind of way, my notion of heroism comes closer to stoicism than anything else....

Kruk: Small victories. Like in "Parker's Dog" (*Heroes),* where these dissolute characters lead a sort of dead-end life, but ... a kind of attention is paid, and even the dog is a symbol of an attempt to get beyond this miserable existence ... I see the animal as often being a kind of sacrifice, in your stories. Because the animal is innocent, dumb .... the bear, or the dog, or the horse.... as seen in "Dancing Bear" (*Man Descending*) "Parker's Dog," "Man on Horseback" ....

Vanderhaeghe: Right. Because the animal is something that virtually anything can be done to. I mean the SPCA [Society for the Prevention of Cruelty to Animals] will get after you and all the rest of it, but a domesticated animal has a kind of dependence that is—damn near total. There are human beings who respond well to weakness....

Kruk: With tenderness....

Vanderhaeghe: Yes. And there are human beings who become—predatory, in the face of weakness. I would argue that the powerless—particularly powerless children, people at the bottom of the totem pole—often act out their rage on something that's a little lower. A boy is taught to be powerful ... if you are thwarted, if in fact you become prey to greater power: a bully, maybe your own father ... you replicate that, often, in behaviour to others, or to other things. Now there may be even something—and I'm always very sceptical about biological arguments—but there may be something to the influence of pure, plain testosterone.

Kruk: The intellectual pendulum's swung back and forth on this issue of gendered behaviour vs. sexual difference, so many times.... One critic has said, "Masculinity is power." Do you agree with that?

Vanderhaeghe: Certainly, an expectation of power ... but there are different kinds of masculinity.

I mean, there's power in terms of violence, power in terms of money—someone like Conrad Black: how much money do you need? Male culture is by and large competitive. And the response to that competition is hierarchy of some kind. Someone like Hemingway, who said, "I've knocked off all my contemporaries; now I'm going after the big guys."

Kruk: Another thing I've noticed in your writing is that you do deal with boys, or very young men, quite a lot. The age ten to twelve seems to pop up frequently—Charlie in "The Watcher", the boy in "Reunion", twelve-year-old Daniel in *Homesick*. Billy of "Cages" and "Drummer" is a teenager. And even the focus of *The Englishman's Boy*, is half on a teenager ... who reminds me of a Huck Finn gone to seed! Is there some attraction to the boy, or is it something you fall into, naturally?

Vanderhaeghe: I think I fall into it, and I also believe that "the child is father to the man." I'd add one other thing: the age of eleven is the golden age for males ... before the onslaught of puberty. Yet you're old enough to be given a great deal of freedom—at least, in a small town.

Kruk: Finally, what is the role of region in your writing? Clearly, there's an emphasis on the prairie as landscape and culture ... in many of the stories. *The Englishman's Boy* couldn't have come from somebody who hadn't known the big expanse, the big sky. Do you think there's any way in which you could be considered part of a prairie tradition?

Vanderhaeghe: Yes and no. I mean, I obviously exhibit a lot of characteristics that identify prairie writing ... but I'm always a little bit uncomfortable with the term "regional," because *all* writing is regional.

Kruk: I talked with Alistair MacLeod about that, and we agreed that "regional" has come to be a political term, usually equivalent with "marginal"....marginal to the centres—say, Toronto, or Montreal. Choosing to be in other parts of the country, at different times, can marginalize you.

Vanderhaeghe: Well, I think that still holds true, that there are great disadvantages to living where I live. There are also great advantages.... Being a Westerner, I tend to write about the West.... It's what I'm familiar with, what I know best. I think if I had left when I was twenty, or twenty-one or twenty-two, that would have been one thing. But to leave when I was, say, thirty-five: I would have been caught in a no-man's-land.

Kruk: Because you were already formed—your identity, your voice.....

Vanderhaeghe: Yes. And I would have been relegated to writing about the past ... I think that happened to W.O. Mitchell a bit; I think he got ... frozen in time. And I don't know if I ever would have learned another society well enough to write it with any authenticity. And just maybe not always—getting things. I always felt, living in Ottawa, I didn't always get it. I mean, it's not a huge leap from Saskatoon to Ottawa, but it did feel—vaguely foreign.

Kruk: I think every province is so distinct, in Canada. It's what we're blessed with—or burdened with, too. So much variation. And I think if you feel deeply, your roots go deep.

Vanderhaeghe: Yes. I'm pretty rooted to this place. I mean, who knows, maybe sometime I'll leave, but ... I don't have any expectations.

Kruk: I'll end with a delightful line from a review of *Man Descending* by Isabel Huggan. Describing the "richness" of your prose, she writes, "He seems to be the kind of man who, were he making a cake, would use real butter instead of margarine and put in an extra spoonful just for good measure."[4] Any comment from the writer as baker?

Vanderhaeghe: No, I'll just say, "Thank you, Isabel." I don't mind that at all!

Saskatoon, Saskatchewan: January 1999

Notes

1 Azure, K. "Interview with Guy Vanderhaeghe," *The Sheaf* (16 June 1983) 5, 8. Quote p. 5.

2 Forceville, Charles, "*My Present Age* and the 'Ed'-Stories: The Role of Language and Storytelling in Guy Vanderhaeghe's Fiction." In *External and Detached: Dutch Essays on Contemporary Canadian Literature,* eds. Charles Forceville, August J. Fry, Peter J. De Voogd (Amsterdam: Free Univ. Press, 1988) 53-61.

3 Hillis, Doris, "Guy Vanderhaeghe" in *Voices and Visions: Interviews with Saskatchewan Writers* (Moose Jaw, Sask: Coteau, 1985) 20-35. Quote pp. 30-31.

4 Huggan, Isabel, "real butter", rev. of *Man Descending, Brick: A Journal of Reviews* 21 (Spring 1984) 13-14. Quote p. 14.

Author Notes

ALFORD, EDNA.

Rooted in the prairies, Alford was born in 1947 in Turtleford, Saskatchewan, and has lived in Saskatchewan and Alberta. She attended the University of Saskatchewan, majoring in English. Perhaps more significantly, she won scholarships to the Saskatchewan Summer School of the Arts, where her teachers included Jack Hodgins and fellow Westerners W. P. Kinsella, Rudy Wiebe, and Robert Kroetsch. It was due to these writing workshops, among others, that she began creating her moving and challenging stories. *A Sleep Full of Dreams* (1981) treats the struggles of elderly women living in a nursing home with honesty and compassion. It is a linked collection, or short story cycle, which presents the reader with a look at a variety of different characters, prairie "pioneers" who are now residents of the Pine Mountain Lodge. The young attendant who observes them, Arla Pederson, is a connecting presence in all but two of the stories ("Under the I," "Half Past Eight"). On the basis of this work, Alford co-won the Gerald Lampert Memorial Award for best new Canadian writer. Alford also co-founded Alberta's *Dandelion* magazine, in 1975, with her friend Joan Clark. *The Garden of Eloise Loon* (1986), a more diverse and disturbing collection, is unified by its themes of madness, social or psychic fragmentation, and the dangers of what Alford calls "compartmentalization." Here the nightmare of nuclear war becomes as fit a topic for fiction as the loss of a parent: " I don't like the separation of art from the rest of the world. We have all these different specializations and they're not speaking to each other; the arts, I think, have the capacity, have the power, to do that" ("Writing 'For Our Psychological Survival'").

Although at first glance a realist writer, Alford likes to introduce hints of the surreal or fantastic into her well-documented worlds, as she admits that "these categories really blur for me... [F]or example, dreams, all of the things that happen psychologically to people, or psychically to people, all of those things to me are real" ("Writing"). One reviewer says of *Garden*, "Her stories exploit a wide variety of voices and techniques in order to produce a kind of elegiac mixture of violence and introspection that is very powerful" (Mierau). In 1988, she was given the $10, 000 Marian Engel Award for Fiction. *Kitchen Talk* appeared in 1992, edited by Alford and poet Claire Harris. An anthology of prose and poetry by Canadian women, it "uses the kitchen as a creative metaphor in the lives of women and their families from different cultural perspectives" (Hancock). Alford sees feminism as "fundamental" to her work and comments, "As a woman writer, part of the excitement for me is that women haven't been able to express themselves in the way that men have, for so long, that there's this incredible energy—and material. But also still a lot of work" ("Writing"). Alford's stories have been prominently anthologized in Canada and have been translated into German and Spanish. CBC Radio produced her play *Blue Canadian Rockies* in 1993. Active in the Western writing community, Alford has been a member of the Saskatchewan Writers' Guild, a fiction editor at *Grain* magazine, and sits on the editorial board of Coteau Books. Alford has specialized in freelance editing, including editing short story collections by Canadians Bonnie Burnard, Geoffrey Ursell and Diane Warren. Presently, she is the Director of the Writing with Style Program at the Banff Centre for the Arts. She is also in the process of finishing a third collection of stories and a first collection of poems.

References

Hancock, Geoff. "Alford, Edna." *Oxford Companion to Canadian Literature.* 2nd ed. General ed. Eugene Benson and William Toye. Toronto: Oxford UP, 1997. 27-28. Quote p. 28.

Mierau, Maurice. "A Good Harvest." Rev. of *A Stone Watermelon,* by Lois Braun and *The Garden of Eloise Loon*, by Edna Alford. *NeWest Review* 13.5 (Jan. 1988) 17.

"Writing 'For Our Psychological Survival'": see this volume.

BIRDSELL, SANDRA.

Born in 1942, Birdsell was raised in small-town Manitoba, one of eleven children. She has devoted her career to documenting, with both sympathy and honesty, the lives of "ordinary" people-- especially women-- struggling with daily hardship and questions of identity, creativity, community and loss. "I think, as a woman, I have important things to say about being a woman, but I want it to be treated as mainstream literature," she declares ("Falling into the Page"). Birdsell's working-class background, and typically Canadian mixed ethnic and religious heritage (from her father, Metis Catholic; from her mother, Russian Mennonite) seems to support her fiction's gritty realism, although unexpected touches of the surreal, or supernatural, also enlarge her vision. Like Findley, she is largely self-educated, and was a married mother before she began writing seriously. A workshop with Robert Kroetsch at the University of Manitoba helped her to discipline and develop her talent; with his support, she received a grant to write the stories that became *Night Travellers* (1982), a very well-received collection that won the Gerald Lampert Award. *Ladies of the House* (1984) followed soon after, for the two collections overlapped in composition, closely related by their focus on the Lafreniere sisters of Agassiz, Manitoba. It was not surprising, then, that these linked collections were put together as *Agassiz Stories* in 1987, and in a U.S. edition, as *Agassiz: A Novel in Stories*, a further indication of Birdsell's deliberate genre-blurring. *Ladies* has also been translated for a francophone Canadian audience as *Agassiz: nouvelles* (Montreal: du Roseau, 1990). To subsidise her fiction writing, Birdsell has written scripts for CBC television, as well as the theatre. In 1986, she helped to adapt William Kurelek's *A Prairie Boy's Winter* (1986) for the stage. She has also written her own play, *The Revival* (1987), drawing again on the Lafreniere women for inspiration. In 1989, *The Missing Child* appeared, winning the W. H. Smith / *Books in Canada* First Novel Award.

Birdsell uses the motif of a flood (a familiar one in her work) to symbolize both a purging of society and a possible rebirth into a better reality in *The Missing Child*. The title seems to suggest a loss of innocence or absence of hope. This theme of absence is picked up again in *The Chrome Suite* (1992), which looks back to the 1950s and the early losses of its protagonist, Amy Barber. This second novel was nominated for a Governor-General's Award. Birdsell has also won a

National Magazine Award for Short Fiction, a 45 Below Award in 1986 (being chosen as one of ten "most promising writers below the age of 45"), and the Marian Engel Award (1993). In 1997, she returned to story writing with the subtle and powerful *The Two-Headed Calf,* also nominated for a Governor General's Award. Not a linked collection, it nevertheless has a consistent focus on the voices of Canada's outsiders—Metis, Mennonites, Russian immigrants—written with a keen attention to time and place. Yet again, amid the alienation and pain of everyday life, magical moments occur. A woman stops to examine the spring snow, for instance, and thinks "All this time I have been walking back and forth to work, I have been walking on crystal ... the roof of a crystal palace.... The symmetry of frozen water, the randomness of beauty made her throat tight" ("Phantom Limbs," *The Two Headed Calf*). As well, Birdsell has published a book for children, *The Town that Floated Away* (1997). Her third novel, *The Russlander* (2001) took seven years to research and write. It explores her maternal heritage through the story of a Mennonite community in Russia, early in the twentieth century, and the shattering events that led some of them to Canada. A Canadian bestseller, *The Russlander* was also nominated for the prestigious Giller Prize.

References

Birdsell, Sandra. "Phantom Limbs," *The Two-Headed Calf.* Toronto: McClelland and Stewart, 1997. 119-40. Quote p. 140.

"Falling into the Page": see this volume

CLARK, JOAN.

A Scottish-Canadian Maritimer by origin, like MacLeod, Clark was born in Liverpool, Nova Scotia in 1934, and raised in small communities of Nova Scotia and New Brunswick. But thanks to her husband's Air Force career, she has also been an Albertan for twenty years and spent time up North (Winisk, Hudson Bay). In in another defining regional shift, since 1985, Clark has made St. John, Newfoundland her home. She received her B.A. in English from Acadia University and studied Education at University of Alberta. Clark has worked as a teacher, though she now dedicates her time fully to her active writing career. In our conversation, she remembers the impact on her of Canadian literary "foremothers": "Obviously I do admire the work of many men—I like Guy Vanderhaeghe, Timothy Findley and so on—I admire their work, but it was the *women*, the fact that women were doing this, these women who had children! That's always been there, that's had *such* an influence on me" ("Letting it Rip"). Clark began to write while living in Alberta, where she co-founded (with Edna Alford) *Dandelion*, that province's first literary magazine. Her early stories and poems were published in journals such as *Dandelion*. Her first books, however, were children's narratives—the novel *Girl of the Rockies* (1968), the picture book *Thomasina and the Trout Tree* (1971) and *The Hand of Robin Squires* (1977), a novel which was translated into Swedish, Danish and French. This output led to her being pigeon-holed as a writer of children's literature, a category often dismissed as inferior, Clark notes with indignation. But her insistence on the imaginative integrity of the story, whether written for adults, teens or younger children, is amply demonstrated by the careful and intelligent writing found in all her projects.

From a High Thin Wire (1982), Clark's first adult book, is a linked collection, comparable to Birdsell's *Night Travellers* and Alford's *A Sleep Full of Dreams*. Her honesty and commitment to the unspoken truths of women's lives comes through even more dramatically in *Swimming Toward the Light* (1990), which follows one woman's turbulent journey towards greater self-knowledge—personally and artistically. Three more children's books came between these two publications, however; *The Leopard and the Lily* (1982), a dream-like parable, and the young adult stories, *Wild Man of the Woods* (1986) and *The Moons of Madeleine* (1987). Her time spent near Hudson Bay, in close contact with Natives, inspired her to write *The Victory of Geraldine Gull* (1988), a courageous work which presents the struggle of Geraldine, an Ojibway woman, to achieve "victory" over her foes in whatever way she can. The novel was nominated for the 1989 Governor-General's Award and the W. H. Smith / Books in Canada First Novel Award and won the Canadian Authors' Association Award for that year. Her residence in Newfoundland and her exploration of the historical Viking site at L'anse aux Meadows inspired her next, ambitious adult novel, *Eriksdottir: a tale of dreams and luck* (1994). *The Dream Carvers* (1995), her children's novel on a similar theme, received three Awards (The Hibernia Book Award, Mr. Christie Award for best Canadian children's book, Geoffrey Bilson Award for historical fiction for young people) and was shortlisted for the Red Cedar Award. Most recently, her dedication to writing compelling fiction for younger readers earned her the 1999 Vicky Metcalf Award (a $10 000 prize). Clark has also been presented with the Marian Engel Award (1991) and an honourary doctorate from Memorial University. In 2000, *Latitudes of Melt* appeared. This novel uses the Titanic disaster to link Ireland and Newfoundland through the life journey of its mysterious heroine, Aurora. It was nominated for the International IMPAC Dublin Literary Award. Another book for younger readers, *The Word For Home*, has just been published (2002).

References

"Letting It Rip": see this volume

FINDLEY, TIMOTHY.

Born 1930 in the wealthy district of Rosedale, Toronto, Ontario to an established family of Anglo-Irish origins, Findley briefly attended private school, although—due to a sickly childhood—he never completed high school. An actor for fifteen years, he participated in the first Stratford Shakespearean Festival season in 1953, with Tyrone Guthrie and Alec Guinness, before going to the Central School of Speech and Drama in London. A year later, he toured Britain and America in *The Matchmaker.* Encouragement for early writing efforts from its playwright, American Thornton Wilder, proved pivotal, for while Findley continued to act, he began to shift his ambitions towards *literary* performance. His first novel, *The Last of the Crazy People (*1967) which concerns a watchful outsider, his attachment to animals, and an act of seemingly irrational violence, established themes which Findley continued to explore. His Governor General's Award-winning work, *The Wars* (1977), follows a sensitive young soldier of World War One as he rebels against military authority and its codes of destructive masculinity. *Famous Last Words* (1981) tackles the Second World War, and treats the "aesthetics of fascism," as Anne Geddes Bailey describes it; *The Butterfly Plague* (first written 1969; revised 1986) was an earlier attempt to probe this connection, using the Hollywood film industry as context.

Lorraine York notes that many of Findley's male figures search "for a way of being male that will not align [them] with the paternal authoritarianism of fascistic ideologies." Yet other novels, like *Not Wanted on the Voyage* (1984), *Headhunter* (1993) and *The Piano Man's Daughter* (1995), do not centre on male protagonists but rather on unconventional, or alcoholic, female "crazies" who challenge authority figures. Like Carol Shields (*Swann*), Findley has also used the "mystery" genre for his own subversive purposes, in *The Telling of Lies* (1986). A novella, *You Went Away* (1996), returns to the familiar backdrop of the Second World War and explores a boy's loss of innocence. Findley's three story collections, *Dinner Along the Amazon* (1984), *Stones* (1988) and *Dust to Dust* (1997) are perhaps more diverse in offering different snapshots of "gender rebels" of both sexes, and, more daringly in the later "Minna and Bragg" stories, the special tensions of living as a gay man in contemporary society. Findley's interest in performance and in making "the perfect gesture" extends logically into the media of theatre, television and film. He has written five plays, *Can You See Me Yet?*

(1977), *Sir John A—Himself!* (1979), *The Stillborn Lover* (1993), *The Trials of Ezra Pound* (1995) and *Elizabeth Rex* (with Paul Thompson, 2000); all but *Trials* have been produced in Canada and *Elizabeth Rex* earned him another Governor General's Award. In addition, Findley has written two memoirs, *Inside Memory: Pages From a Writer's Workbook* (1990), and *From Stone Orchard: A Collection of Memories* (1998), gathering columns Findley wrote for the country living magazine, *Harrowsmith*. Among his numerous awards are the Canadian Authors' Association Award for Fiction (1985), Periodical Marketers of Canada: Best Magazine Fiction (1988), the Government of Ontario Trillium Award (1989, for *Stones*), the Banff Centre for the Arts National Award, the Order of Ontario, the Order of Canada, and being named *Chevalier de l'Ordre des Arts et des Lettres* in France. His ninth novel, *Pilgrim*, the story of a man who cannot die, appeared in 1999, followed by *Spadework* (2001). Findley was recently honoured with a tribute at the 2001 International Festival of Authors in Toronto. A sixth play, *Shadows* (2002), premiered at Stratford's fiftieth anniversary season. Unfortunately, the author did not live to see it: Timothy Findley died June 21, 2002, aged 71.

References

Bailey, Anne Geddes. *Timothy Findley and the Aesthetics of Fascism.* Vancouver, B.C.: Talonbooks, 1998.

York, Lorraine. "Findley, Timothy." *The Oxford Companion to Canadian Literature.* 2nd ed. General ed. Eugene Benson and William Toye. Toronto: Oxford UP, 1997. 403-5. Quote pp. 404-405.

HARVOR, ELISABETH.

A New Brunswicker by birth, born in 1936 in St. John's to artistic Danish parents, Harvor has lived in Quebec and Ontario as well. Her first choice of career, nursing, was abandoned—though it provides rich memory material for her writing—and after immersing herself in early marriage and motherhood, Harvor returned to school to do a qualifying year, then an M.A., in English (Concordia,1986). After a late start, she has grown in confidence and acclaim as an award-winning story writer and poet. In 1965, she won the CBC New Canadian Writing Award for one of her short stories. Her first collection, *Women and Children* (1973, re-issued in 1991 as *Our Lady of All the Distances*), garnered high praise, including this comment from Alice Munro, an early influence: "Absolutely some of the best, richest, subtlest, craziest, finest writing ever about marriage, kids, sex ... LIFE." (backcover) Her next collection, *If Only We Could Drive Like This Forever* (1988) continued to mine the deep veins of human intimacy and vulnerability she exposes so well. As Jane Rule puts it in a review, "such intimacy makes the reader share vulnerability with the characters rather than sit in comfortable distance and judgment." Her work has been published in American and Canadian journals, including the prestigious *New Yorker* magazine, and anthologized fifteen times. Harvor has taught creative writing at many schools, including Concordia, York University, the Maritime Writers Workshop and the Humber School for Writers. Teaching poetry inspired her own poetic growth; she has won The League of Canadian Poets' National Poetry Prize twice, in 1989 and 1991. Her two collections of poetry are *Fortress of Chairs* (1992), which won the Gerald Lampert Memorial Award, and *The Long Cold Green Evenings of Spring* (1997).

Harvor has also supported herself by working as writer-in-residence in libraries and universities across the country, from Ottawa to New Brunswick to Montreal (Concordia) to Saskatoon. A third collection of stories, *Let Me Be the One* (1996) was short-listed for the Governor-General's Award. Here, Harvor is bolder than ever in making her focus women in states of vulnerability, loneliness and desire—still mother-obsessed, still prey to philandering husbands and cruel children. Her wit, as well as her honest look at social-sexual interactions, is readily apparent in the opening of "How Will I Know You?": "When she stood in the doorway to his cubicle on cold and sunny Monday morning in early spring, feeling newly shiny and slim and reading him some of the winning entries from a *Globe and Mail* contest for invented mistakes that drunken or incompetent sign-painters might make—HAZARDOUS FOOTBATH, SMALL APARTMENT FOR RUNT, HOSPITAL NOT RESPONSIBLE FOR YOUR LONGINGS—he laughed, looking with surprised alertness into her eyes, and then just before noon, on his way past her desk, he dropped a note on her letter tray...." Recently, she edited the anthology of new writers called *A Room At the Heart of Things* (1998). Harvor's first novel, *Excessive Joy Injures the Heart,* was published in 2000. A reviewer for *Quill and Quire* declared, "Intricately textured with surreal juxtapositions and small encounters, fragile humour and fear, *Excessive Joy* extends Harvor's distinguished career as a short-story writer and poet"(Garvie). In 2000, she also received the Alden Nowlan Award for her body of work.

References

Garvie, Maureen. Rev. of *Excessive Joy Injures the Heart. Quill and Quire* 66.10 (October 2000) 38-39. Quote p 39.

Harvor, Elisabeth. "How Will I Know You?" *Let Me Be the One*. Toronto: HarperCollins, 1996. 30-47. Quote p. 30.

Rule, Jane. "Characters in Conflict between Duty and Desire." Rev. of *If Only We Could Drive Like This Forever,* by Elisabeth Harvor, *Globe and Mail* 12 Mar. 1988: C15.

HODGINS, JACK.

The rural hamlet of Merville, Vancouver Island, British Columbia, is the birthplace of Hodgins, who was born there in 1938 to Irish-Canadian parents. His sensitivity to borders, margins and what has been described as an "island mentality," has often been attributed to this circumstance of origin. Hodgins attended the University of British Columbia, where he studied Creative Writing with Earle Birney. He also trained as a teacher, and taught high school English in Nanaimo, B.C. between 1961 and 1981. For a few years, Hodgins lived in Ontario, as Visiting Professor at the University of Ottawa (1981-83), but soon after chose to return to the West Coast. Today he teaches Creative Writing at the University of Victoria, back on his beloved Island. His first publication was the story, "Every Day of His Life"; along with nine others, it made up his debut work, *Spit Delaney's Island* (1976). Scholar David Jeffrey calls it, "A superb collection of stories, certainly among the finest achievements in Canadian fiction," adding, it "reveals Hodgins in the full range of his powers and in his unique voice as a writer." His bold first novel, *The Invention of the World* (1977), won Hodgins many admirers. An exuberant comic vision, genuine affection for people, and emphasis on the value of community, define his body of writing. For as Hodgins observes, "The sense of community comes out, quite often, through a sharing of a story" ("'The Voice *is* the Story'"). His "shared stories" include five novels: the Governor General's Award-winning *The Resurrection of Joseph Bourne* (1979), *The Honorary Patron* (1987), *Innocent Cities (*1990), *The Macken Charm* (1995) and a story of returned soldiers turned pioneers, *Broken Ground* (1998).

The Macken Charm treats the Macken family and their mini-community. Another large family, the playful Barclays, is the starting point for his second story collection, *The Barclay Family Theatre* (1981). Like most of his fiction, this work retains the Island as reference point, even if its family members set off into an increasingly bewildering, border-crossing world. According to Peter Buitenhuis, a theme "haunts all of Hodgins's fiction—that of the Platonic view of a world of ideal forms that lies behind and animates the so-called 'real' world." Hodgins has also written a children's novel, *Left Behind in Squabble Bay (*1990); a travel memoir of Australia, *Over Forty in Broken Hill* (1992) and *A Passion for Narrative: A Guide for Writing Fiction* (1994), which draws upon his wealth of experience in teaching and writing. He has travelled to Ireland, and also toured Japan, the inspiration for his story, "The Sumo Revisions" in *The Barclay Family Theatre*. His fiction has certainly travelled well, winning Hodgins the Commonwealth Literature Prize (Canada-Caribbean region), the Canada-Australia Prize, and honourary doctorates from University of British Columbia and B.C.'s Malaspina University College. The stories have been translated into Dutch, Hungarian, Japanese, German, Russian, Italian, Polish and Norwegian. In 1996, he was one of ten Canadian writers invited by the French Minister of Culture to be honoured at the *Les Belles Etrangeres* festival in Paris. *Broken Ground* was nominated for the International IMPAC Dublin Literary Award. Currently, he is completing a third collection of stories, while working on his latest novel and a screenplay based upon *Spit Delaney's Island.* Hodgins's stories continue to attract interest: in March 2001, the world premiere of *Eyes on the Mountain*, an opera co-written by Christopher Donison and Hodgins, took place. It draws on the stories "Every Day of His Life," "Three Women of the Country," *(SDI)* and "Mr. Pernouski's Dream" (*TBFT*) in an interdisciplinary celebration of music, drama and Hodgins's prose.

References

Buitenhuis, Peter. "Jack Hodgins," *Profiles in Canadian Literature.* Series 8 Ed. Jeffrey M. Heath. Toronto and Oxford: Dundurn Press, 1991. 99-105. Quote p. 100.

Jeffrey, David. "Jack Hodgins (1938-   )," *Canadian Writers and Their Works.* Ed. Robert Lecker, Jack David, Ellen Quigley. Fiction Series, vol. 10. Introd. by George Woodcock. Toronto: ECW Press, 1989. 187-239. Quote p. 228.

"'The Voice *is* the Story'": see this volume

MACLEOD, ALISTAIR.

Though his distinctive focus on the people, place and history of Nova Scotia's Inverness county links him securely with Cape Breton, a special place on Canada's cultural map, MacLeod was actually born in 1936 in North Battleford, Saskatchewan, and lived in Alberta until the age of ten. At that point, however, the family moved back to Cape Breton, re-establishing a strong family tie to the area, and marking MacLeod for life in the process. He went on to pursue an academic and teaching career, achieving his Ph.D. in 1968 from the University of Notre Dame. After teaching at the University of Indiana for several years, he was hired by the University of Windsor, where he maintained an academic career, teaching English and Creative Writing, until his recent retirement. Meanwhile, MacLeod slowly built an international reputation with his moving short stories. These have won prizes and been anthologized many times, and "The Boat" and "The Lost Salt Gift of Blood" have been included in the prestigious *Best American Short Stories* and *Best Canadian Short Stories,* as well as *The Best Modern Canadian Stories. The Lost Salt Gift of Blood* appeared in 1976, and was widely recognized both in Canada and internationally. In 1991, it was nominated for the "People's Choice" Award as one of the best books published in the United Kingdom. Ten years later, *As Birds Bring Forth the Sun* (1986) was published to similar acclaim. As one scholar observes, MacLeod "works slowly, but with lapidary sureness, cutting and polishing each word, phrase, sentence and paragraph to achieve rhythms and density characteristic of poetry...." (Mitchell). On the basis of his short fiction, MacLeod has been selected as one of the Modern Library's 200 greatest writers in English since 1950.

Active also as a mentor, MacLeod has taught in the writing program at the Banff School of Fine Arts for seven years; he has been the fiction editor of *University of Windsor Review* for twenty-five years. His stories have been translated into languages as diverse as Urdu (of Pakistan), French, Russian, Norwegian, Italian and Gaelic, for BBC Scotland has broadcast several of his stories on Scottish radio. The connection is obvious: MacLeod's paternal ancestors came to Canada from the Scottish Isle of Eigg in 1791. The Inverness county area where they settled was dominated by Gaelic speakers until roughly the time of the Second World War. Furthering the connection between his ancestral past and his imaginative present, MacLeod has been Canada's Scottish/ Canadian exchange writer (1984-85). As a writer, one of his goals is to attempt to preserve the power of spoken storytelling in his very literate stories, for the simple reason that "Story has obviously existed longer than literacy has" ("'The World is Full of Exiles'"). He has been honoured with doctorates from his alma mater, St. Francis Xavier University (1987) and, aptly enough, new University College of Cape Breton (1991). His first novel, *No Great Mischief* (1999), was over ten years in the writing. It is described as "a story of families, and of the ties that bind us to them. It is also a story of exile and of the ties that bind us, generations later, to the land from which our ancestors came" (book dust jacket). It won the International IMPAC Dublin Literary Award, and has already been translated into fourteen languages. In 2000, *Island: The Collected Short Stories of Alistair MacLeod*, solidified his reputation as one of our most beloved writers in this form. In 2002, he was the recipient of the annual tribute at the International Festival of Authors in Toronto.

References

MacLeod, Alistair. *No Great Mischief.* Toronto: McClelland and Stewart, 1999.

Mitchell, Orm. "MacLeod, Alistair." *The Oxford Companion to Canadian Literature.* 2nd ed. General ed. Eugene Benson and William Toye. Toronto: Oxford UP, 1997. 708-9. Quote p. 708.

"'The World is Full of Exiles'": see this volume.

RULE, JANE.

"A hot-eyed moderate"—the title of her assured 1985 volume of social and literary commentary—and a Canadian "by choice," Rule was born in Plainfield, New Jersey in 1931. She received her B.A. from Mills College, California, attended Stanford University for one quarter and spent a year studying 17th-Century Literature at University College, London. Rule briefly taught at Concord Academy in Massachussets, before immigrating in 1956 to Vancouver, British Columbia. From 1960 to 1976, she found work as both English and Creative Writing Instructor at the University of British Columbia; in 1994, she was recognized with an honourary D. Litt from UBC. Her first novel, *Desert of the Heart* (1964), scandalized her colleagues with its unapologetic and sophisticated focus on a lesbian love affair; twenty years later, it was translated into film as *Desert Hearts* (1985). Rather than backing away from the controversy, Rule insisted on exploding sexual stereotypes by bringing the theme of homosexual relationships and identities into the academy: *Lesbian Images* (1975) is a landmark work in the emerging area of feminist history and gender studies. Her six other novels were written in between teaching; almost all include, but are not restricted to, portraits of women loving women. Yet far from idealizing these portraits in novels *This is Not For You* (1970), *The Young in One Another's Arms* (1977) and *After the Fire* (1989), Rule attempts to expand our understanding of the attainment of community and autonomy by showing how both are yearned for—by gay, as well as straight, couples. And she is not just opposed to sexual stereotypes; Rule pointedly undercuts clichés about the elderly, and children, by creating stubborn individuals from both ends of the generational spectrum, as shown in *Against the Season* (1971) and *Memory Board* (1987). *Contract with the World* (1980) treats the struggle of six artists both to affirm their true feelings as individuals, and to work together to support their social and artistic visions. Critic Richard Cavell observes, "Her work develops out of a conceptual centre which unites the social vision of comedy with the concomitant awareness that comedy ... enacts a double perspective of a utopian society set over and against the society within which the work is written."

Rule's two story collections, *Theme for Diverse Instruments* (1975) and *Inland Passage* (1985), may offer, as she claims, "experiments" in point of view or voice, yet they are an integral part of her body of work, showing Rule's continuing concern with challenging notions of "community" or on a smaller scale, "family"— at times with a deft humour, at times with a cutting edge of satiric anger. *Outlander* (1981), a combination of stories and essays addressing the gay community, goes even further in terms of challenging people's narrow perceptions about the supposedly "deviant." Yet she herself refuses to subscribe to facile counter-clichés, noting in our conversation, "I think people can gain insight or be narrow, from whatever vantage point they're given. I don't think that, because you're a homosexual, you have a better insight into the clichés of gender" (" 'I Don't Need Other People To Say What I Feel' "). Rule has won the Canadian Authors' Assocation Award for Best Novel and Best Short Story (both 1978). Retired from teaching in 1976, and from writing in 1991, Rule continues to participate in her "chosen" community of B.C.'s Galiano Island. Rule has been honoured with the U.S. Gay Academic Union Litrature Award (1978), and, more recently, the Order of British Columbia (1998).

References

Cavell, Richard. "Jane Rule." *Profiles in Canadian Literature.* Series 7 Ed. Jeffrey M. Heath. Toronto and Oxford: Dundurn Press, 1991. 159-66. Quote p.160.

"'I Don't Need Other People to Say What I Feel'": see this volume

SHIELDS, CAROL.

Born 1935 in Oak Park, Illinois, USA, Shields has dual Canadian/American citizenship, but has made her home—since 1957—in Ottawa, Winnipeg, and, most recently, Victoria, British Columbia. Shields studied at Hanover College, then University of Ottawa, where she obtained her M.A. in English; her thesis, *Susanna Moodie: Voice and Vision,* was published in 1976. Until recently, Shields has been affiliated with the University of Manitoba as an academic and also acted as Chancellor for University of Winnipeg. Shields developed slowly but surely as a writer; she began in poetry (*Others* 1972, *Intersect* 1974, *Coming to Canada* 1995) and crafted four deceptively quiet novels, *Small Ceremonies* (1976), *The Box Garden* (1977), *Happenstance* (1980) and *A Fairly Conventional Woman* (1982), before trying out the fictional "experiments" that were published as *Various Miracles* in 1985. Encouraged by the support she received for "telling it slant" in these quirkily postmodern stories, she examined the life of a seemingly unremarkable woman, who was also a poet, in *Swann: A Mystery* (1987). Her fascination with biography recurs more profoundly in her award-winning *The Stone Diaries* (1993), an oblique examination of the life and times, spanning the twentieth century, of Daisy Stone Goodwill. A second collection of stories, *The Orange Fish* (1989), was chosen by the Christian Science Monitor as best short fiction work of the year. Her comic romance, *The Republic of Love* (1992), was also well-received.

Shields's interest in exploring people in groups, and the interaction of public spaces with private lives, brought her naturally into writing plays: *Departures and Arrivals* (1990), *Thirteen Hands* (1993), *Fashion Power Guilt and the Charity of Families* (with daughter Catherine Shields, 1995) and 1998's *Anniversary* (with David Williamson). She also collaborated on the epistolary novel, *A Celibate Season* (1991), with Blanche Howard, writing half of the letters between a married couple temporarily separated by a career move. *Shields's* ninth novel, *Larry's Party* (1997), boldly but lovingly enters the male territory to demonstrate both its uniqueness and its familiarity to "the opposite sex," for as she argues about gender difference: "Of course our experiences are necessarily limited—this is part of the human conundrum—but observation and imagination may lead us to what we intuitively know, and have known all along" ("The Same Ticking Clock"). Shields has won many honours in Canada, the United States and Britain: most notably the Governor General's Award and the Pulitzer Prize for *The Stone Diaries,* which was also on the short list for Britain's Booker Prize and received the *Prix de Lire* in France. Her frequently-anthologized stories have won the CBC Award (Second Prize) and two National Magazine Awards. She is an Officer of the Order of Canada, a member of the Order of Manitoba and most recently, a *Chevalier de l' Ordre des Arts et des Lettres* of France. A third collection of stories, *Dressing Up for the Carnival,* appeared in 2000. Returning to women's biography, Shields wrote a monograph on Jane Austen (2001) and co-edited (with Marjorie Anderson) a collection of thirty-four reflective pieces by women, *Dropped Threads: What We Aren't Told* (2001). Prolific Shields produced a tenth novel, *Unless,* in 2002. Addressing the title, the heroine observes "Unless you're lucky, unless you're healthy, fertile, unless you're loved and fed, unless you're clear about your sexual direction, unless you're offered what others are offered, you go down in the darkness, down into despair. *Unless* provides you with a trap door, a tunnel into the light, the reverse side of not enough." *Unless* was recently nomiated for the Orange Prize. Carol Shields died July 2003, after a courageous battle with breast cancer.

References

Shields, Carol. "The Same Ticking Clock." *Language in Her Eye: Writing and Gender. Views by Canadian Women Writing in English.* Ed. Libby Scheier, Sarah Sheard and Eleanor Watchtel. Toronto: Coach House, 1990. 256-59. Quote p. 259.

—. *Unless.* Toronto: Random House, 2002. Quote p. 224.

VANDERHAEGHE, GUY.

The only child of English and Belgian parents, Guy Vanderhaeghe was born in Esterhazy, Saskatchewan in 1951 and had a typical rural upbringing, perhaps inducing an early sympathy, in the writer-to-be, for outsiders and unlikely "heroes" of all types. He received an M.A. from the University of Saskatchewan in History, a subject that continues to fuel his imagination, as seen in the brilliant treatment of the West as myth and experience in his internationally-acclaimed novel, *The Englishman's Boy* (1996). While crafting his narrative art through the writing of short stories, Vanderhaeghe supported himself by working as an archivist, researcher, freelance writer/editor and high school teacher. His first publication, *Man Descending* (1982), received instant admiration, winning the Governor General's Award for Fiction. Its poignant blend of gritty characters speaking their own truths, and energetic prose, suggested that here was a fresh contributor to the Canadian "prairie tradition," although Vanderhaeghe's influences, he maintains, are also international. His second published collection, *The Trouble With Heroes* (1983), was actually a compilation of earlier work, ranging widely in setting, though sharing a focus on men and their struggle for their own definition of heroism in what one critic calls Vanderhaeghe's "uniformly affirmative vision of the stubbornness of the human spirit" (Staines). *My Present Age* (1984), nominated for Britain's Booker Prize, picks up the clever "loser," Ed, from the final two stories of the first collection, and creates a black social satire around his own "descent" into total alienation.

Despite his strong showing in the short story form—his stories have been anthologized and given prizes in Canada and the U.S., and "Home Place"(*Things As They Are?)* was published in the *London Review of Books*--Vanderhaeghe modestly feels that his greatest talent lies in the bigger form of the novel: "It always seemed to me that the short story owed more to a poetic sensibility than it did my own consciousness, which I think is more or less shaped around narrative" ("'A Vernacular Richness'"). His attraction to narrative led him to create in *Homesick* (1989), a three-part narrative addressing the uneasy reunion of a father, daughter and grandson in 1960s Saskatchewan, and their different yearnings for the healing of home. A third collection of polished stories, *Things As They Are?* (1992) seemed to play with the border between realism and fantasy, or faith and lucidity, as Vanderhaeghe puts it. The creation of dramatic voices, and the potential of collaborating with the local theatre community, drew Vanderhaeghe to write two plays, both set and staged in Saskatchewan. *I Had a Job I Liked. Once.* (1992) won the 1993 Canadian Author's Association prize for the best drama published that year; *Dancock's Dance* (1996) premiered at Persephone Theatre in 1995. He seemed to push through into another literary dimension with *The Englishman's Boy*, which won the Governor General's Award, the Saskatchewan Book of the Year Award and was shortlisted for the Giller Prize. The novel shows "his ear for well-turned dialogue, his sensitivity to language and sparse rhythms, and his apparently effortless evocation of time, place and character," according to David Staines. Internationally, Vanderhaeghe has won the Geoffrey Faber Memorial Prize of Britain (for *Man Descending)* and has been short-listed for the 1998 International IMPAC Dublin Literary Award (for *The Englishman's Boy*). In 1997, he received an honourary D. Litt. from the University of Saskatchewan. His fourth novel, *The Crossing,* appeared in 2002.

References

Staines, David. "Guy Vanderhaeghe." *The Oxford Companion to Canadian Literature.* 2nd ed. General ed. Eugene Benson and William Toye. Toronto: Oxford UP, 1997. 1150-52. Quotes p. 1151.

"'A Vernacular Richness'": see this volume.

INDEX TO THE CONVERSATIONS

Names of Authors, Artists and Other Public Figures

Alford, Edna	133, 212
Anderson, Sherwood	51
Atwood, Margaret	36, 38, 82, 93, 107, 110, 122, 203
Auden, W.H.	178, 179
Bentall, Barney	216
Birdsell, Sandra	171, 212
Black, Conrad	229
Boll, Heinrich	46
Borson, Roo	122
Brod, Harry	83, 140
Bryant, Anita	183
Burroughs, William	87
Callaghan, Morley	69, 82, 106, 167
Callwood, June	185
Carey, Barbara	117, 122
Carmen, Bliss	107
Carson, Ed	196, 202
Carver, Raymond	81, 170
Cather, Willa	184
Cheever, John	83, 87, 211
Chekhov, Anton	209, 215
Coles, Don	117, 122
Colette	107
Connolly, Cyril	217
Conrad, Joseph	128
Dante	181
Davenport, Guy	193
Davies, Robertson	149
Deitch, Donna	183
Delbaere, Jeanne	143
Dickens, Charles	69
Donne, John	178, 179
Du Maupassant, Guy	81
Duncan, Sandy	97
Engel, Marian	36, 46, 70, 79, 107, 110, 110, 178, 202, 204
Erdrich, Louise	46
Erskine, Albert	51
Faulkner, William	43, 150, 162, 215
Findley, Timothy	69, 183, 185, 207
French, Dayv James	122
Gabriel, Barbara	90, 91, 185
Gallant, Mavis	36, 195, 203, 204, 209
Gardner, Ava	91
Garrod, Andrew	163
Gass, William	193
Gasset, Ortega	213

George, Boy	91
Gibson, Graeme	96
Goldie, Terry	91
Greene, Graham	208
Grier, Barbara	176
Griffith, D.W.	208
Hardy, Thomas	171
Harris, Claire	37
Harvor, Elisabeth	204
Hemingway, Ernest	107, 194, 202, 229
Henry, O.	81
Hodgins, Jack	50, 132, 162, 223
Huggan, Isabel	231
Hutcheon, Linda	92
Janes, Percy	164
Johnson, Pauline	107
Jones, Thom	211
Joyce, James	43, 215
Kaufman, Michael	87, 88, 89
Kipling, Rudyard	81
Kirkonnell, Watson	106
Kroetsch, Robert	49
Lang, K.D.	91
Laurence, Margaret	36, 46, 52, 67, 69, 70, 93, 133, 204, 212
Leacock, Stephen	149, 252
Lessing, Doris	46, 107, 115
Levine, Norman	82
MacKenzie, William Lyon	68
MacKinnon, Ken	168
MacLennan, Hugh	69
MacLeod, Alistair	141, 152, 230
Madonna	91
Mailer, Norman	83
Mansfield, Katherine	51, 200, 209, 211, 215
Marlatt, Daphne	197, 216, 217
Maugham, Somerset	87
McClelland, Jack	161
McCullers, Carson	36, 107
McInnis, Nadine	122
Metcalf, John	74
Mitchell, W.O.	149, 231
Moodie, Susanna	197
Morris, Wright	155
Morrison, Toni	46
Mortimer, Penelope	107
Munro, Alice	36, 54, 67, 68, 70, 74, 82, 93, 107, 108, 109, 110, 122, 133, 162, 169, 178, 182, 183, 195, 196, 197, 203, 209, 211, 212
Nabokov, Vladimir	120
Nash, Ogden	106

Newhart, Bob	97
O'Brien, Edna	102, 107, 120
O'Connor, Flannery	36, 43, 51, 162
Oates, Joyce Carol	114
Olds, Sharon	121
Ondaatje, Michael	83, 98
Pratt, E.J.	107
Proust, Marcel	87
Quarrington, Paul	207
Raddall, Tom	69
Rich, Adrienne	179, 184
Richards, David Adams	171
Richler, Mordecai	149, 167, 168
Roth, Philip	118, 122
Roy, Gabrielle	52, 59
Rule, Jane	135
Schuster, Marilyn	186
Seton, Ernest Thompson	82
Shakespeare	179, 181
Shields, Carol	116, 119, 149
Singer, Isaac Bashevis	46
Staines, David	154
Stein, Gertrude	83, 84, 89
Steinem, Gloria	183
Styron, William	83
Taylor, Elizabeth (actress)	91
Taylor, Elizabeth (writer)	107
Thomas, Audrey	36
Thompson, Kent	109
Tregebov, Rhea	117, 122
Turner, Lana	91
Twigg, Alan	88
Valgardson, W.D.	162
Vanderhaeghe, Guy	69, 162
Walker, Alice	46
Warhol, Andy	91
Warren, Robert Penn	51
Watson, Sheila	36
Waugh, Evelyn	208
Webb, Phyllis	179
Welty, Eudora	51
West, Vita Sackville	184
Wilde, Oscar	87
Wilder, Thornton	77, 95
Williams, Tennessee	86, 87
Wilson, Ethel	36
Wiseman, Adele	36
Wolfe, Thomas	95, 107
Woolf, Virginia	184
Yeats, W.B.	178, 179

Titles of Stories, Books and Other Media

After the Fire	173
"The Age of Unreason"	104, 115
AnaHistoric	216, 217
Arc	122
"As Birds Bring Forth the Sun"	169
"At Mrs. Warder's House"	38, 39
The Atlantic Monthly	211
Bad Behaviour	121
Bear	111, 178
The Beggar Maid	108
"The Bid"	35, 39
A Bird in the House	67, 197
"Blessed are the Dead"	179
"Bloodflowers"	162
"The Boat"	168
The Body Politic	183, 184
"Boundary Lines"	49
The Breast	118
Broken Ground	126, 130, 135, 137, 153
"Cages"	212, 218, 222, 229
The Canadian Forum	117
Cat's Eye	70, 203
"A Chair for George"	188
Chatelaine	174
Children are Civilians Too	46
"The Closing Down of Summer"	164, 165, 166
"Clothes-line"	122
"Colour Wheel"	64
"Companionship"	31, 39
"The Concert Stages of Europe"	133, 142
Contract with the World	188
Dance of the Happy Shades	203
"Dancing Bear"	228
Dancing in the Dark	37
David	69
"A Day at the Front, A Day at the Border"	109, 119
"Daybreak at Pisa"	78, 79
"The Dead"	215
Desert Hearts	183
Desert of the Heart	123
Despair and the Critic	123
"Dinner along the Amazon"	78
The Dinner Party	39
"Disorder and Early Sorrow"	118
The Divine Comedy	188
The Diviners	204
"Dreaming of Jeannie"	54
"Drummer"	212, 222, 229

Dubin's Lives	108, 120
"Dulce"	178
"Dulse"	108
The Englishman's Boy	207, 208, 216, 217, 229, 230
A Fairly Conventional Woman	199, 200
"Fall Cleaning"	30
Famous Last Words	91
The Fire-Dwellers	37
"The Flood"	49
"The Forest Path to the Spring"	120
Fortress of Chairs	115, 123
"From a High Thin Wire"	67
From the Fifteenth District	*203*
"The Garden of Eloise Loon"	34, 35, 40
The Garden Party	215
The Ghost Writer	118
"Ghostkeeper"	120
"A Gift of Mercy"	79
Girl of the Rockies	63
The Glass Menagerie	85
The Globe and Mail	132
"Going to Russia" (Harvor)	115
"Going to Russia" (Vanderhaeghe)	218
The Golden Notebook	115
The Hand of Robin Squires	63
The Handmaid's Tale	203
Happenstance	199
"Head"	35, 43
Headhunter	78, 98, 183
"Heart Trouble"	109
"Hello Cheeverland, Goodbye"	78
"Herr Madman"	107, 115
"Home Movie"	174
Homesick	217, 218, 221, 229
The Honeyman Festival	202
Howard's End	118
The Hoyer	30
Huckleberry Finn	214
The Hudson River	109
"In Case of Rapture"	34, 45
"In the Middle of the Fields"	120
In the Skin of a Lion	98
"Inland Passage"	179
Inside the Easter Egg	178
Intolerance	208
"Invasions '79"	142
The Invention of the World	139, 145, 146
"Island"	168
The Ivy Crown	120
Jesus of Montreal	48

The Joke	55
"Journey to the Lake"	49
K in Love	122
"The King is Dead"	224
"King Walsh"	222
Kitchen Talk	37, 47
La Dame aux Camellias	94
"La Danse Russe"	120
"La Vie Boheme"	122
The Ladder	174, 183
"Ladies and Gentlemen, The Fabulous Barclay Sisters!"	133
"Lady with a Lapdog"	215
The Land of Dizziness	123
The Last of the Crazy People	96
The Late Bourgeois World	122
"Lemonade"	78
Lesbian Images	184
"Lies in Search of the Truth"	119
Light in August	215
"The Lineman"	45
Lives of Girls and Women	67, 197, 212
"Loneliness Has Its Claims"	212, 221
Look Homeward, Angel	95
"The Lost Salt Gift of Blood"	170
The Lowest Place on Earth	104, 109, 115, 123
The Macken Charm	148
"The Madonna Feast"	64
"Man Descending"	213
"The Man in the Brooks Brothers' Shirt"	121
"Man on Horseback"	218, 224, 227, 228
Mating	120
"Milk Bread Beer Ice"	196
"Minna and Bragg"	79
The Missing Child	48, 55, 56, 57, 58
The Montrealer	203
My Childhood	52
"My Country Wrong"	180
"My Present Age"	213, 216, 217
"The Name's the Same"	79
A New Life	108
The New Yorker	109, 211
Nine Short Stories	81
No Clouds of Glory	110
No Great Mischief	159
Of the Farm	120
"The Orange Fish"	198
The Orchard Keeper	208
"Other People's Troubles"	142
"Out of the Silence"	78

"Pain Was My Portion"   109, 111
"Parker's Dog"   228
"The Peace of Utrecht"   108
The Piano Man's Daughter   94
"The Plague Children"   151, 156
A Pocketful of Canada   106
"The Prodigal"   218
The Proving Grounds   122
"Real Life Writes Real Bad"   79, 80, 95
"The Red Dress"   203
Redbook   173, 174, 175
Reflections in a Golden Eye 107
"The Religion of the Country" 142
"Rembrandt's Hat"   120
The Resurrection of *Joseph Bourne* 157
"Reunion"   225, 229
The Road Past Altamont   52
The Robber Bride   93
A Romantic Weekend   121
Room Temperature   118
"Rosa"   122
The Sacrifice   37
"Sam, Soren and Ed"   212, 213
The Saturday Evening Post   211
Saturday Night   117
Seize the Day   120
"Separating"   131
Short Story Masterpieces   51
"Simon's Luck"   108
Sister Carrie   107
"The Snob"   69
"Spit Delaney's Island"   131, 144, 153
The Stone Angel   107, 204
"Stones" (Birdsell)   49
"Stones" (Findley)   80
A Streetcar Named Desire   86
"The Students' Soiree"   101
"The Sumo Revisions"   151, 153
Sunshine Sketches of a Little Town 148, 212
Surfacing   110
Swann: A Mystery   192, 194, 195, 205
"A Sweetheart"   104, 105
"The Teller's Cage"   105
"Things As They Are?"   218, 228
Thomasina and the Trout Tree 63
"Three Women of the Country"   142
"Today is the Day"   197
Toronto Life   174
"Toronto Street"   54
"Transfer"   41, 42

The Trials of Ezra Pound	79
"Under the I"	32
The Victory of Geraldine Gull	63
"Vision"	169
"Voice-Over"	120
Waiting for the Barbarians	52
War and Peace	214
"The Watcher"	212, 221, 229
The West Coast Review	197
West Mall	164
When She Was Good	122
Who's Afraid of Virginia Woolf	88
Wild Animals I have Known	82
"The Wild Plum Tree"	49
Wilderness Tips	110
"Winter Dog"	167
"Wire Kiss"	122
The Woman Destroyed	107
Women and Madness	39
The World According to Garp	93
"The Wreck of the Julie Plante"	106
Wuthering Heights	167
You Can't Go Home Again	95